WHY? BECAUSE. BECAUSE WHY?

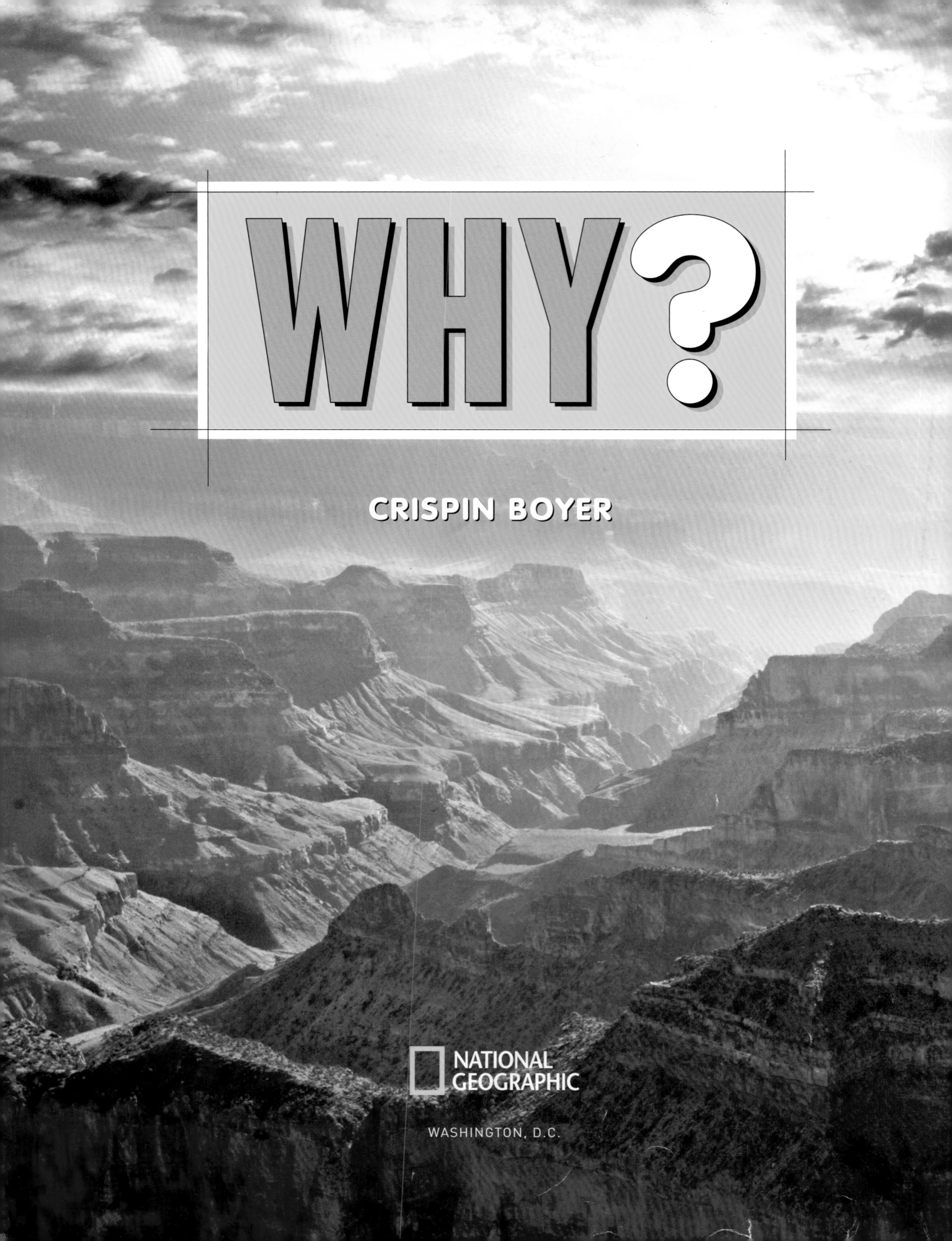

WHY?

CRISPIN BOYER

NATIONAL GEOGRAPHIC

WASHINGTON, D.C.

CONTENTS

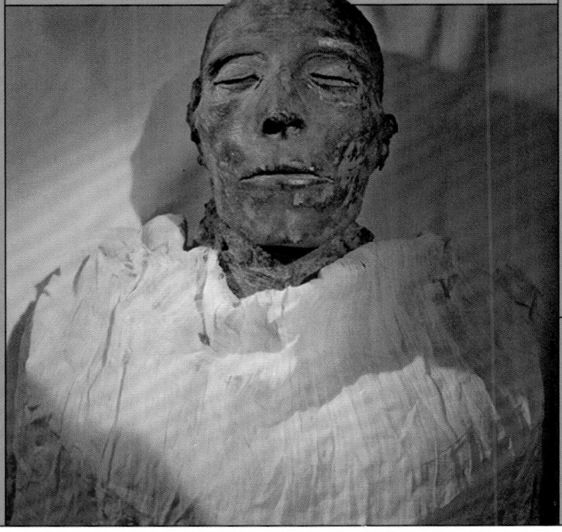

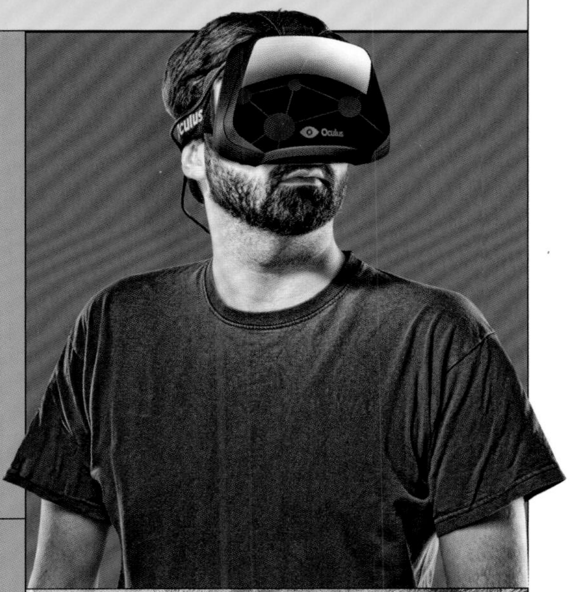
Oculus

WHY is the sky blue? Why is your snot yellow? Why do skunks smell like the worst thing EVER? Why do we ASK WHY?

You have questions. This book has answers—over a thousand of them—spread across hundreds of topics. Some are serious, some are silly, some are strange, and some answer Q's you never thought to ask. Many put to rest those nagging questions that pop into your noggin at the strangest times and keep you awake at night. Reading *Why?* will help your mind unwind.

This book has so many answers, in fact, that we've no time to waste. The sky is blue because air molecules in our atmosphere filter blue light out of the color spectrum. Snot gets its yellow (and eventually green) color from a chemical in your white blood cells, which your body unleashes to fight infection. Skunks reek because they have glands in their butts loaded with an icky musk. And why do we ask why? Well, that answer is a little complicated. We'll get to it—and many, many other mysteries—soon enough. Just keep in mind that discoveries are being made all the time and that theories are constantly evolving. While this book packs in the most up-to-date answers now, things might be different ten years from now. In the meantime, keep *Why?* handy for when you need instant answers, want to stump your parents, or just want to sleep at night.

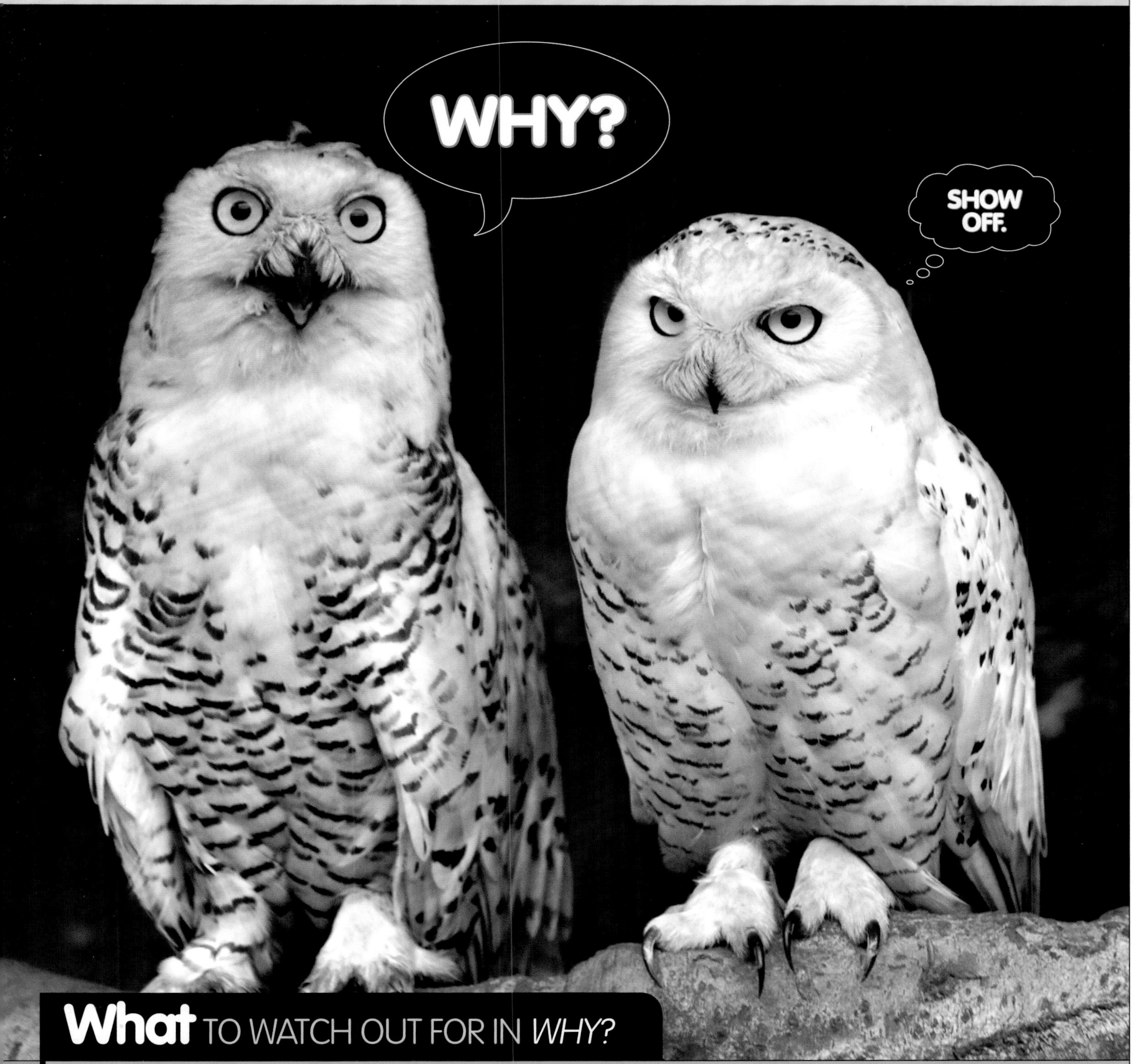

What TO WATCH OUT FOR IN *WHY?*

QUESTIONS

The bulk of this book, naturally, is made up of questions and their corresponding answers. Each page is packed with Q's related to a topic, and answers often lead to more questions. Oh, and just because the book is called *Why?* doesn't mean questions that begin with "who," "what," "when," "where," and "how" don't get their fair share.

SAY WHAT?!

Watch for weird-but-true facts scattered among all the questions.

MYTH MASHED

Surprise! Some well-established "facts" are actually fiction. Myth Mashed blurbs show that what you think is true isn't always so.

PERSONS OF INTEREST

Meet the very important people—explorers, scientists, celebrities, and pioneers—who played a big part in the topics and questions at hand.

Q:TIPS

From time to time, you'll find advice related to each chapter's topics and answers.

SILLY QUESTION, SERIOUS ANSWER

Go ahead: Ask anything. Why did the chicken cross the road? Why can't you find a pot of gold at the end of the rainbow? No question is too wacky for *Why?* Even the craziest Q's get the scientific treatment throughout the book.

YOUR **BODY**

THIS CHAPTER HAS a lot of heart, and guts, and brains, and maybe even a kidney or two—and it's all yours! From aging to zits, bad breath to B.O., brain function to ice-cream headaches, the pages that follow will get under your skin and shine a light between your ears. Prepare yourself: Things are about to get personal.

1

WHY ME?

WHY do I look the way I LOOK?

Everything you see in the mirror—from your height to your hair color to the dimple (or lack thereof) on your chin—is written into nearly every cell of your DNA, spiraling chains of proteins found in every cell in your body. Think of DNA as your body's instruction manual. It tells your cells how to grow into organs, hair, teeth, fingernails, your tongue, and every single other part of your body. Stretches of DNA (called genes) are like pages in that instruction manual. Genes control what you will look like, plus less obvious traits such as whether you have perfect vision or the ability to curl your tongue.

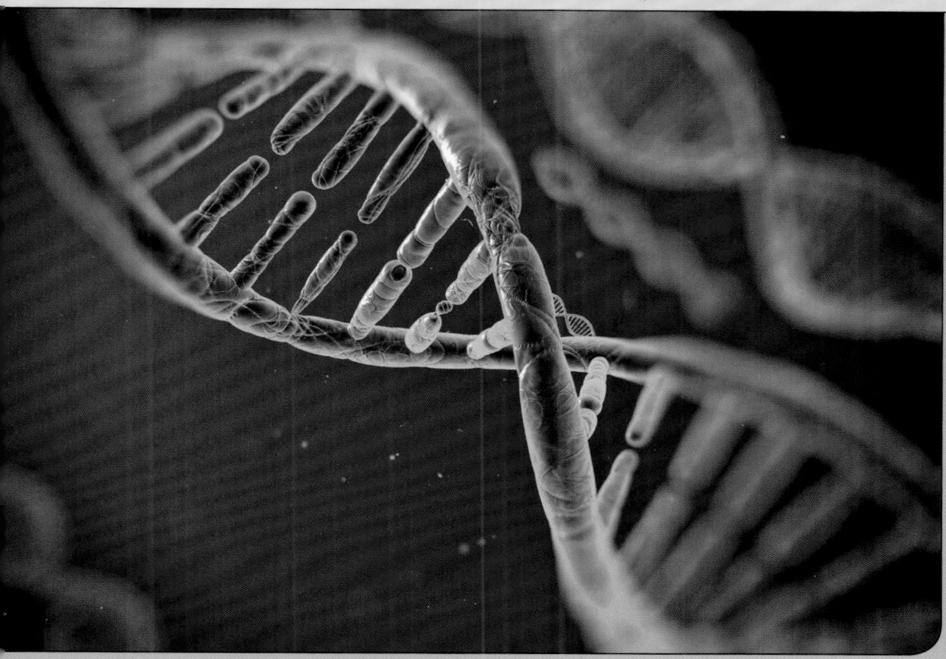

Where did I get my genes?

While you admire your good looks in the mirror, don't forget to thank your parents. Genes come in pairs: one from Mom and the other from Dad. It's the combinations of genes that bring about—or "express"—various physical traits (in a process called heredity). Some genes are more influential on your appearance than others. The genes for dark hair are dominant over the genes for red and blond hair, making dark hair more common.

Do animals have DNA?

Yes, all of them do, actually. And not just animals. Every living thing on Earth—including single-celled bacteria, trees, and plants—has DNA in its cells. You might expect to share many genes with a chimpanzee or bonobo, our closest living relatives, but did you know you also share genes with that banana the chimp is chomping?

Why do some kids look less like their parents than other kids do?

You can't always guess a child's appearance just by looking at his or her parents. The study of genes—called genetics—is achieving breakthroughs all the time, but much about heredity remains mysterious. Combinations of genes can affect other genes, leading to unpredictable characteristics or features that lurk in the genetic background for several generations. Our genes are also riddled with so-called junk DNA that doesn't seem to express itself in any noticeable way. Environment and diet also play a large role in shaping a person's weight, skin tone, and other physical characteristics.

How similar AM I GENETICALLY TO ...

... A CHIMPANZEE? 96–99%

Humans and chimps split from a common ancestor between 13 and 6 million years ago.

... A FRUIT FLY? 60%

Consider this the next time you swat that itty-bitty bug buzzing around your cantaloupe: You and that fly are related! (So are you and the cantaloupe.) Fruit flies and humans share many basic genes, along with some genes that might make you more vulnerable to cancer. In fact, scientists are studying fruit flies for clues to beating cancer.

... MY PET DOG? 82%

Dogs might be "man's best friend," but read on for the shocking truth.

... MY PET CAT? 90%

It turns out humans share more genes with felines than with Fido.

... A BANANA? 50%

No, this doesn't mean you're half banana. All life-forms on Earth share fundamental features and functions at the cellular level. Sharing half our genes with a banana just shows that we evolved from a common ancestor more than a billion years ago.

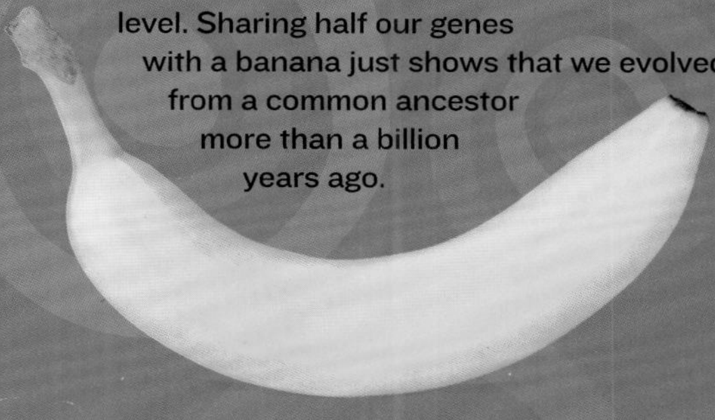

WHY DO I have ...

... a heart?

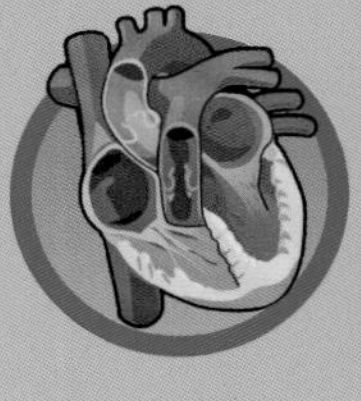

Your body's engine, the heart pumps blood to every cell in your body.

... blood?

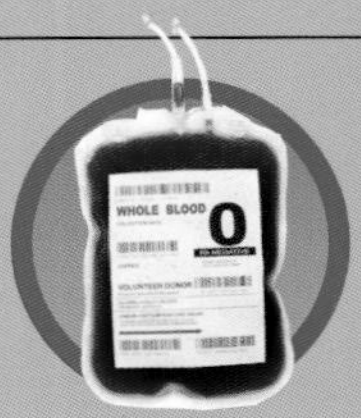

A mix of special cells and liquid "plasma," blood delivers all the good stuff (oxygen vitamins, minerals, and chemicals called hormones) to the cells in your body and carries away all the bad stuff (carbon dioxide and other waste) for disposal. Red blood cells transport oxygen, while white blood cells fight infection. Special cells called platelets seal the leak when blood vessels break—a process called clotting. An oxygen-carrying protein called hemoglobin is what gives blood its red color.

BODY BUILDING

350	About the number of bones in the body at birth
206	Number of bones in an adult (many bones fuse together during growth)
20 FEET (6 M)	Length of the small intestine
60,000 MILES (96,560 KM)	Length of blood vessels
1.3 GALLONS (5 L)	Average volume of blood in an adult's body

... lungs?

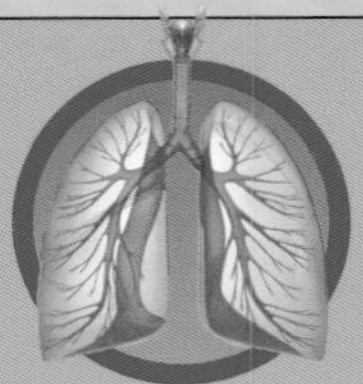

Each breath you inhale fills these balloon-like organs with oxygen, which is absorbed into your blood; each exhalation expels carbon dioxide waste from your blood.

... skin?

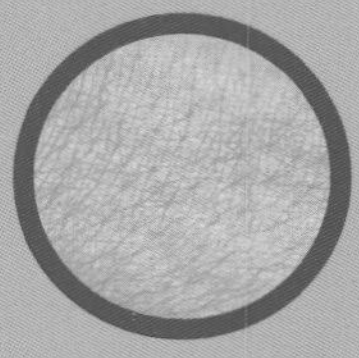

Skin holds your insides in and protects your tissues from ultraviolet radiation from the outside. Skin is your body's largest organ. It is made of layers of cells that march to the surface and flake off from friction. The outermost layer is entirely dead.

... tonsils?

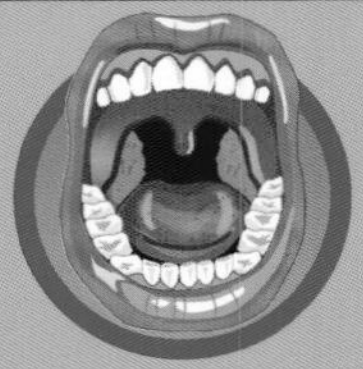

These two meatball-shaped masses of tissue at the back of your throat are part of your lymph system, which includes a network of nodes that work like little security guards to battle infection.

... an appendix?

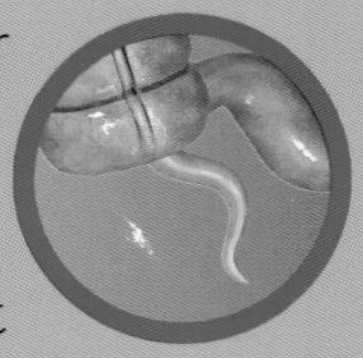

This skinny tube in our digestive system is mostly useless today and can actually endanger your life if it becomes inflamed. Scientists suspect that the appendix, which replenishes essential bacteria in our guts, was an important organ back before germ-fighting medicines helped humans overcome constant bouts of diarrhea.

... a stomach?

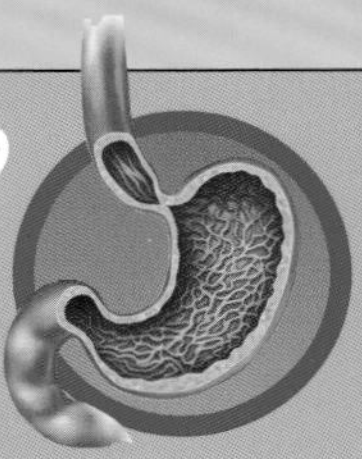

This expandable organ stores everything you eat and starts breaking down food with powerful acids.

... intestines?

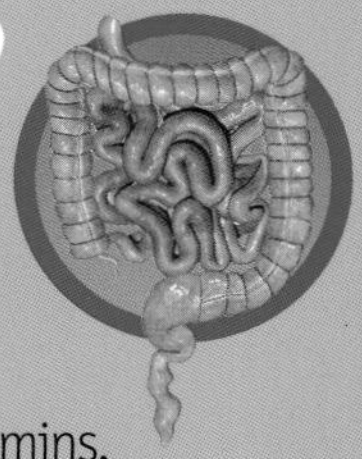

The bulk of food digestion takes place in your small and large intestines, two tubes that absorb all the vitamins, minerals, and other nutrients from everything you eat.

... a liver?

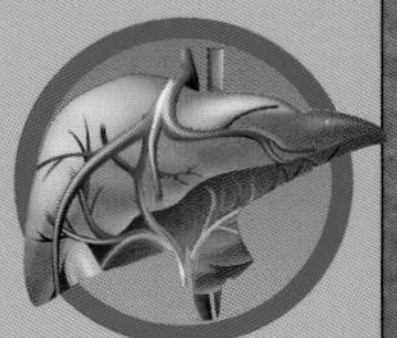

Your body's biggest internal organ, the liver is like a complex chemical-processing plant. It converts nutrients from the small intestine into fuel your body can use. It makes bile, an essential substance for digestion. It cleans your blood of toxins and removes damaged red blood cells.

... kidneys?

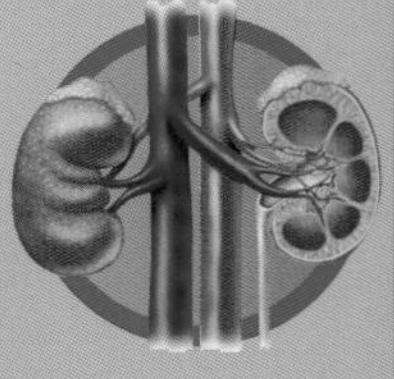

This bean-shaped organ is so essential to good health that your body comes with a second one for free! Each kidney is crammed with more than a million microscopic filters—called nephrons—that skim the waste chemicals and other gunk from your blood.

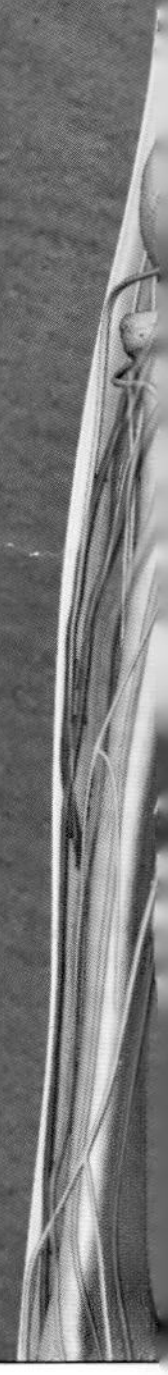

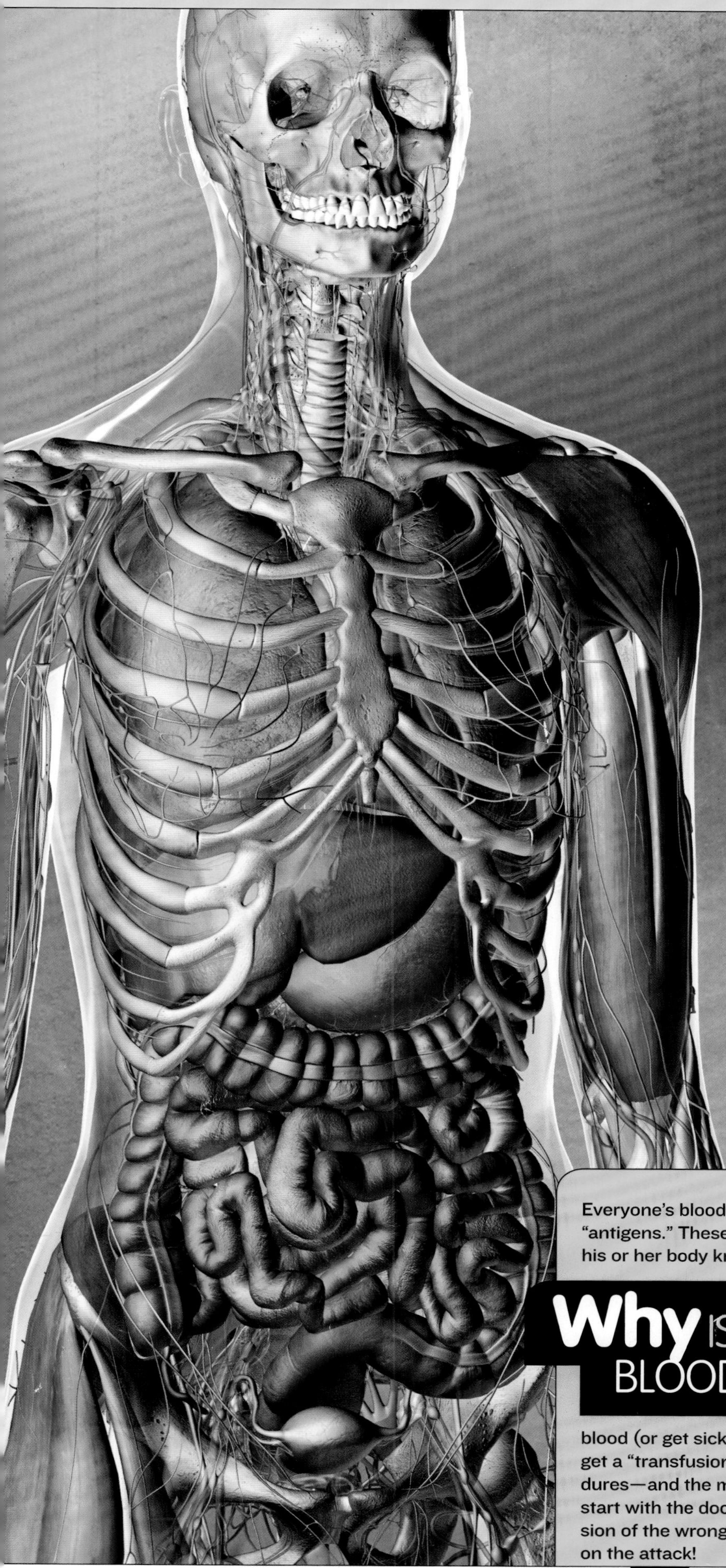

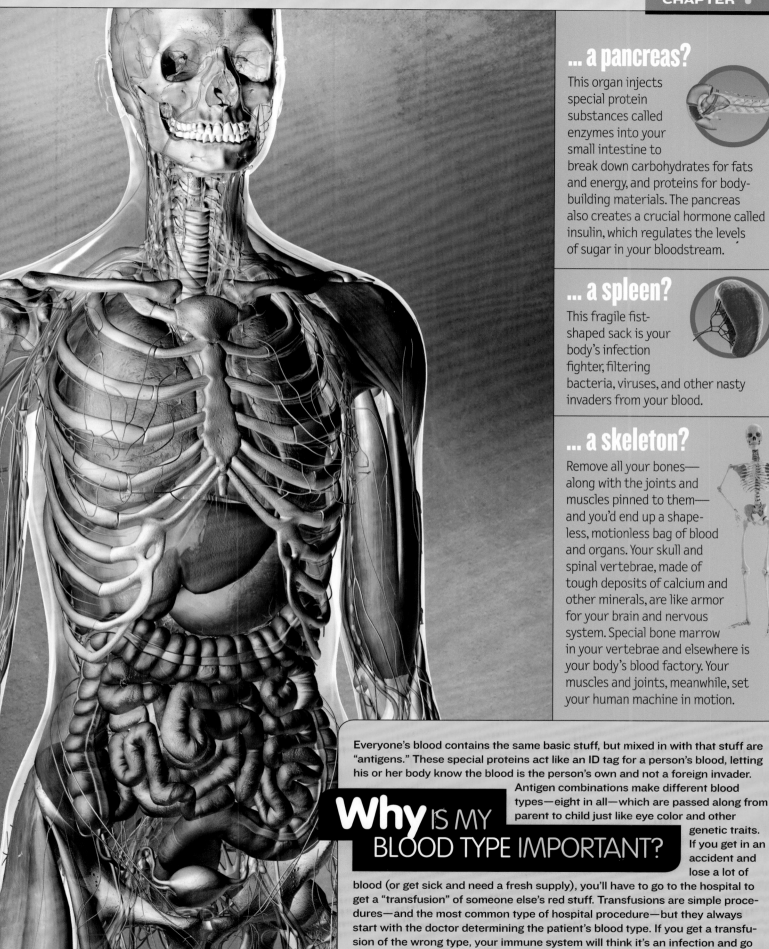

... a pancreas?

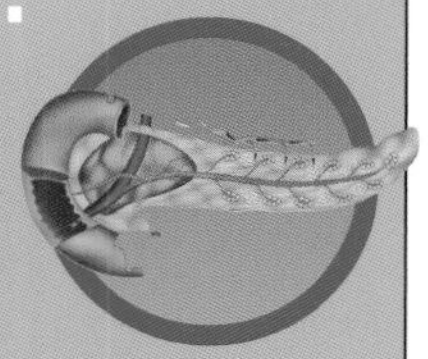

This organ injects special protein substances called enzymes into your small intestine to break down carbohydrates for fats and energy, and proteins for body-building materials. The pancreas also creates a crucial hormone called insulin, which regulates the levels of sugar in your bloodstream.

... a spleen?

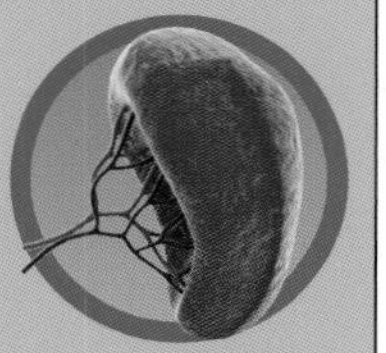

This fragile fist-shaped sack is your body's infection fighter, filtering bacteria, viruses, and other nasty invaders from your blood.

... a skeleton?

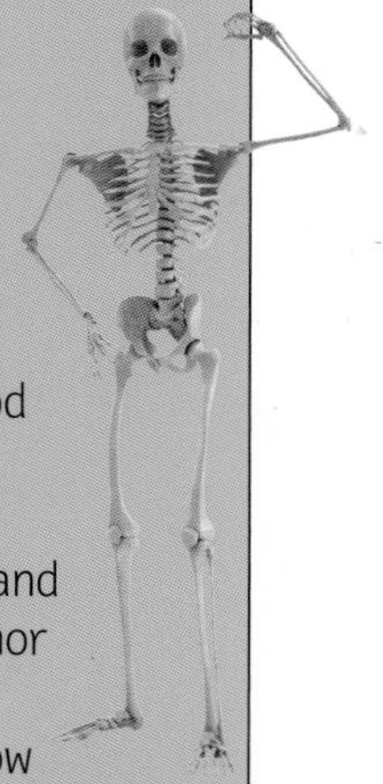

Remove all your bones—along with the joints and muscles pinned to them—and you'd end up a shape-less, motionless bag of blood and organs. Your skull and spinal vertebrae, made of tough deposits of calcium and other minerals, are like armor for your brain and nervous system. Special bone marrow in your vertebrae and elsewhere is your body's blood factory. Your muscles and joints, meanwhile, set your human machine in motion.

Why IS MY BLOOD TYPE IMPORTANT?

Everyone's blood contains the same basic stuff, but mixed in with that stuff are "antigens." These special proteins act like an ID tag for a person's blood, letting his or her body know the blood is the person's own and not a foreign invader. Antigen combinations make different blood types—eight in all—which are passed along from parent to child just like eye color and other genetic traits. If you get in an accident and lose a lot of blood (or get sick and need a fresh supply), you'll have to go to the hospital to get a "transfusion" of someone else's red stuff. Transfusions are simple procedures—and the most common type of hospital procedure—but they always start with the doctor determining the patient's blood type. If you get a transfusion of the wrong type, your immune system will think it's an infection and go on the attack!

WHY can I SURVIVE without all my organs?

It's a no-brainer that you need your brain and your heart, and you wouldn't last long if your liver failed. But the lungs and kidneys come in pairs, so you could survive if one of them failed. People who've lost their spleens in accidents have gone on to live healthy lives. The tonsils and appendix, meanwhile, are practically useless and are routinely removed when they become inflamed.

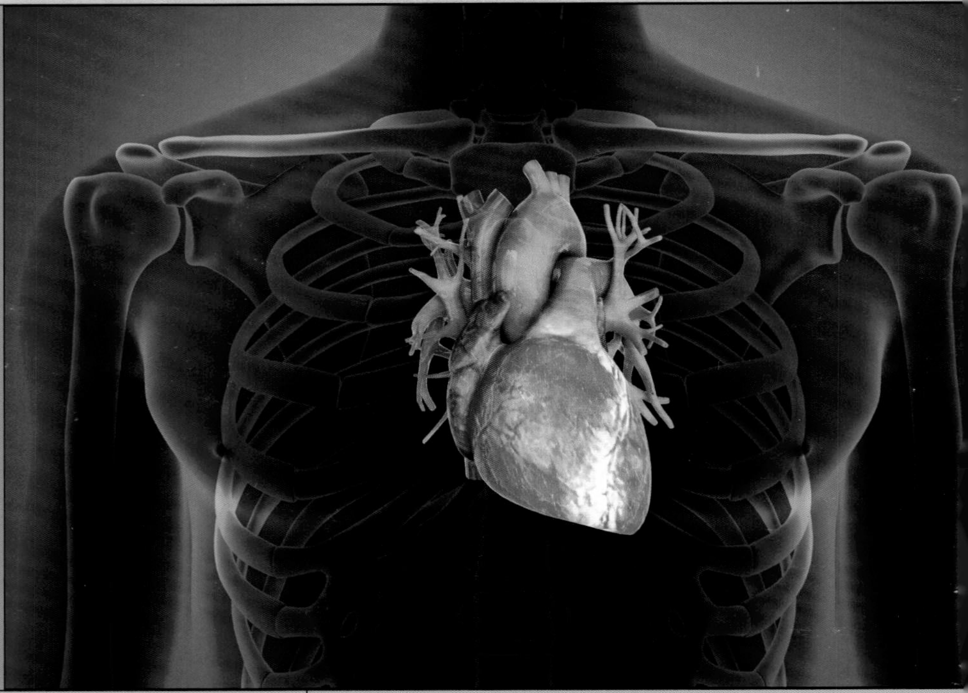

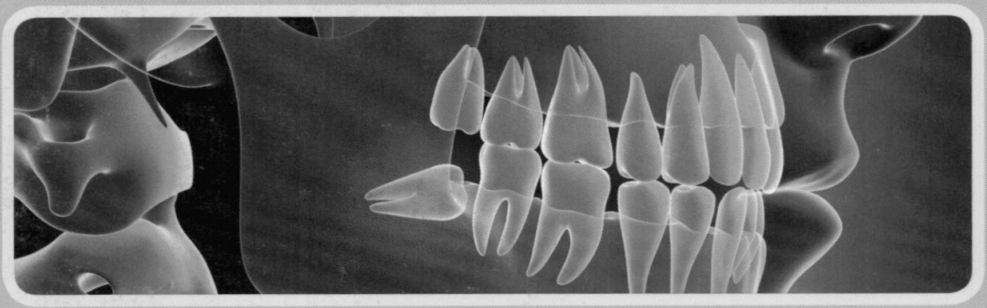

Why are some body parts pointless?

Called "vestigial" organs, these useless body parts are leftovers from our evolutionary ancestors, who actually needed them. Take your wisdom teeth, for example. Today they crowd our mouth and often need to get yanked by the dentist, but our primate ancestors had larger jaws and needed the extra choppers in case some rotted away in the days before tartar-control toothpaste. Our tailbone—or coccyx—is a leftover from animals that needed tails for balance or grasping tree branches.

Why do I have eyebrows?

Humans have evolved to become less hairy in the past six million years or so, but we still have those clumps of fur above our eyes. Beyond their role in our facial expressions, eyebrows act like natural sweatbands, preventing rain and sweat from running directly into our eyes.

Why do men have nipples?

They were there before you were even born. Human embryos in the womb develop according to a blueprint that's the same for males and females. Eventually, the embryos begin to take on features specific to their sex, but not until after they've already developed nipples. Later in life, chemicals called hormones trigger changes in females so that they can nurse their young. Males don't have those hormones, so they're stuck with nipples that are nothing more than chest accessories. Other than a few exceptions (mice, platypuses, stallions), most male mammals have nipples. Nipples don't cause males any harm, which is probably why evolution hasn't given them the ol' heave-ho.

Why do people get goose bumps?

Like your wisdom teeth and your tailbone, goose bumps serve no purpose in modern humans. They're created by itty-bitty muscles in our hair follicles, which raise the bumps as a reflex reaction to a sudden drop in temperature or feelings of panic, anger, or extreme fear. Goose bumps fluffed up the body hair of our much furrier ancestors to help trap heat or make them look larger to threatening animals. Today, goose bumps just make you look like you need to borrow a sweater.

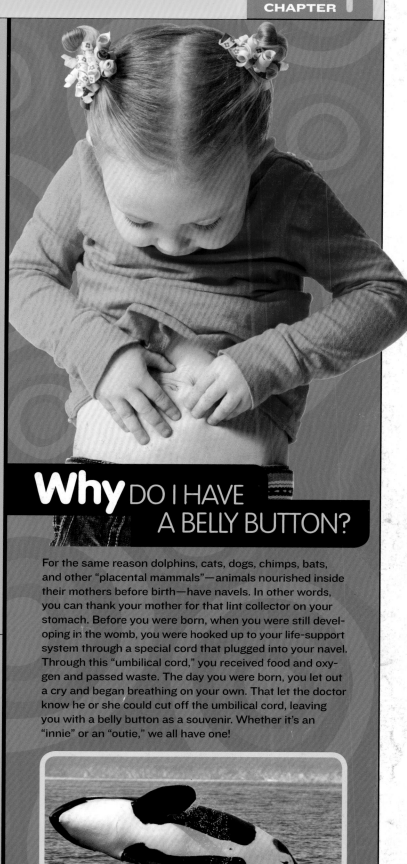

Why DO I HAVE A BELLY BUTTON?

For the same reason dolphins, cats, dogs, chimps, bats, and other "placental mammals"—animals nourished inside their mothers before birth—have navels. In other words, you can thank your mother for that lint collector on your stomach. Before you were born, when you were still developing in the womb, you were hooked up to your life-support system through a special cord that plugged into your navel. Through this "umbilical cord," you received food and oxygen and passed waste. The day you were born, you let out a cry and began breathing on your own. That let the doctor know he or she could cut off the umbilical cord, leaving you with a belly button as a souvenir. Whether it's an "innie" or an "outie," we all have one!

WHY do I ask WHY?

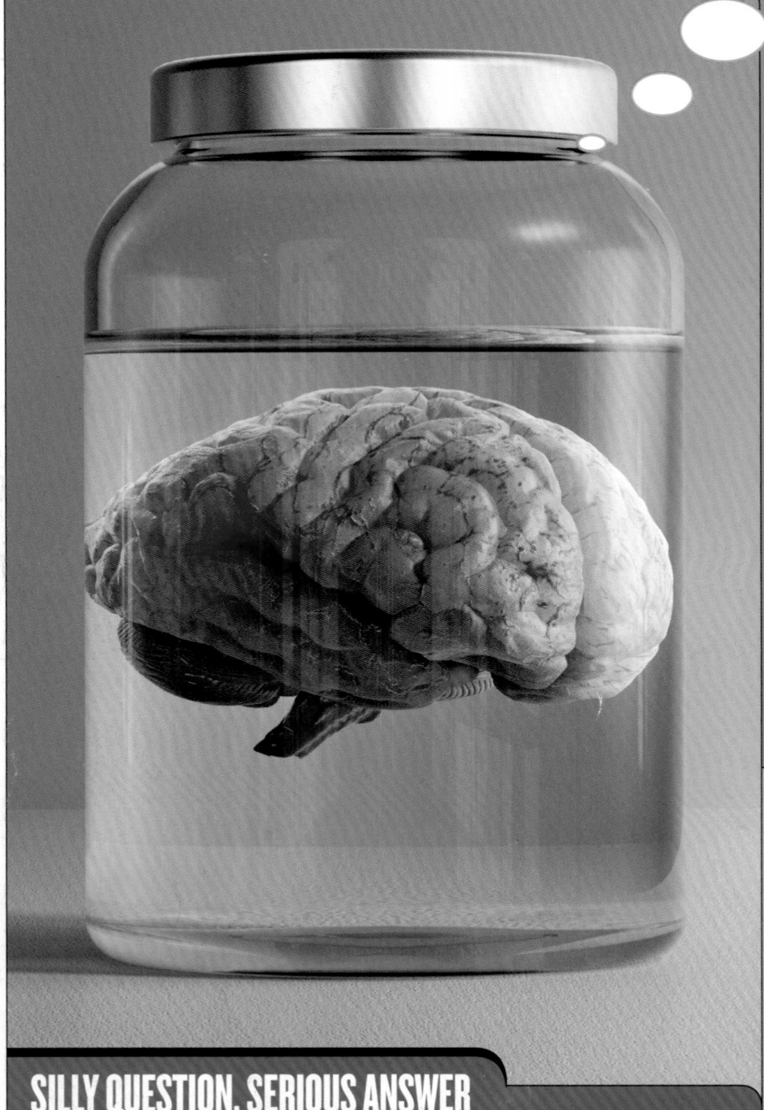

Thank that amazing brain of yours for your uncontrolled curiosity. Not only does this wrinkly mess of gray matter control all your body's automatic functions (breathing, blinking, food processing, the beating of your heart), but it also empowers you to laugh, cry, create, dream, score a three-pointer in basketball, learn, paint, beat your sister at *Mario Kart*, and ask questions. The brain is the master of your nervous system and the source of your personality. No other organ in nature is as mysterious.

SILLY QUESTION, SERIOUS ANSWER

Are gray and white matter really gray and white?

Eh, close enough. Gray matter has some pink and yellowish tints mixed in. White matter is really more pinkish. It turns white when it dies and has been preserved as a lab specimen.

What exactly is between my ears, anyway?

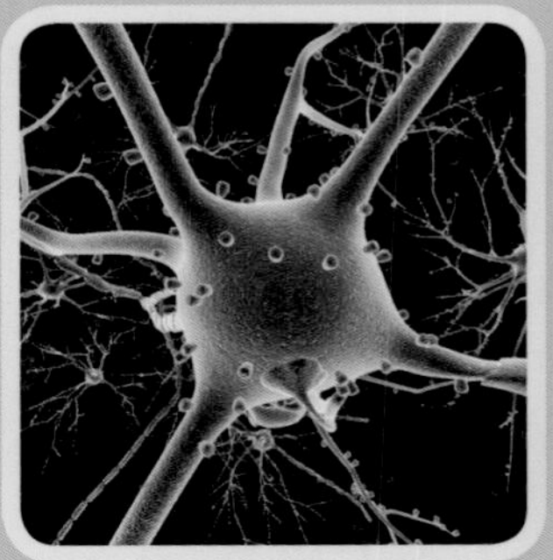

One of your body's largest organs, your brain is three pounds (1.3 kg) of fat and proteins condensed in a mass with a tofu-like texture. Its contents come in two colors ...

GRAY MATTER: Your brain contains about 100 billion nerve cells. Called neurons, they make up your brain's "gray matter."

WHITE MATTER: Your neurons communicate with one another by sending electrical signals and forming chemical connections in a network of nerve fibers called dendrites and axons, which form your brain's white matter. This communication between neurons is what's responsible for your every thought, memory, movement, and automatic bodily function.

Q: tips

HOW CAN I PROTECT MY BRAIN?

You have two lungs and two kidneys, but you have only one brain. Make the most of it—and complement its own built-in safety features—by following these tips:

Wear a helmet

while riding your bike, skateboarding, snowboarding, or engaging in any other potentially dangerous activity.

Don't smoke

Not only is it bad for your lungs, but it can cause neurological damage to your brain as well.

Eat well

A poor diet can lead to illnesses later in life (such as type 2 diabetes and high blood pressure) that can cause shrinkage of the brain.

Exercise your body

Running, playing soccer, and other physical activity releases chemicals that refresh your brain and prime it for learning.

Exercise your mind

Games that test your memory and concentration actually improve your brain's flexibility in processing information and can possibly help you dodge dementia (a disease that affects your mental abilities) later in life.

HOW much of my body's energy does my brain use?

The electrical messages bouncing across your brain at any given time outnumber the messages zipping through the world's telecommunications networks. All that activity requires enough electricity to power a dim lightbulb. That might not sound like much until you consider the brain uses 20 percent of the body's energy but is only about 2 percent of its weight.

WHAT protects my brain from injury?

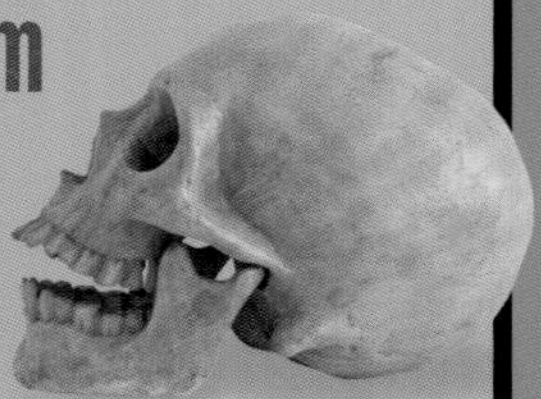

Your brain is a delicate organ that needs all the protection it can get. That thick skull of yours is its first line of defense (being boneheaded is a good thing!), followed by three sturdy membranes called meninges. Fluid fills the gaps between these membranes, cushioning the brain from impacts. A special "blood-brain barrier" made of special cells acts like a security perimeter in the brain's circulatory system, and keeps out anything that might contaminate your sensitive network of neurons.

SAY WHAT?!

WHENEVER YOU get in trouble for doing something totally lame-brained, blame your lame brain. It hasn't finished developing yet! Scientists discovered that the white matter connecting your frontal lobes—which control your decision-making process—to the rest of the brain isn't fully formed until you reach your mid-20s. In other words, your center of good judgment isn't fully wired into your brain yet.

MYTH MASHED

WHY DO WE USE ONLY 10% OF OUR BRAINS?

It's a reassuring idea for anyone who thinks they have superpowers or hidden artistic talents: We could accomplish amazing feats if we could just tap into our unused reserves of gray matter. It's also a total myth. We use nearly every part of our brain all the time. Even a simple activity like brushing your teeth—walking toward the toothbrush, squeezing out just enough toothpaste, keeping track of which teeth you've cleaned as you brush away—activates a small electrical storm across your brain as the various lobes, cortices, and cerebellum work together to brush, rinse, spit, and remember to floss. The activity in your brain never stops, even when you sleep.

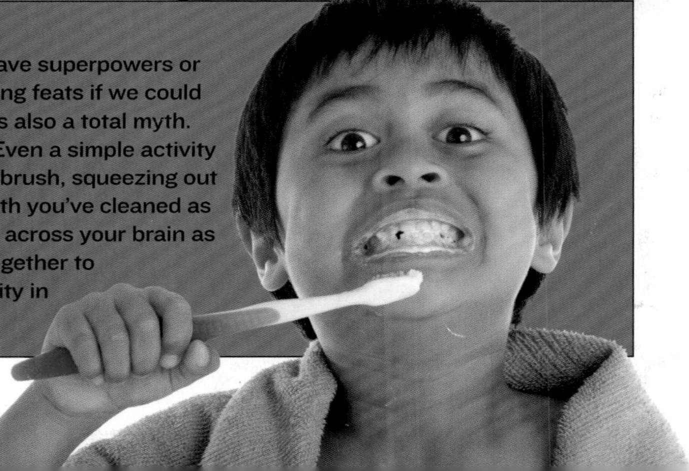

WHY am I SMARTER than, say, a dolphin or a chimpanzee?

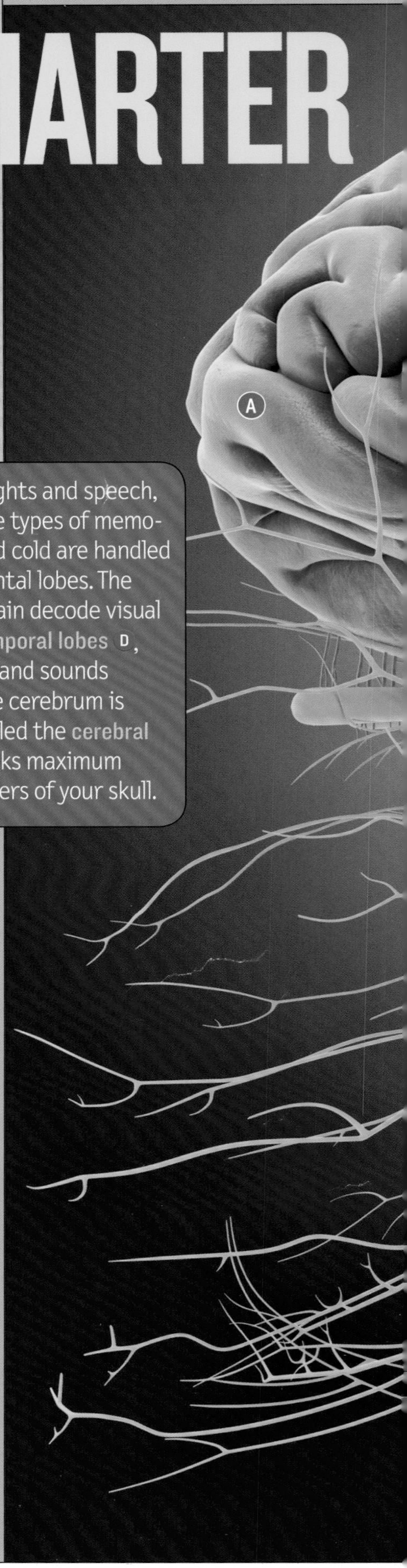

Credit for your uniquely human intellect—your ability to solve algebra problems or play the electric guitar or wonder about the function of your own brain—goes to your **cerebrum**. Accounting for 85 percent of your brain's mass, it's far larger and more complex than the cerebrums of other brainy animals such as dolphins, whales, and elephants. It's also home to your brain's most important lobes—the sub-processors of that supercomputer between your ears.

The **frontal lobes** (A) process your thoughts and speech, as well as learning, emotions, and some types of memory. Your senses of pain, touch, heat, and cold are handled by the **parietal lobes** (B) behind the frontal lobes. The **occipital lobes** (C) at the back of the brain decode visual information from our peepers. The **temporal lobes** (D), near your temples, process memories and sounds transmitted from your ears. The entire cerebrum is enveloped in a layer of gray matter called the **cerebral cortex**. Its deeply wrinkled surface packs maximum processing power into the tight quarters of your skull.

Why does my body move when I want it to?

Your **cerebellum** (E), the second largest part of your brain, coordinates the movement of your muscles and keeps you from tumbling over when you walk.

Why do I remember things?

Every time you experience something new, electrical charges fire through the white matter in your brain, creating chemical links that form a network of pathways out of neurons. Your memories are stored in these connected neurons, and the connections become stronger and expand into other neurons with repeated exposure to the new experience. Practicing a song on the guitar makes the same neural networks fire again and again, becoming stronger and thus making the song easier to play. Spending time with a new friend reinforces old connections and builds new ones as you learn about your pal's habits. As you learn and gain new memories, your brain's structure changes and makes new connections. The brain you have today will be different tomorrow.

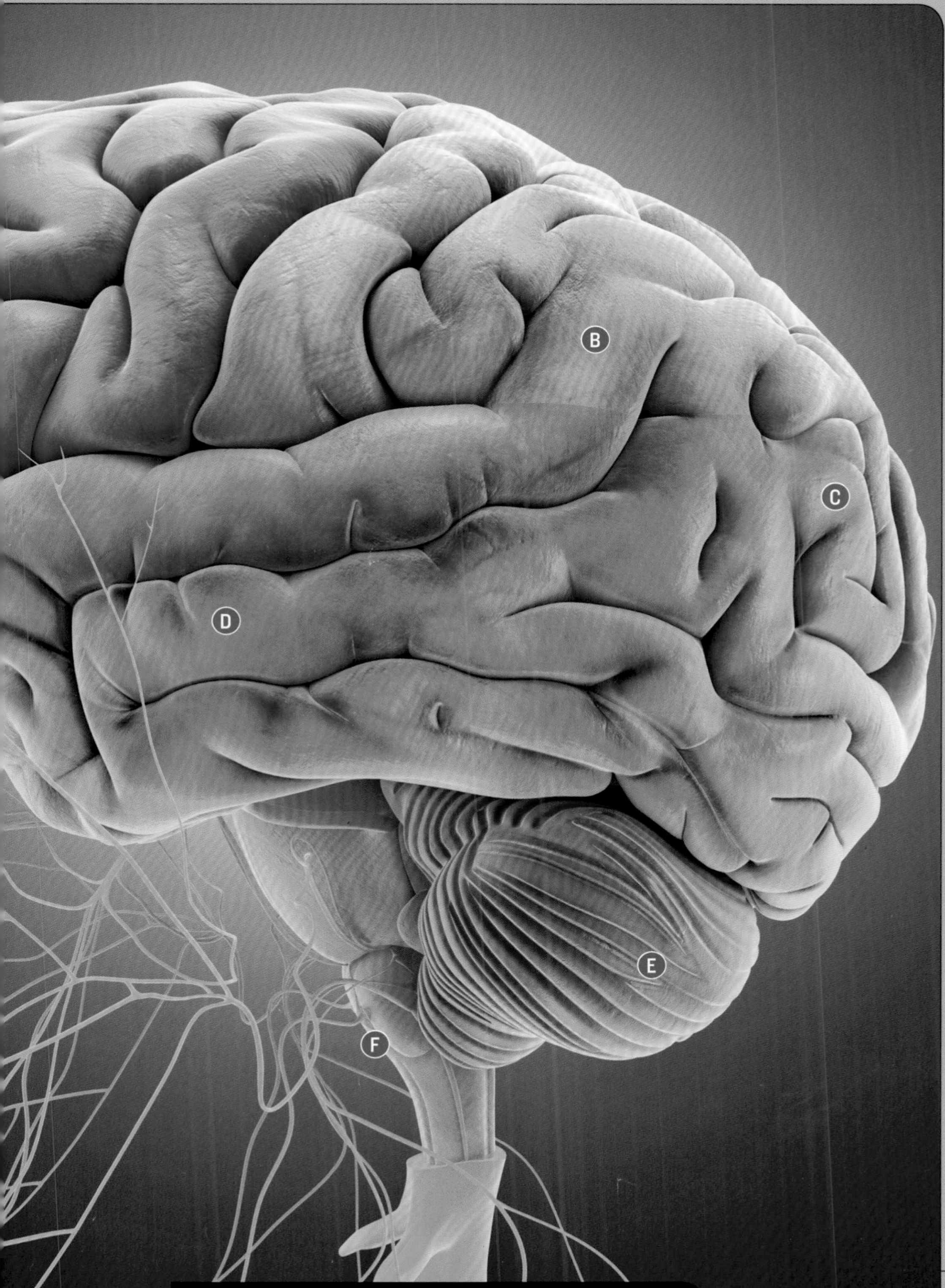

Why do I forget things?

When it comes to retaining memories, your brain is practically a bottomless pit—one that continues to deepen throughout your life. So why did you forget where you put your towel at swim practice? It turns out your brain is equipped with two types of memory ...

SHORT-TERM: Powerful but fleeting, short-term memory is meant to store information—such as phone numbers, email addresses, and other humdrum everyday data, like the location of that towel at swim practice—that you won't need to recall during your golden years. As you'd expect, short-term memories don't linger. They fade even faster if you were distracted at the time the memory took shape (maybe a teammate was talking to you while put down your towel, or maybe you moved the towel many times during practice and your short-term memory can't place its exact location).

LONG-TERM: Experiences move from short-term to long-term memory when they're repeated (such as when you memorize flash cards to study for a test) or accompanied by meaningful emotions and significant sensory input (such as when you scored the winning goal or the day you got your pooch as a puppy). Scientists believe your brain has a limitless capacity for long-term memories, but sometimes you can't recall a particular detail without help from sensory clues (a familiar smell is a powerful reminder) or the recollections of friends involved in the event. Scientists blame such forgetfulness on a flaw in our ability to retrieve memories—a flaw that nonscientists call a "brain fart."

What MYSTERIES REMAIN ABOUT THE BRAIN?

SOME BIG ONES! Although scientists are mapping out the brain's neural network and have a decent understanding of which parts do what, they still don't know where your mind—aka your consciousness, personality, and everything else that makes you you—fits into the puzzle. Maybe someday you'll solve that mystery—if you put your mind to it.

Why do I breathe without thinking about it?

Credit goes to your F brain stem, the autopilot for your most important automatic functions: breathing, blood pressure, and heart rate.

WHY do we YAWN?

Everybody yawns—even unborn babies in the womb—and yet researchers aren't quite sure why we do it. Although humans yawn more often when we're tired or bored, scientists have ruled out sleepiness or lack of oxygen (which would cause sleepiness) as causes. Instead, they suspect yawning might help us keep a cool head. As with a supercomputer, the brain needs to stay cool to function properly. Each yawn pumps air into sinus cavities in the head, cooling the brain in the process. And because the brain and body are slightly warmer just before bed, we tend to yawn when we're tired.

Why do we need to sleep?

Video games, track meets, chemistry class—your waking hours are crammed with activities and tasks that give your noggin a real workout. All that processing causes chemicals to clutter your brain. A good night's sleep clears your head—literally. While you snooze, your brain goes into housekeeping mode, flushing the toxins and preparing itself for a busy day of math classes, socializing, and beating your brother in basketball.

How much sleep do I need?

That depends on your age. Kids between 5 and 12 need about 11 hours of sleep. Older kids and adults can get by with 7 or 8.

IS YAWNING contagious?

Absolutely! In fact, yawning is so contagious that even reading about yawning can make you yawn. (Go ahead and get it out of your system.) Studies have shown again and again that people who see other people yawn—even in videos—are more likely to yawn.

WHY IS YAWNING CONTAGIOUS?

Yawns don't catch on among children younger than five or among people with emotionally dampening disorders. That leads researchers to believe contagious yawning is just another way humans reinforce social bonds between people. Humans are social and emotional animals. We tend to understand and feel the emotions of friends and even strangers. Yawning falls into that category. When we see someone yawn, we yawn.

IS YAWNING CONTAGIOUS FOR OTHER ANIMALS BESIDES HUMANS?

You bet, at least among higher primates such as chimpanzees and bonobos (for the same reason as for humans, researchers suspect). Even more surprising, experiments show that dogs catch yawns from watching people!

Why do I get sleepy?

Whenever you try to defeat drowsiness to finish one more Harry Potter chapter, you're actually locked in a losing battle over bedtime with your brain stem. This chunk of gray matter at the base of your brain regulates your sleep, along with other automatic bodily functions such as breathing and the ticking of your heart.

What happens if I don't get enough sleep?

Doctors believe that a good night's sleep comes with many benefits, including improved creativity and mental sharpness. Avoid going to bed and you'll soon suffer the consequences: crankiness, clumsiness—even hallucinations if you miss a few days. Your brain will go on strike, and easy tasks will become supremely difficult until you turn in and switch off.

Q: tips

How CAN I GET A GOOD NIGHT'S SLEEP?

- Keep to a sleep schedule. Set a bedtime and a wake-up time and stick to them.
- Relax with a book before bed, but don't keep your smartphone within reach. It's a certified sleep stopper.
- Don't fall asleep with the television on.
- Don't eat any big meals or chug any large drinks within two hours of bedtime.
- Getting plenty of sun exposure during the day helps you sleep at night, so spend some waking hours outside!

WHY do we DREAM?

Scientists aren't really sure.

Studies suggest that dreams help us cope with painful memories. Dreaming might also make us smarter and more creative during our waking hours. So if you're feeling drained, grabbing 40 winks—and a few vivid dreams—might recharge your brain.

Why do some people snore in their sleep?

Because something is keeping the air from moving freely through the passages behind their noses and mouths. Maybe they have bad sleep posture, or maybe they've put on weight or have a sinus infection. Sometimes, snoring is brought on by age. Whatever the reason, snoring can get loud. A woman in England once snored loud enough to drown out the sound of a low-flying passenger plane!

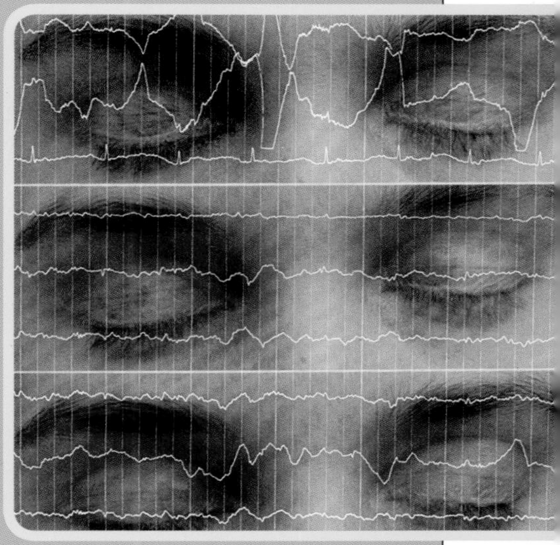

Can we control our dreams?

Sleep experts say we can seize control of our dreams and do all sorts of fantastical things—fly, relive favorite memories, eat a mountain of ice cream—but only after we realize we're actually dreaming. Achieving this deep-sleep state, known as lucid dreaming, isn't easy. Wannabe dream masters practice every night for years and still never achieve success. A variety of masks and headbands promise to help sleepers reach a lucid state by flashing tiny lights above the eyelids. Sleep researchers, meanwhile, are researching other methods of triggering dreams.

How long do I need to sleep before I start to dream?

Dreams don't start until you reach a state called REM (rapid-eye-movement) sleep, roughly 90 minutes after your head hits the pillow.

NIGHT SIGHTS

COMMON dream THEMES

WHAT DOES IT MEAN

when I dream about ...

... flying?

Life's going great. You feel like you have the freedom to accomplish anything!

... falling?

You feel nervous and unprepared. Did you forget to study for today's science test?

... appearing naked in public?

You feel vulnerable. Maybe you told a lie or overshared personal info.

... finding new rooms at home?

You're excited about new or unexpected opportunities in your life.

... getting chased by something?

You're putting off some unpleasant task or approaching a big deadline.

WHY are my eyes Green or Brown or ...

Just like the shape of your nose and the color of your hair, your eye color is determined by the genes you inherit from your parents. Those genes determine how much melanin—a colored chemical matter—you have in each **IRIS** Ⓐ, which is the colorful part of your eye. The more melanin you have, the darker your eyes. Less melanin makes for lighter eyes, which is why fair-skinned people often have light blue or gray eyes.

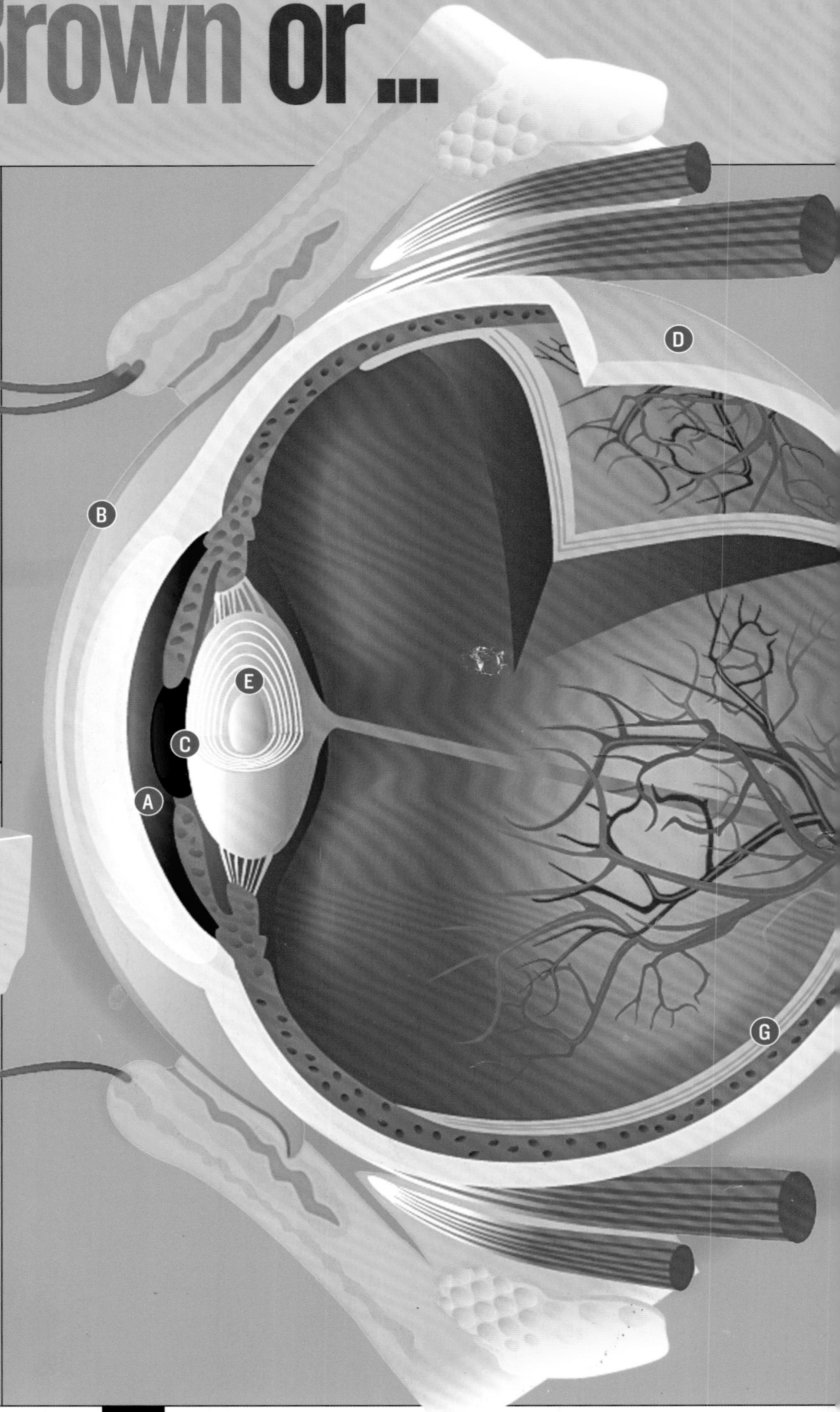

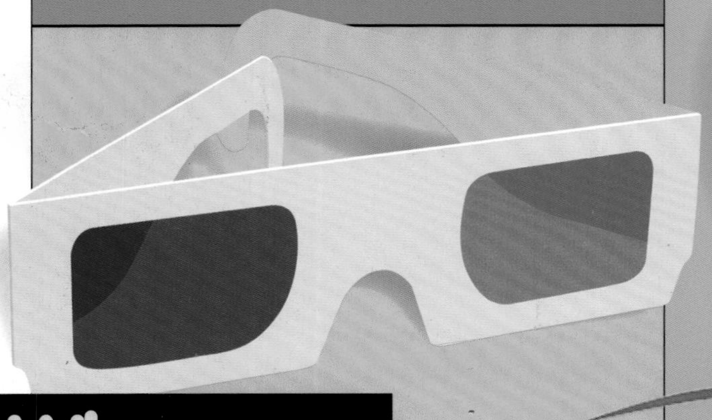

Why DO I SEE IN 3-D?

Like all human beings, you have "binocular vision," meaning both your eyes face toward the front and provide your brain with two slightly offset images. Your brain processes the differences in these two images to create a perception of depth, or a three-dimensional view.

What does each part of my eye do?

CORNEA B The eye's protective, transparent cover, the cornea is similar to the protective glass on a camera lens. It bends the light entering your eye to pre-focus the image before it reaches your lens.
PUPIL C Muscles in the iris control this hole in the center, which, like a camera's shutter, allows light to enter the eye and strike the lens. In bright sunlight, the pupil contracts to let in less light. In darkness, it opens wide to let in as much light as possible.
SCLERA D The whites of your eyes, sclera form a protective cover about the size of a Ping-Pong ball.
LENS E Like a projector in a movie theater, the lens focuses light onto the retina. It's suspended in a muscle that changes the shape of the lens to focus on objects near and far faster than any computerized camera.
OPTIC NERVE F This cable carries visual information from your retina to the brain. Your brain processes the information and translates it into what you're actually seeing.

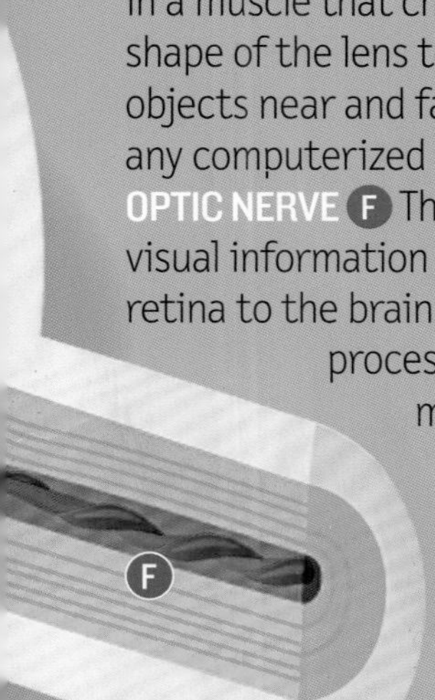

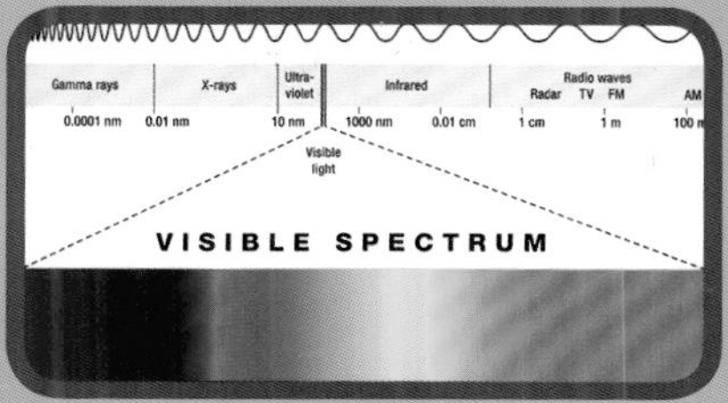

Why do I see in color?

Your **RETINA** G is covered with millions of special cells called rods and cones that process light from the lens. Cones detect colors (people who are color blind are missing cone cells for a particular color), while the rods process light information. Scientists can guess at how animals perceive vision by counting the rods and cones in their eyes. Cats, for instance, have eight times as many rods as humans but far fewer cones, which explains their excellent night vision and their relative color blindness.

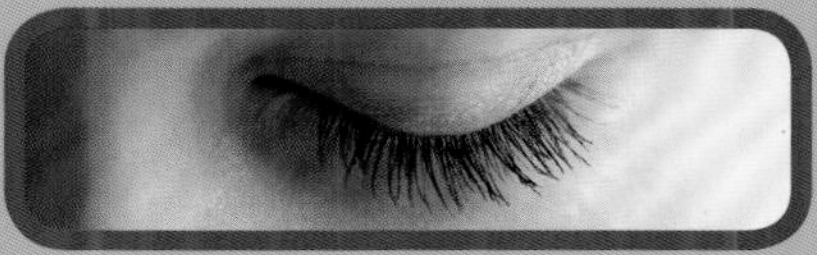

Why do I have eyelashes?

These fine hairs are our eyes' first line of defense, shielding them from dust and dirt.

SAY WHAT?!

CHICKENS HAVE terrible night vision, but they're capable of seeing colors—including vibrantly purple ultraviolet colors—that humans cannot. Researchers think chickens and other birds inherited their visual capabilities from their dinosaur ancestors. Because most dinosaurs weren't nocturnal (active at night), they developed exceptional color perception and motion-detection vision for hunting in broad daylight.

Why DO SOME PEOPLE HAVE TWO DIFFERENTLY COLORED EYES?

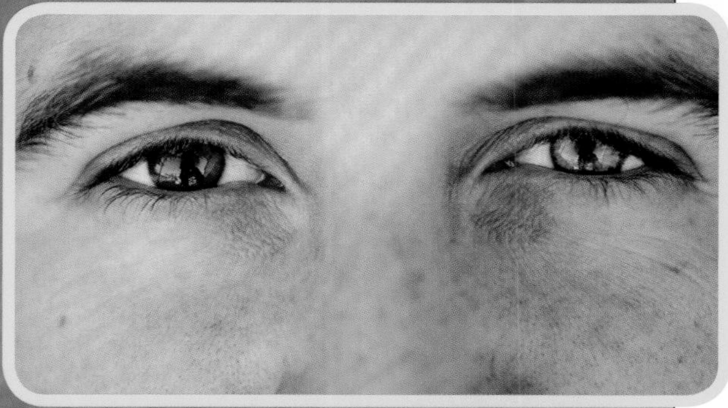

Sometimes, a person's melanin pigment doesn't spread evenly to each iris, which can lead to one eye being darker than the other or even splashes of color in each iris. This extremely rare condition—known as heterochromia—doesn't affect a person's vision.

How COMMON IS MY EYE COLOR?

WHY are my tears SALTY?

Sodium chloride— the most common type of salt—is in all your body's fluids: blood, sweat, and (yep) tears. Your tears contain a little less than one percent salt.

Why do my eyes sting when I swim in the ocean but not when I cry?

Because seawater contains about three times more salt than your tears. The higher concentration of salt can cause a mild stinging in your eyes even if you wear a mask.

Why do I cry?

That depends on the kind of crying you're talking about. Our eyes produce tears of three types ...

BASAL TEARS flow constantly to keep our eyes from drying out. Our bodies produce about five to ten ounces (148 to 295 mL) of basal tears each day.

REFLEX TEARS protect our peepers from irritants in the air, such as smoke and dust.

EMOTIONAL TEARS flow when our brain registers sadness or stress, which triggers the release of body chemicals called hormones that turn on the waterworks. Some scientists believe that emotional tears help rid our body of bad chemicals that build up during stress—which is why you feel better after "having a good cry." With the possible exceptions of elephants and gorillas, humans are the only animals that shed tears of this type.

Why do I blink?

Humans blink automatically to flush away the stream of cleansing tears produced by ducts in the corners of our eyes. Adults blink about 15 times per minute, but our rate of blinking slows when we read (which is why our eyes tire after tackling a long book) or focus on a distant object. No matter how hard we try not to blink, the need to flush the eyes eventually trumps our willpower—as anyone who's lost a staring contest will tell you.

Why do some people need to wear glasses or contacts?

Your eyes are amazing machines, but it takes only one small imperfection in the shape of your cornea or the lens to cause fuzzy focusing. Doctors call these imperfections astigmatisms, and they're often inherited from parents. Glasses and contact lenses (or corrective surgery) can fix the problem.

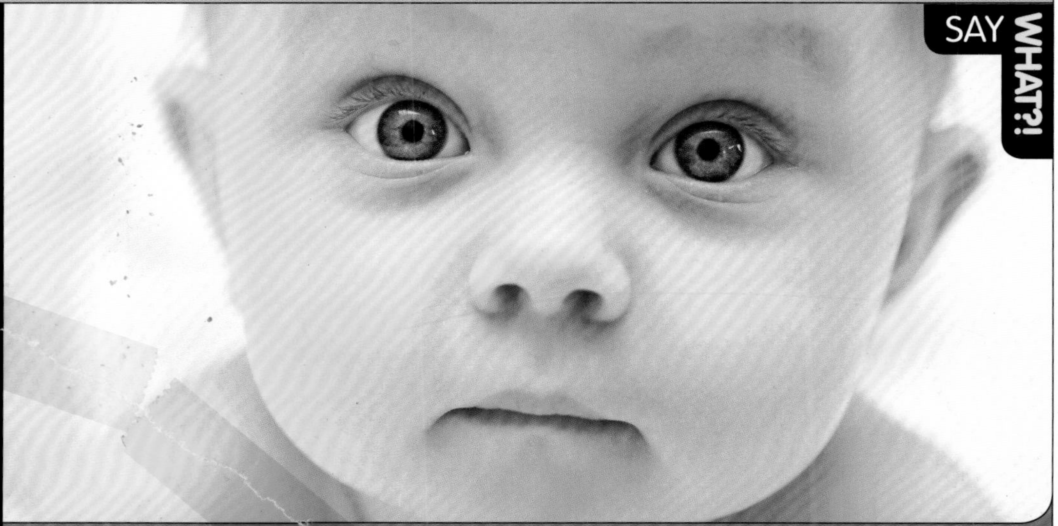

SAY WHAT?!

NEVER START A STARING CONTEST WITH A BABY.

Infants blink only about two times per minute.

WHY do I have 10 FINGERS?

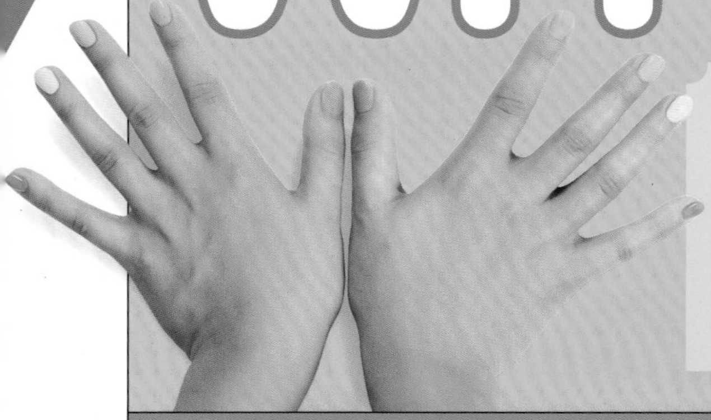

Scientists have several ideas why humans can high-five each other instead of, say, high-four or high-six. One theory suggests four fingers and a thumb on each hand are the perfect number and length to grip objects firmly. (Another study suggests we can grasp most things with just our thumb and index finger if necessary; the other four fingers are spares.)

The process of evolution determined the most beneficial number of fingers and toes for our survival. Pandas, after all, have thumblike digits to help them grasp bamboo shoots, while some birds have quadruple digits for perching and tucking away during flight. Occasionally, babies are born with extra fingers and toes (a condition known as polydactyly), but those additional digits have never offered enough of an edge to survive to later generations. In other words, evolution determined that five fingers per hand are just right for humans.

Why do I have thumbs?

Having no thumbs would make you all thumbs, fumbling to tie your shoes or assemble a hamburger. (Don't believe us? Tape one of your thumbs against the side of your hand and see how hard life becomes.) We inherited a fully "opposable" thumb—named for its ability to close tip-to-tip against our other fingers—from our primate ancestors around two million years ago. These ancient relatives needed handier hands to help get a grip on simple tools. So give a thumbs-up to your thumbs. They're the mains reasons you can text with one hand and build a burger without fumbling the bun.

Why do I have fingerprints?

Those whirls, swirls, loops, and arches on your fingertips (and toes, in case you didn't know) are unique to you—even if you have an identical twin—and they remain unchanged throughout your entire life. In fact, the faint ridges known as fingerprints form before you're even born. Fluids in the womb put pressure on your developing digits, which, combined with your rate of growth and genetic makeup, create one-of-a-kind designs.

Okay, but WHY do I have fingerprints?

Ah, you want to know the point of those fingertip designs (well, besides incriminating crooks who forget to wear gloves). Scientists have put forth all sorts of possible reasons. Fingerprints might magnify the hand's ability to detect vibrations, for example, or improve our sense of touch. They also might work like tire treads to help us grip objects. Speaking of which ...

Do other animals have thumbs besides us?

Lots of them, although the exact number depends on your definition of "thumbs." Apes and many monkeys have opposable thumbs just like us, while smaller primates, pandas, and koalas have thumblike digits and claws that help them grip plants and prey.

Why do my fingers wrinkle when I've been swimming?

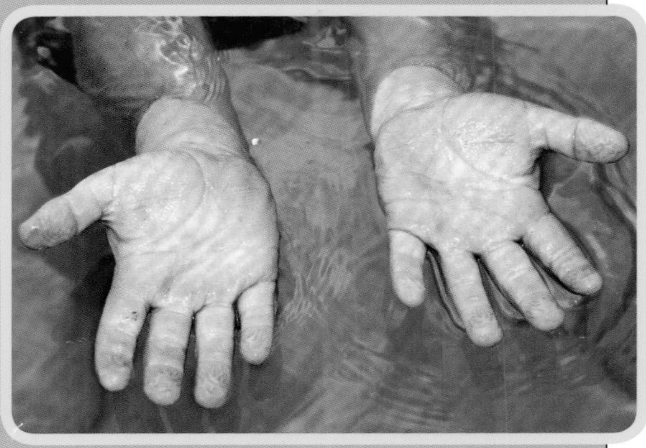

You might think that playing in the pool or soaking in the tub makes your fingertips and toes waterlogged and soggy. Not so! The prune effect is caused by blood vessels shrinking just below the skin—an automatic reaction triggered by your nervous system when it senses long exposure to water. Scientists think people evolved this reaction to improve their grip and traction in wet environments. After all, pruny fingers make it easier to snag slippery fish.

Why CAN I POP MY KNUCKLES?

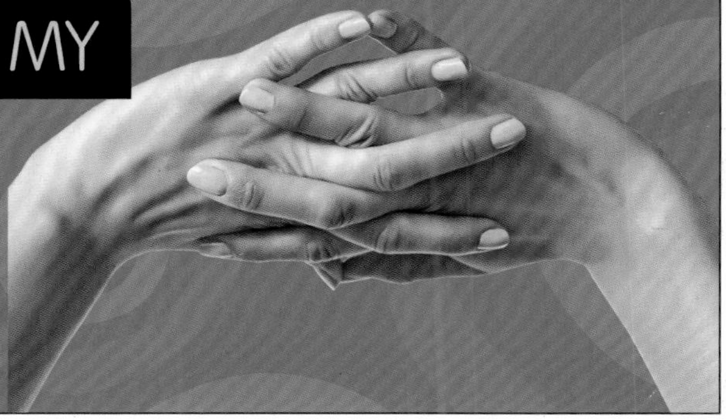

When you move or bend your fingers, you occasionally squeeze tiny air bubbles that form in the protective fluid around your body's joints. Those popping bubbles create an audible crack.

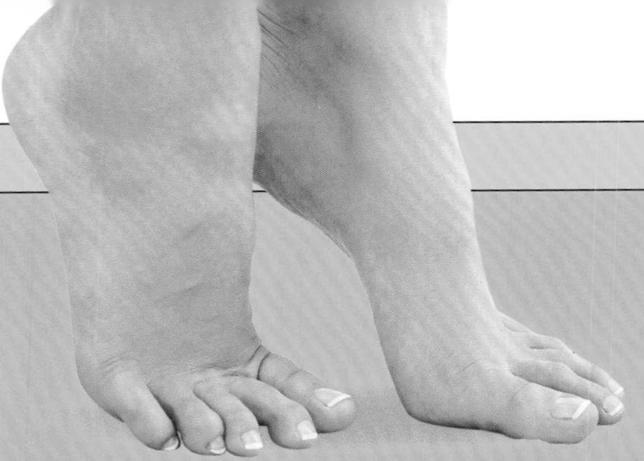

WHY do I have FINGERNAILS? (AND TOENAILS)

Humans evolved with flattened fingernails instead of the thicker, sharper claws found on most mammals. Researchers think that fingernails and toenails helped our ancestors climb trees, peel fruit, and use simple tools. And fingernails are still useful today! Their color and condition offer clues about your overall health. Nail polish turns them into fashion accessories. You use them to pop open the tops of soda cans. And nothing makes a better back-scratcher than a nice set of nails!

What are fingernails made out of?

Believe it or not, that armor plating at the tips of your fingers is made of the same stuff as your hair and skin, a protein called keratin. It's also in the hooves and horns of animals.

Do animals have fingerprints like us?

It should come as no surprise that gorillas, chimpanzees, and other higher primates closely related to humans have fingerprints. But if you look closely at a koala's paws, you'll see tiny swirling ridges on the skin of its fingers and toes. They're fingerprints, and every koala has a unique set. That means animal detectives would have no problem tracking down koala crooks!

SAY WHAT?!

YOUR TONGUE IS IMPRINTED with unique patterns just like your fingerprints.

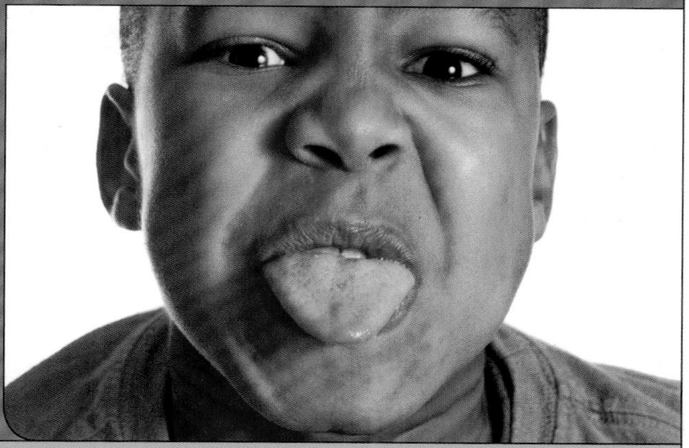

What would happen if I never trimmed my nails?

Fingernails grow slowly—roughly a hair's width a day—but that growth adds up over the long term. Let yours grow wild and you might eventually beat the Guinness World Record set by Melvin Boothe, whose untamed claws reached a combined length of more than 32 feet (nearly 10 m).

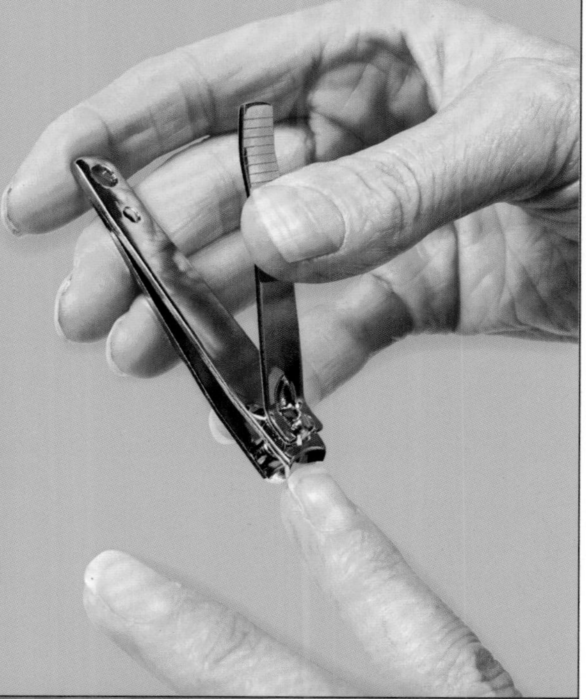

THE power OF TEN

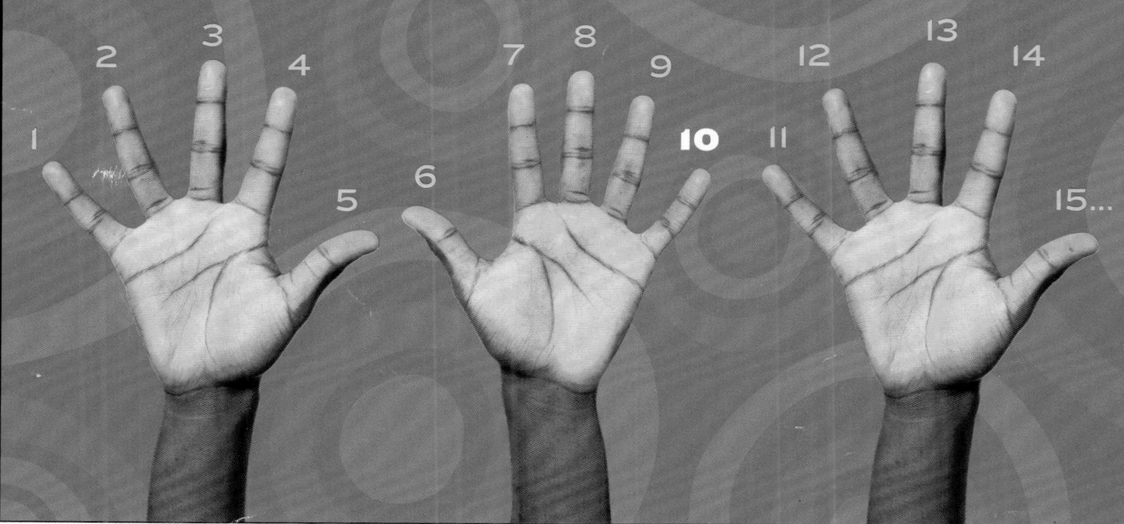

Our decimal number system—which is based on the numbers one through ten—was inspired by the ten fingers (and toes) of our ancestors. That's why the word digit means "finger" in many languages. If we had evolved with, say, seven fingers, we'd have a number system based on seven numbers (once we counted to seven, we'd move right to eleven). And it would seem totally natural to us.

WHY do I have a sense of TASTE?

Scientists have determined that the human tongue is attuned to several flavors: sweet, salty, bitter, sour, savory (think soy sauce), and possibly fat.

Telling the difference between these tastes was crucial to our prehistoric survival. Bitter flavors, for instance, may have signaled a poisonous plant. Sour tastes indicated a spoiled supper. Sweet, savory, and fatty flavors were tied to foods with a lot of energy.

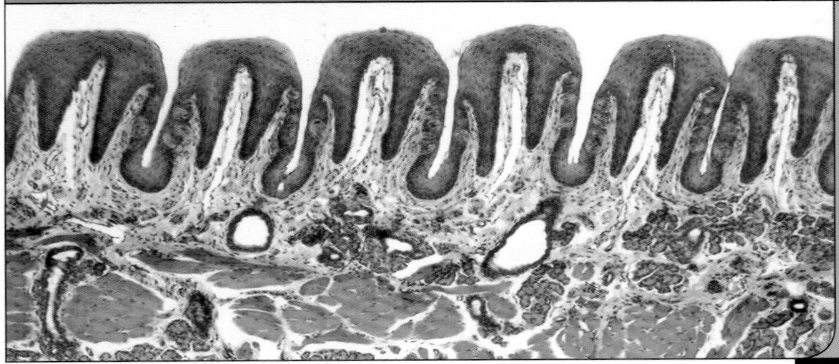

Okay, but... How do I taste my food?

Your tongue bristles with tiny bumps called taste buds: chemical receptors that interpret flavors and transmit that information to your noggin. Our sense of smell also greatly enhances the flavor of our food.

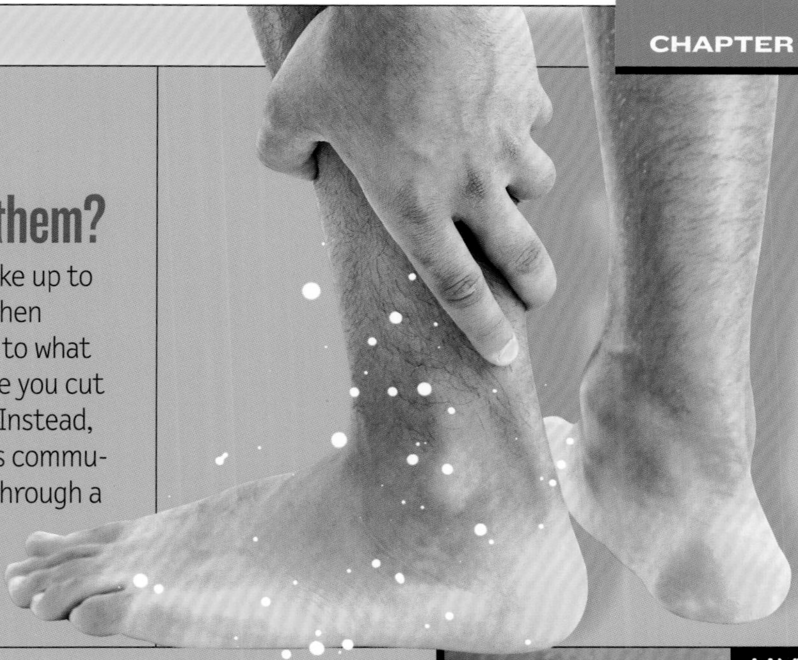

Why do my arms or legs get tingly when I lie on them?

Roll onto your arm in your sleep and you'll likely wake up to find it numb and lifeless, as if it wants to sleep in. Then comes the sensation of pins and needles. Contrary to what you might think, limbs don't go limp simply because you cut off their blood supply when you lie on them wrong. Instead, you're pressing on nerves and cutting off the limb's communication with the brain. Roll off and the nerves go through a sort of "reboot," sending pulses to the brain that you perceive as that tingly feeling. The lazy limb comes back online in short order.

Why do I start sneezing when I step into sunlight?

You must have a "photic sneeze reflex," a condition that causes you to sneeze uncontrollably when suddenly exposed to bright light. About one in five people have it, although scientists aren't sure why.

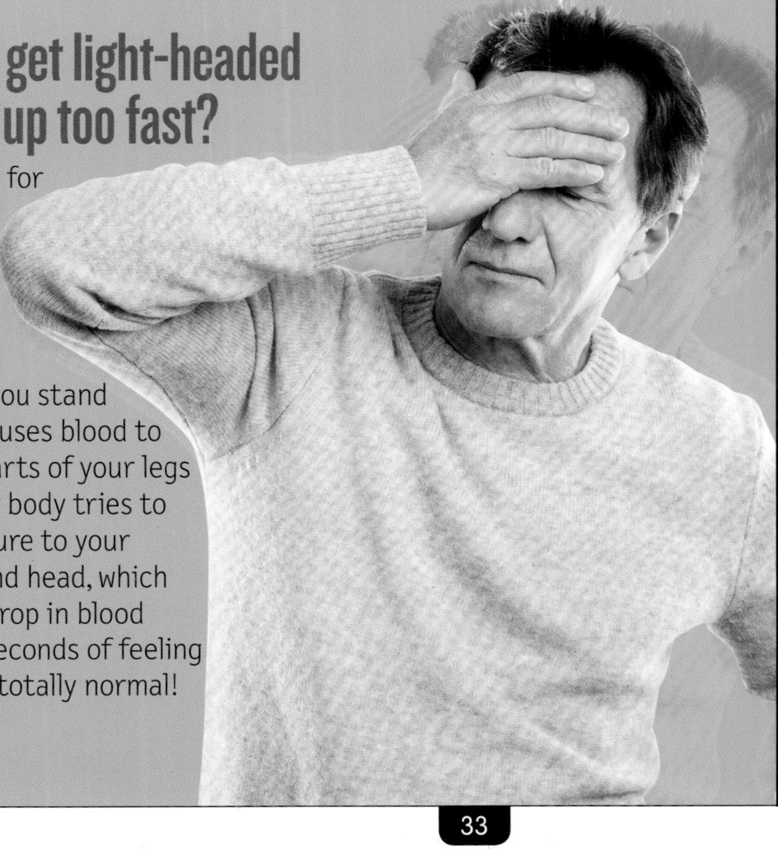

Why do I get light-headed when I stand up too fast?

Doctors have a name for that fuzzy feeling in your head when you leap to your feet from a sitting position: "orthostatic hypotension." When you stand up quickly, gravity causes blood to settle in the lower parts of your legs and lower torso. Your body tries to equalize blood pressure to your upper torso, arms, and head, which results in a sudden drop in blood pressure and a few seconds of feeling faint. Fear not—it's totally normal!

MYTH MASHED

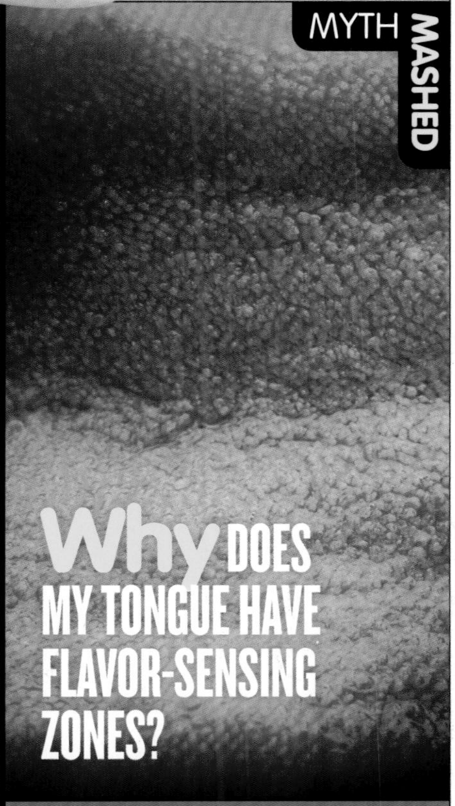

Why DOES MY TONGUE HAVE FLAVOR-SENSING ZONES?

It doesn't! People used to think that different clusters of taste buds around your tongue were tuned into different flavors (sweet and salty in the front, bitter in the back), but recent studies debunked this "taste bud map." With only slight variations, every taste bud on your tongue is capable of sensing all the flavors. The center of your tongue, meanwhile, is a tasteless place, free of taste buds.

WHY do I get dizzy when I SPIN?

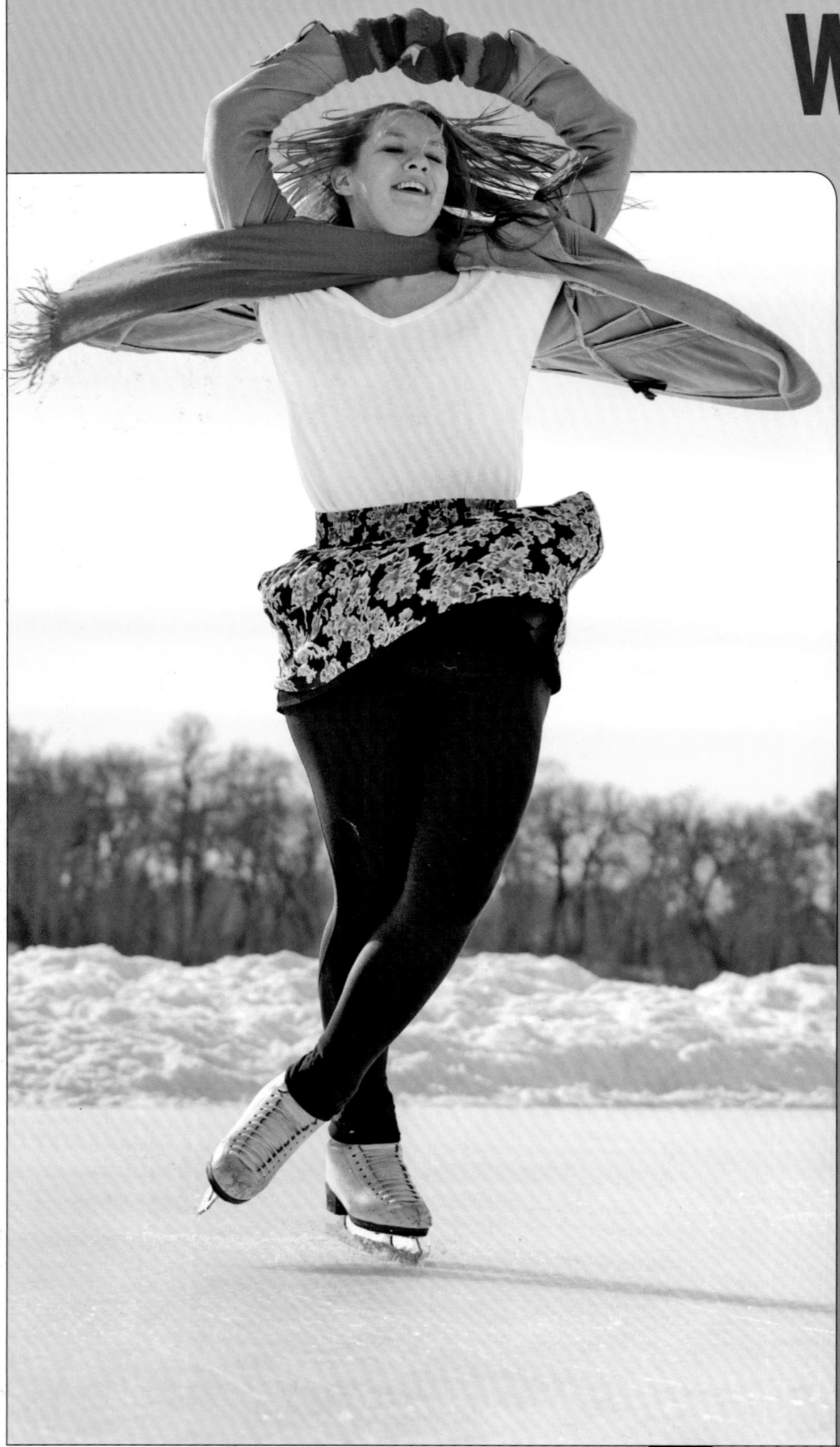

Your ears do more than just hear your brother's burps and act as earring supports. They contain special organs that help you detect your motion, tell up from down, and keep you from tumbling when you trip. Whenever you move or tilt your head, fluid moving through canals in your inner ear interacts with tiny hairs along the canal walls, telling your brain that you're in motion. When you spin in circles, the fluid spins right along with you. Stop and the fluid keeps spinning, sloshing against the hairs and making your brain think you're still spinning—which causes the feeling of dizziness.

Why do my ears pop on a plane (or when I'm riding up a mountain)?

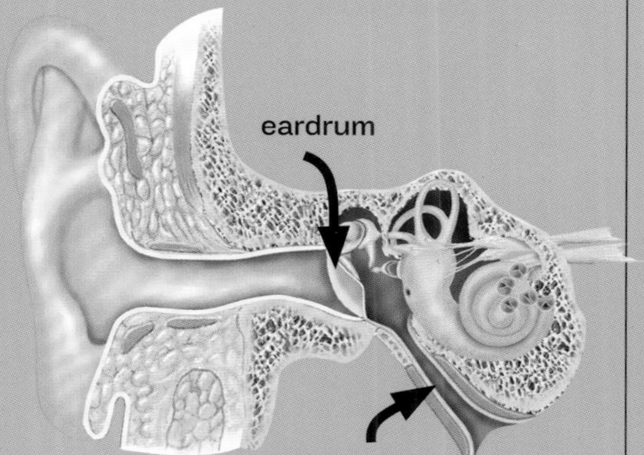

Plane cabins are pumped with air to simulate altitudes of around 7,000 feet (2 km) rather than sea level, and it takes 20 minutes or so for a plane to reach its cruising altitude and interior pressure setting. That means passengers typically experience a gradual decrease in air pressure at the beginning of a flight and a gradual increase at the end, provided the destination airport is lower than 7,000 feet (2 km). That gradual change in pressure is similar to what you feel when cruising up or down mountain roads or riding up or down a tall building in a fast elevator.

Behind your eardrums are small air-filled chambers that connect to your throat through tiny tubes. When the air pressure outside your eardrum changes, air moves through the tiny tubes to equalize the pressure inside your head. That movement of air creates a popping sensation. Sometimes, if you have a cold or allergies gumming up your noggin's empty spaces, your ears won't equalize quickly enough, causing louder pops and bursts of pain as air presses against your eardrum.

Why do my ears hurt when I dive underwater?

For the same reason that your ears might ache when you take off in a plane: The pressure outside your ear (in this case, water pressure) is greater than the air pressure inside your ear, causing your eardrum to bend painfully inward. Changes in water pressure happen much more rapidly than changes in air pressure, however, and your ears will begin to ache in as little as 5 feet (1.5 m) of water.

SAY WHAT?!

YOU GET DIZZY when you spin, but dolphins don't. That's how they can get away with lightning-fast underwater loops, barrel rolls, and other flip-through-the-air acrobatics that would make humans lose their lunch.

Q: tips

How CAN I STOP MY EARS FROM POPPING WHEN I'M FLYING OR UNDERWATER DIVING?

- Chewing gum during takeoff and landing on a plane helps equalize your ears during the periods where the pressure changes the most rapidly.
- If you don't have any gum, try moving your jaw back and forth, sniffing rapidly, or yawning.
- If you need to travel with a cold or allergies, ask your parents about taking a decongestant before your flight to help clear your ear tubes.
- Some people can clear their ears underwater by moving their jaws.

WHAT are GERMS?

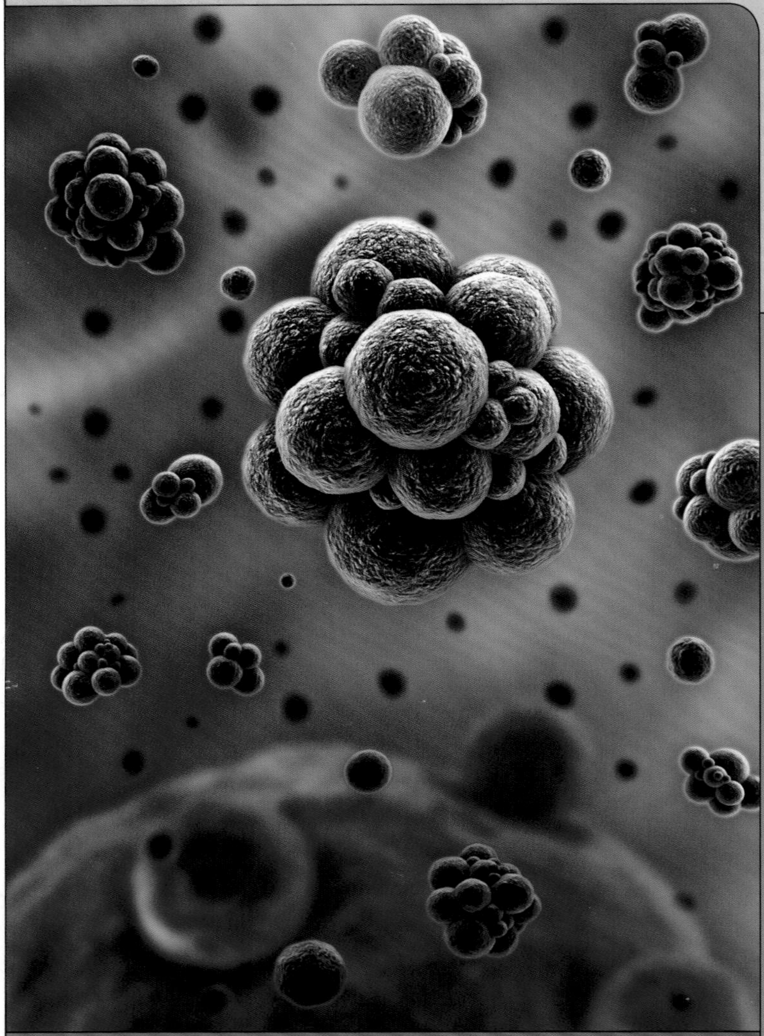

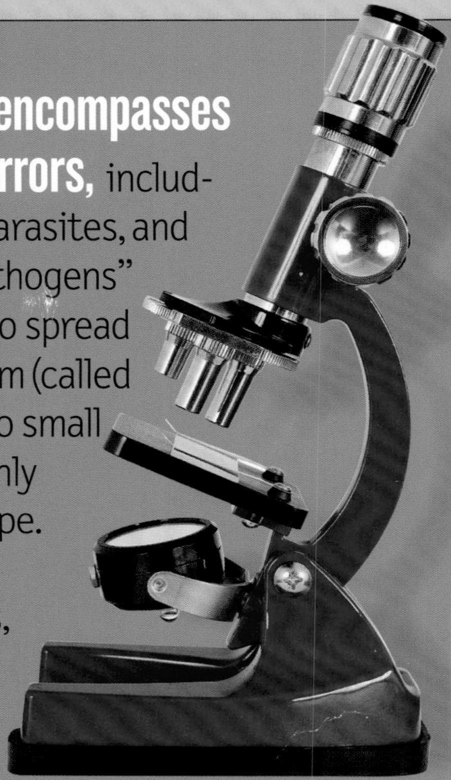

The term "germ" encompasses an army of tiny terrors, including viruses, fungi, parasites, and bacteria. These "pathogens" all have the ability to spread from victim to victim (called a host). Germs are so small you can see them only through a microscope. They look like spiky blobs, oozing spirals, hairy hot dogs, or other microscopic monsters.

Why ARE GERMS BAD FOR US?

These microorganisms hitch a ride into our bodies on the food we eat, in the air we breathe, or through a variety of other methods. Once they've invaded our personal spaces, germs reproduce and create toxic waste, which triggers our body's most repulsive reactions. They make us sniffle, upchuck, run to the toilet, break out in rashes and fevers, and suffer even more unpleasant symptoms.

How do we get sick from ...

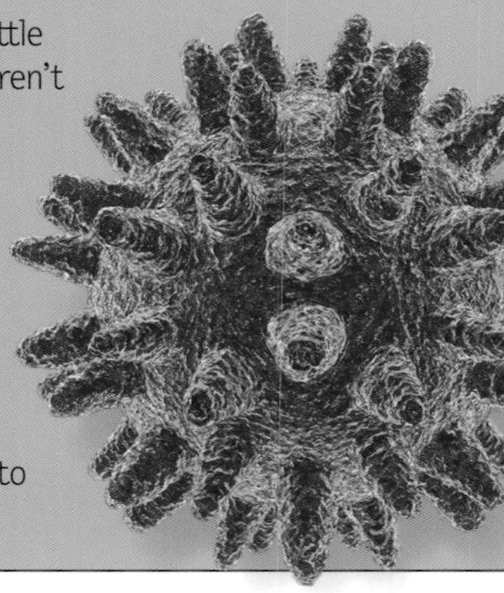

... viruses? Most viruses are frail little things (unlike bacteria and fungi, viruses aren't even alive) that can multiply only inside a living host (including animals, plants, and even bacteria). There they spread, overwhelming and attacking the host's immune system and causing all sorts of nasty symptoms. Colds, flus, chickenpox, immune disorders, and measles are caused by viruses. Among the worst is Ebola, which triggers bleeding and is fatal to more than half the people who catch it.

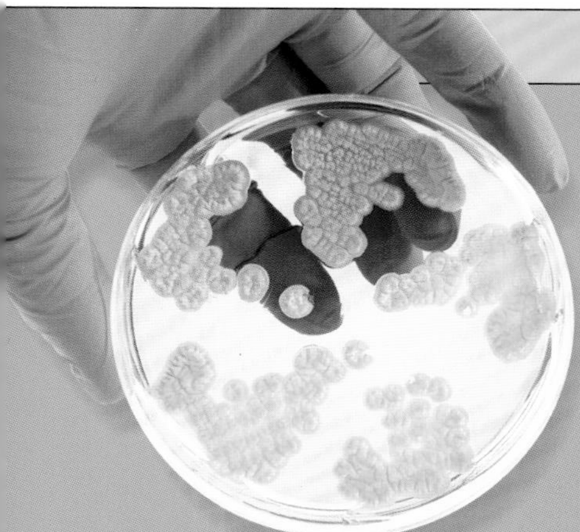

... fungi?

Fungi are microscopic molds, yeasts, and other plantlike pathogens that thrive in wet, warm places like our armpits, our belly buttons, and the dank spaces between our toes. They feed on our sweat and dead tissues and produce stinky wastes that irritate our skin.

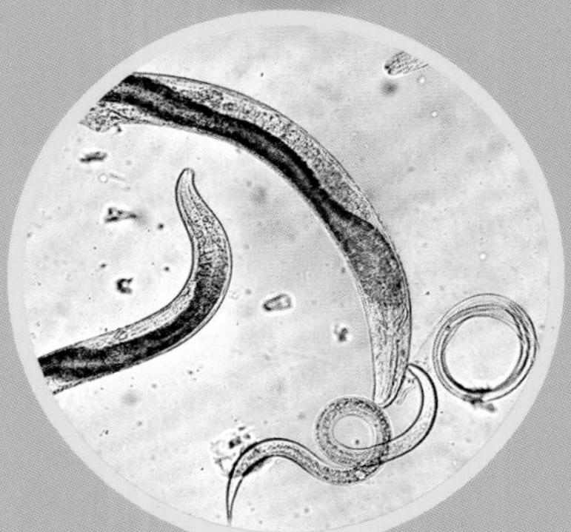

... parasites?

This ghastly germ group includes itty-bitty insect larvae, amoebas, and one-celled organisms called protozoa that live in nasty food, damp soil, or dirty water. Parasites depend on a living host for their survival. They sneak into our bodies in tainted water and food, causing us all sorts of gastro-intestinal gripes: diarrhea, vomiting, upset stomachs, and worse. Malaria—a common diseases that causes chills, shaking, and fevers—is spread by a parasite passed in mosquito bites. These life-sucking relationships are often the stuff of nightmares.

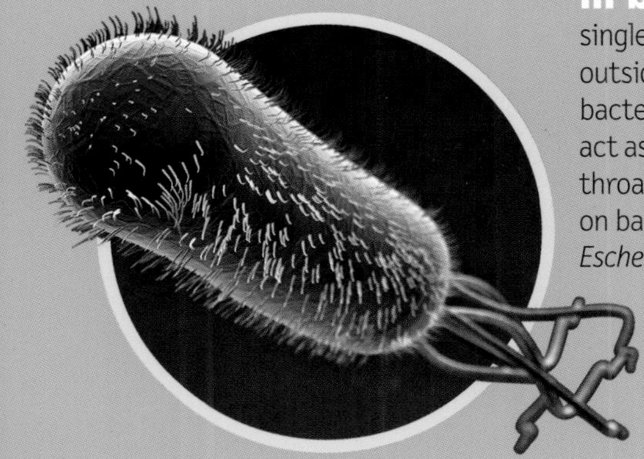

... bacteria?

Unlike viruses, bacteria are living single-celled organisms that can reproduce both outside and inside the body. Like all living things, bacteria create waste—microscopic poops that can act as a poison inside the host. You can blame sore throats, ear infections, and tooth-tartar buildup on bacteria. One of the most famous bacteria is *Escherichia coli*. This rod-shaped microbe lives deep in your intestines, the body's busiest bacterial neighborhood. Harmful ones make you puke for days. Helpful *E. coli* strains produce an important vitamin. That's right—some bacteria are actually good for you!

How many bacteria are inside my body right now?

Your body is built of trillions of itty-bitty living blobs, called cells, that work together to make you *you*. But for every cell you call your own, ten foreign bacteria cluster around or near it. You're a microbe metropolis! Scientists call these communities of foreign bacteria your body's "flora," and no two people host the same mix of microorganisms. In fact, scientists are beginning to think of your flora as just another organ.

That's a lot of bacteria! Can I see any of them?

No, they're microscopic. But you can certainly smell them. Like any living thing, bacteria eat, reproduce, die, and create waste, which can make your life stink—literally! (Bacteria are the source of bad breath and body odor.)

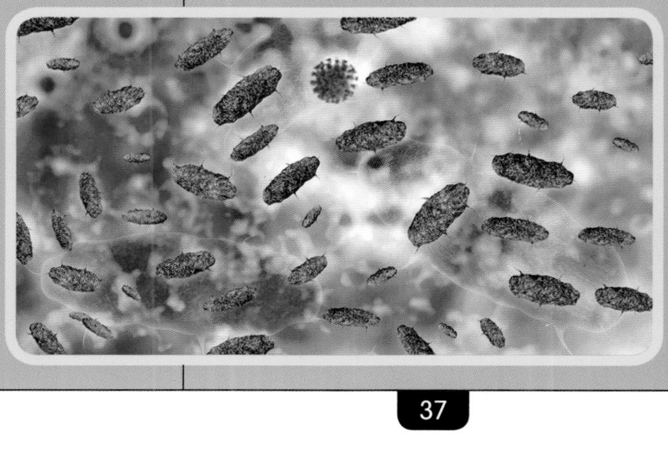

SMALL WONDERS

THE benefits OF BACTERIA

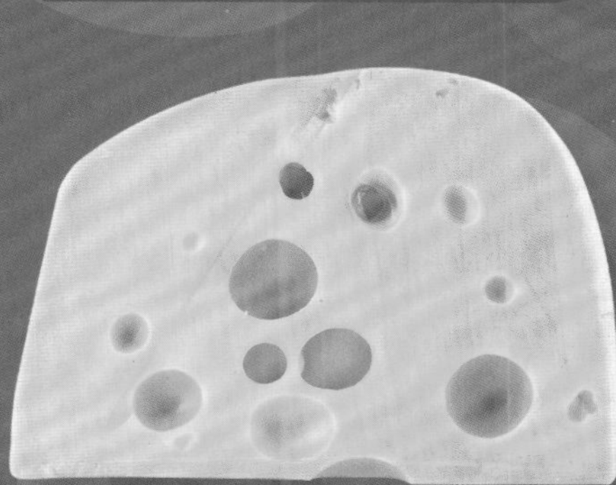

Your gut reaction might be to wrinkle your nose at the thought of bacteria inside your guts, but it turns out that many so-called good bacteria are essential to your health, the survival of life on Earth, and the making of tasty foods. Behold, the benefits of our microscopic allies ...

Health Boosting

Your body's microbes support your immune system, which fights sickness.

Plant Feeding

Blue-green algae and other types of bacteria convert the nitrogen in the air into compounds plants can use.

Food Processing

Microbes in our innards play a huge role in the digestive process, helping us absorb nutrients and vitamins from our food.

Food Making

Bacteria are a vital ingredient in the process of turning milk into yogurt and tasty cheeses. The holes in Swiss cheese are created by carbon dioxide bubbles exhaled by bacteria during the cheese-making process.

Planet Cleaning

Bacteria break down dead animals and plants, which "decompose" into nutrients for the living.

WHY do I SNEEZE?

Sometimes dust, flakes of dead skin, pollution, microbes, or your own booger buildup from a cold find their way into your nose's air passages. When mucous membranes in the lining of your nose detect these intruders, they send an urgent message to your brain: Unleash a sneeze!

How do I sneeze?

You don't have to do anything. Sneezing is a lightning-fast involuntary reaction, in which your chest, stomach, throat, and face muscles work together to blast particles from your nasal passages. The whole process lasts less than three seconds, and it propels spit, boogers, chewed food, and other particles from your nose and mouth at nearly 100 miles per hour (mph) or 161 kph.

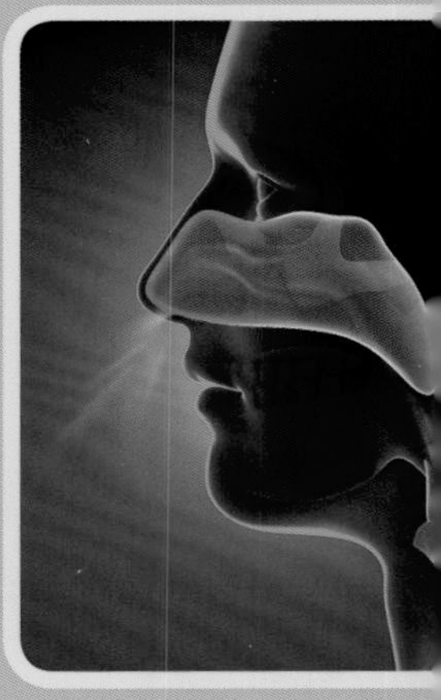

Why WOULDN'T MY EYEBALLS LAUNCH FROM MY HEAD IF I DIDN'T CLOSE THEM WHEN I SNEEZED?

MYTH MASHED

Fear not! Right before you unleash a sneeze, your brain automatically signals your eyes to shut tight. You have no control over the process, and your blinkers stay firmly in place.

Why do I upchuck when I get sick?

If you catch a stomach flu (usually a virus in your guts), swallow food spoiled by bacteria, or simply pig out until your body rebels, your stomach will kick into reverse to eject whatever's causing the trouble. Your guts churn, your head spins, and your throat begins to burn. Before you know it, *blaaargh!* You've launched your lunch! Clammy skin, waves of uneasiness, and a queasy feeling known as nausea usually precede puking, giving you a heads-up to hang your head over the toilet. Motion sickness—a condition brought on by winding roads, rocking boats, or back-to-back rides on the Tilt-a-Whirl—can lead to hurling, too.

Why does throw-up burn my throat?

Your stomach contains powerful acids that help break down food, and some of this sour-tasting gastric juice gets pumped up and away when you puke. Although a wave of spit and mucus helps protect your throat and mouth when you vomit, you'll still feel the burn. Particularly forceful barfing sessions will propel puke into your sinuses and out your nose, producing an eye-watering sting. Nasty!

Q: tips

How CAN I AVOID GERMS?

- Wash your hands with soap and water for at least 20 seconds after you touch any potentially infected surface or person.
- Don't touch your face after touching an infected surface. It's a surefire way to get sick!
- Get vaccinations for all the major germ-based illnesses from your doctor. A vaccine contains trace amounts of (or weakened) microbes that trigger your body into making "antibodies" to fight against specific diseases, making you immune to them.
- Be careful about sharing food or drinks with sick friends.
- If you get sick, remember: The inside of your elbow makes a great sneeze shield. You might coat your arm in snot, but at least you'll avoid infecting everyone in your launch zone!

Why hasn't medical science found a cure for the common cold?

You'd think curing a case of the sniffles would be a cinch for the scientists who invented artificial hearts and defeated lethal diseases like smallpox and polio. But eliminating the common cold is tricky because it's actually caused by more than 200 evolving viruses that all produce the same symptoms (whereas smallpox was caused by just one virus).

Why does my nose run when I get a cold?

Your nasal membranes make mucus—aka snot—and this sticky substance serves as security against germs, dust, and pollen particles that would make breathing difficult if they reached your lungs. Moved along by tiny nostril hairs called cilia, snot pummels and pushes invading particles toward the exit—your nostrils—or dumps them down your throat. Your body produces nearly two gallons (7.6 L) of mucus each week. You usually swallow all that snot without giving it a second thought. Catch a cold virus or come under an allergy attack, however, and the membranes pump up the volume. Your nose turns into a leaky snot faucet. You start coughing up globs of phlegm—a type of mucus produced in your throat and lungs. A hacking cough and runny nose are your body's ways of flushing all the bad stuff.

How are germs spread?

Every time an infected person coughs or sneezes, he or she spreads sickness. One sneeze alone can launch thousands of germ-jammed droplets nearly 20 feet (6 m), potentially infecting anyone in the blast radius. Bacteria and some viruses can survive for a short time on door handles, bathroom counters, and other surfaces.

Where do boogers come from?

Snot is sticky for a reason—it collects all the crud that gets up your nose. Once snot reaches the nostrils, it dries into crumbly little boogers for easy disposal. Polite people blow them into tissues; everyone else engages in rhinotillexis, the technical term for nose-picking.

WHY do I need to EAT?

This answer is obvious to anyone who's skipped breakfast and felt like the walking dead for the rest of the day.

Your body is a high-performance machine, and like any machine, it needs gas to go. That fuel comes in the form of nutrients—vitamins, minerals, carbohydrates, and fat—in your food. Through the process of digestion, your body turns carbohydrates into energy and proteins into building blocks to help you grow taller, build muscle, prevent illness, and have healthy hair, teeth, and skin. As you'd expect, healthy foods make the best fuel. Eat nothing but junk food and you'll ruin your engine.

How long could I go without eating?

That depends on many factors. Are you healthy? Skinny? Will you need to struggle until your next meal or just laze under a palm tree? People have survived more than ten weeks without food, but they had water and didn't need to move around too much. Starvation takes a horrible toll on the body, however, causing awful symptoms, from extreme weakness to hallucinations to spasms. And that's not even counting the pain. Ever forget to pack a lunch? Pangs of starvation are a hundred times worse than those of hunger.

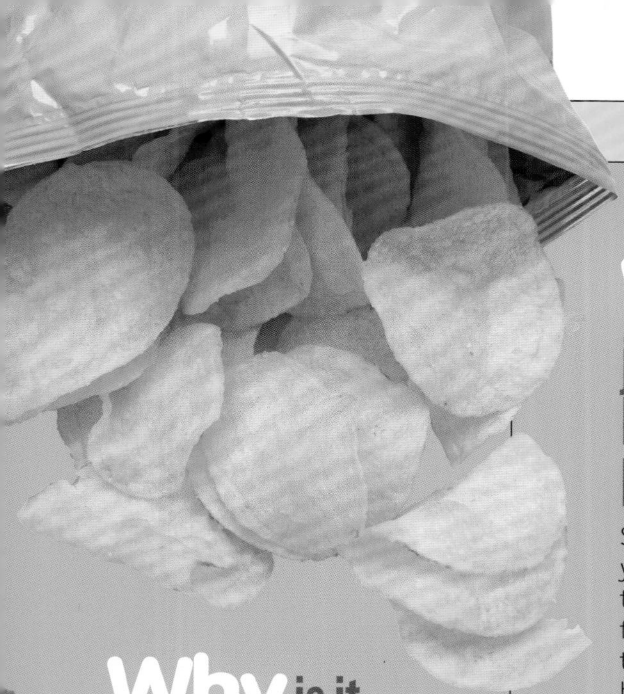

Why is it so hard to eat just one potato chip?

It's not the potato in the chip that drives your taste buds wild—it's the chip's salty flavor. Your body craves salt because it needs it to survive. (Salt helps your tissues stay hydrated and serves other vital functions.) Too much of a good thing can be bad, however. Consuming too much salt can lead to heart disease and other health risks.

Why does junk food taste better than healthy food?

Salt isn't the only substance your body craves. The human tongue prefers sweet, salty, and fatty flavors to the more subtle tastes of veggies, whole grains, beans, and other good-for-you foods. Sweet fruits and fatty meats pack a lot of energy, which was essential to our ancestors in the age before Twinkies, fast-food restaurants, and 24-hour convenience stores. Our bodies still crave these high-calorie foods (which is why they taste so good). Companies that make breakfast cereals, potato chips, candy bars, and other junk food are well aware of our cravings and tailor the tastes of their foods to trigger our addiction to sweets, salts, and fats.

Why does chopping onions make me cry?

Slicing into an onion releases a cloud of chemicals that react to form a burning chemical with a real mouthful of a name: syn-propanethial-S-oxide. Your eyes unleash reflex tears to hose off the irritants.

So, how can I hold back those tears?

Wear safety glasses if you don't want to tear up while slicing an onion. You'll look a little silly, but that beats looking like a crybaby.

Why DO I GET A HEADACHE WHEN I EAT SOMETHING COLD TOO QUICKLY?

Doctors have a name for that burst of brain pain that comes from gulping a cold treat on a hot day: "sphenopalatine ganglioneuralgia." The phenomenon is better known as brain freeze or an ice-cream headache—two names that do a great job of describing exactly what's happening in your head. Your mouth and tongue are loaded with blood vessels, including arteries at the back of the throat that circulate blood straight to your brain. Chugging an icy treat unleashes a mini-blizzard in your mouth, so the arteries near your throat constrict to protect your brain from an extreme temperature change. You feel that contraction as a brain freeze.

SO, HOW CAN I BEAT BRAIN FREEZE?

Go slow when you eat or drink something cold on a hot day. That'll help you avoid triggering an ice-cream headache in the first place. If you feel one coming on, jam your tongue against the top of your mouth, or drink something warm to counteract the effects of the frozen treat.

Why do I need to drink?

Proper hydration—drinking enough liquids—is even more important to your body than proper nutrition. Your body needs water to keep from overheating, lubricate the tissues, absorb nutrients, and flush waste.

How long can a person survive without water?

A healthy person can survive only five or six days without water—fewer days in hot climates.

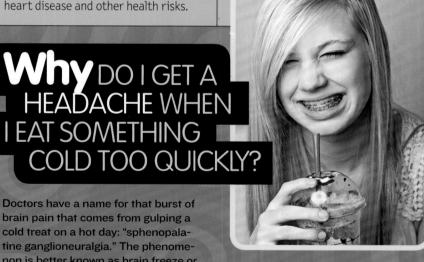

WHY does my belly GROWL when I get hungry?

Actually, your stomach and small intestines rumble all the time—even when you're not hungry—as food is moved through the digestive process. It's just that the rumble is louder when your belly's empty and not muffled by pizza crusts and burger bites.

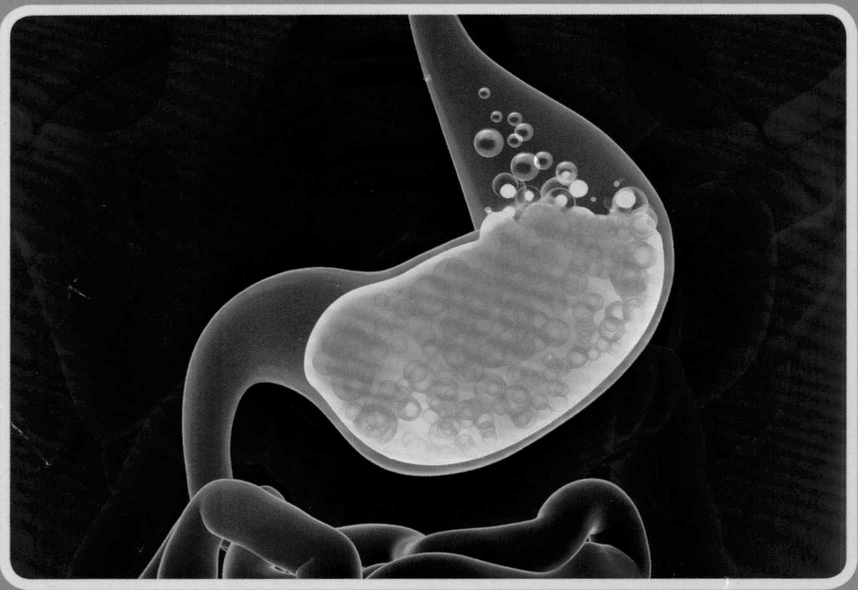

Why does my mouth water when I smell dinner?

Because your body is gearing up for digestion, the process that converts food into energy (and into some yucky stuff, too, but we'll get to that in a bit). Glands in your mouth secrete a watery substance called saliva (aka spit), which contains chemicals that help melt chewed food into slimy gobs of mush—each called a bolus—for easier swallowing. Your tongue herds every bolus to the back of your throat and drops it into your esophagus, a pipe that squeezes everything you eat into your stomach.

Why can I swallow food even when I'm hanging upside down?

When it comes to your digestive system, what goes down usually does not come up. Muscles in your food pipe (the esophagus) and stomach push everything you eat on to its next destination in the digestive system (which is why astronauts can snack in orbital free fall).

How does my body digest food?

The process of digestion that started in your mouth continues in your stomach. This expandable organ is lined with mighty muscles that pummel your food. A sea of gastric juices, meanwhile, dissolves your dinner into a thick paste called chyme (pronounced kyme), which dribbles slowly to its next port of call, the small intestine, where the bulk of digestion takes place. This 20-foot (6-m) tube coils through your abdomen and teams with other organs (along with colonies of bacteria) to absorb nutrients from everything you eat. It's followed by the large intestine, which sops up chyme's excess water and minerals.

Where DOES NUMBER TWO FIT INTO THIS PROCESS?

When enough processed digested food reaches your rectum—the launch chamber of the digestive system—you start to get that pressing feeling. Quick, grab a good book and find yourself a toilet!

What's in number two?

By the time that burger and fries you ate yesterday reaches the end of the large intestine, it's officially poop-in-waiting—a dry mass of indigestible fiber and dead bacteria (which is the source of excrement's eye-watering odor). Your poo is colored brown from waste iron and dead blood cells in your intestines.

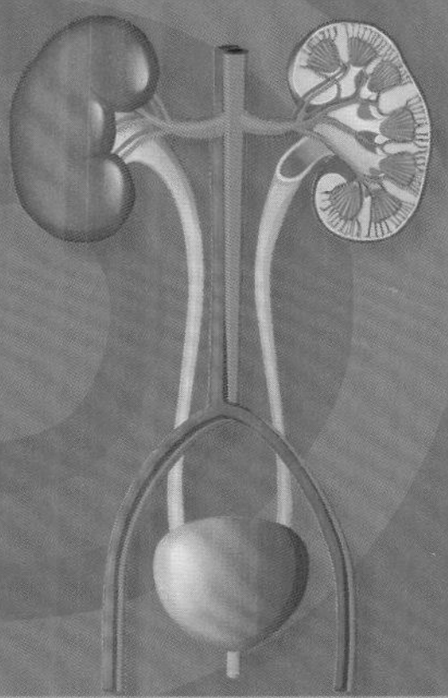

Why do I have to go number one?

All the bad stuff collected by your kidneys, along with any excess fluid, drains into a stretchy pouch called the bladder. As the bladder fills, it balloons in size until it reaches capacity—about a pint (473 mL) of fluid. A full bladder sends your brain into yellow alert and your legs scrambling for the nearest bathroom.

What's in number one?

Urine is made of water, urea (a waste product also found in sweat), salts, and other waste chemicals. A digestion-aiding chemical called bile gives pee its light yellow color, which becomes darker if you're thirsty. Oh, and, by the way...

Urine can turn reddish if you eat beets or blackberries.

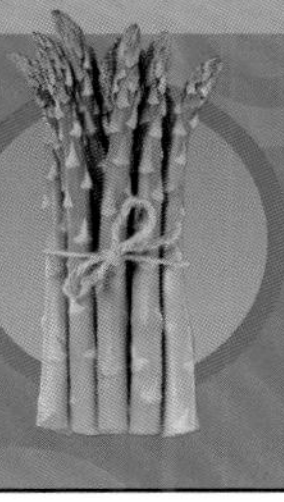

Gobbling down asparagus can make your pee extra smelly.

WHY do I TOOT?

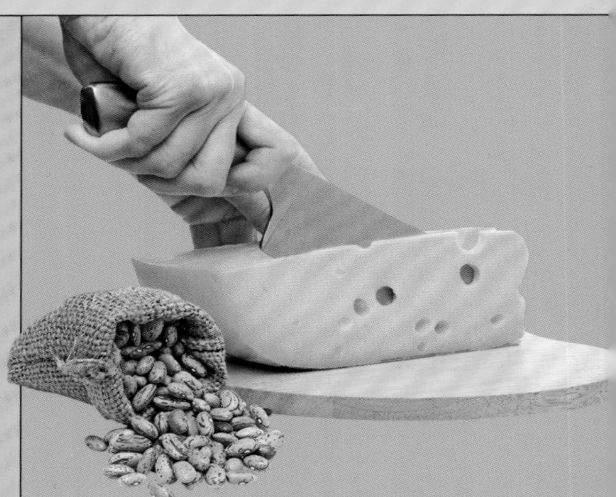

How often do people pass gas?

Between 13 and 21 times a day. You can up your flatulence frequency by munching on more dairy and wheat products, vegetables, and of course, beans.

No need to be speak in code—everybody passes gas. Most of your body's foul fog is pumped out by the billions of bacteria that live in your large intestine, aka your body's flatulence factory. These microorganisms excrete stinky gas as they help break down the food you eat. They cut all the cheese; you take all the blame.

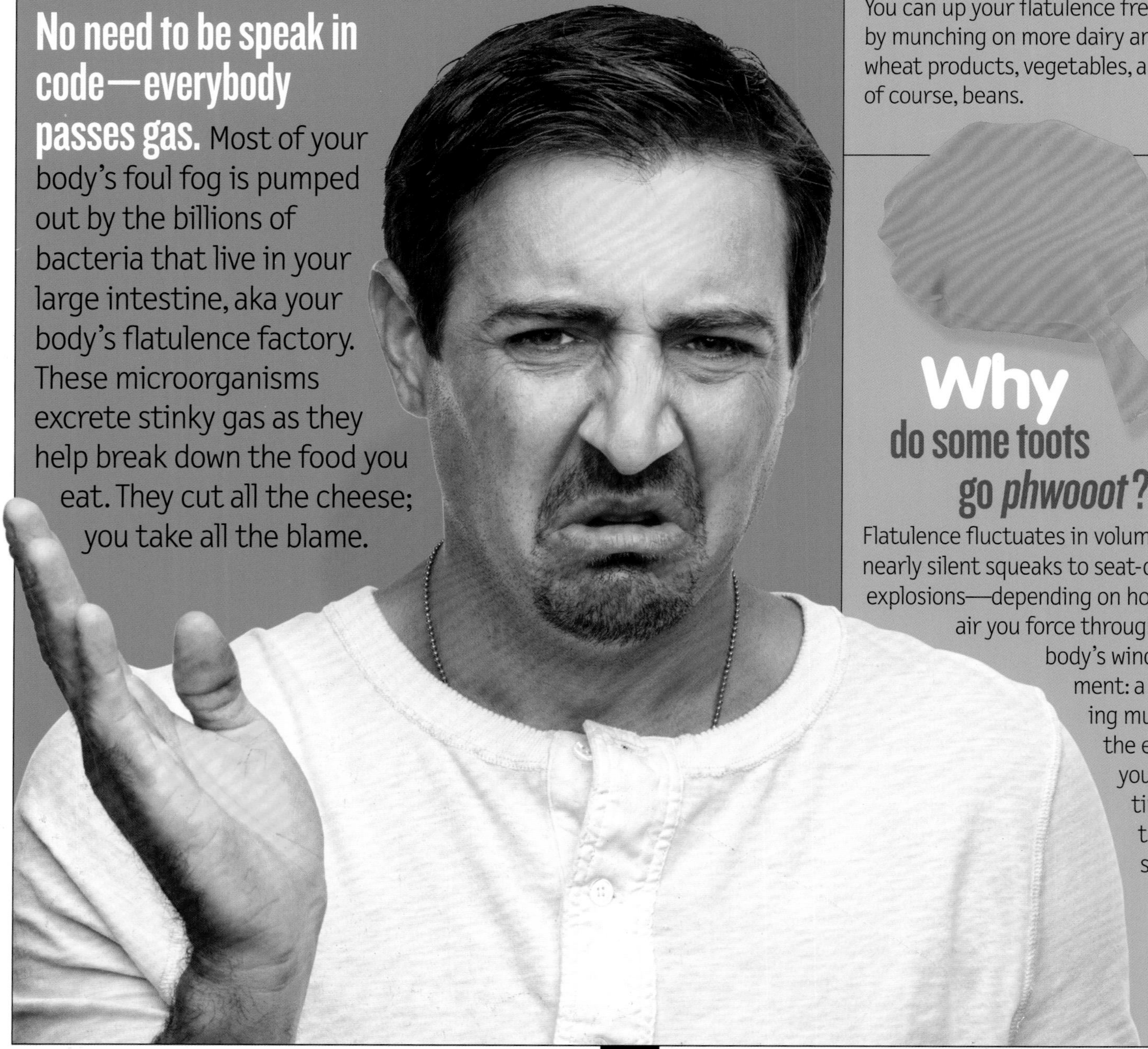

Why do some toots go *phwooot*?

Flatulence fluctuates in volume—from nearly silent squeaks to seat-quaking explosions—depending on how much air you force through your body's wind instrument: a puckering muscle at the end of your intestines called the anal sphincter.

Why do some toots make everyone around you go pee-yew?

What do you expect from air shared from your derriere? Although 99 percent of your flatulence is made of odorless gases, the remaining one percent can put tears in the eyes of passersby. Food-munching bacteria in your guts produce skatole (the source of poop's particular odor) and sulfides that give toots that rotten-egg aroma.

Is it possible to trigger a toot?

Sure, if you're a "flatulist"—a type of entertainer who can pass gas on command. The most famous professional tooter was Joseph Pujol, a 19th-century French "farto-maniac" who entertained royalty with his gas-summoning abilities. He could imitate thunderstorms and even play the flute with his "wind instrument."

Why do I burp?

You gulp a bit of air into your stomach every time you eat, drink, talk, chew gum, or yawn. When your belly balloons to its maximum capacity, it releases the bubbles back up your food tube (your esophagus) and out your mouth and nose. The result: *Brrraaap!* My, what a loud upper esophageal sphincter you have! (That's the flexible flap at the tip of your food tube that vibrates as it releases swallowed air from your stomach.)

How often do people burp?

Between 25 and 30 times each day. More if they drink bubbly beverages such as soda.

Q: tips

How can I get rid of the hiccups?

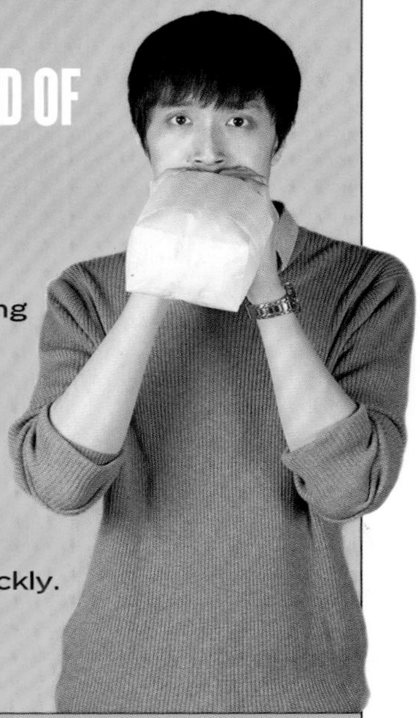

Hiccup remedies don't work for everyone, but here are some common techniques worth trying the next time your diaphragm gets stuck on repeat ...

- Hold your breath for 10 seconds.
- Breathe into a paper bag for 20 seconds.
- Drink a glass of cold water quickly.
- Put sugar under your tongue.
- Tickle the roof of your mouth.

But why don't burps stink like gas passed from your other end?

Burps get only the budget tour of your digestive system, dipping no deeper than your stomach, so they're mostly nothing but hot air. As a result, belches typically emerge from your mouth fragrance-free—unless you've eaten a spicy meal. What better way to let everyone know you had leftover pepperoni pizza for breakfast?

Why do I get the hiccups?

Hiccups happen when your diaphragm—a sheetlike muscle at the bottom of your chest that helps you suck air into your lungs—goes a little haywire, usually after eating too much or too quickly or when you get nervous. The diaphragm spasms, jerking air into your throat to make the familiar *hic-up* sound.

SAY WHAT?!

HATE THE HICCUPS? Imagine the ordeal of Iowa farmer Charles Osborne. He hiccuped every day for nearly 70 years (doctors think he damaged the hiccup-controlling part of his brain). Before he passed away in 1991, Osborne received thousands of letters with homemade remedies. One buddy even fired a double-barreled shotgun just out of sight, hoping to scare away the hiccups. (It didn't work.)

WHY do I get ZITS?

You body is covered with millions of hair follicles that pump out protective oils, but it takes just one clog to create a dreaded blemish. Bacteria, dead skin, oil, and white blood cells that gave their lives fighting infection combine into a repulsive white pus that erupts when you give the pimple a squeeze (which you should never do, unless you want to memorialize that zit with a scar).

Why do I sweat when I get hot or when I exercise?

Sweat is secreted from glands in your skin to cool your body and flush away waste. It's nature's air-conditioning!

Why does my sweat stink?

Sweat doesn't smell like anything until it's tainted by microorganisms living on your body. Your sweatier parts—your armpits and feet—offer a banquet for bacteria, which produce stinky micro-poop. Hence, B.O.—pee-yew!

Why do I get bad breath?

Blame the bacteria in your mouth. They made a midnight snack of the leftovers stuck on your teeth and between your gums, raising a royal stink with their secretions.

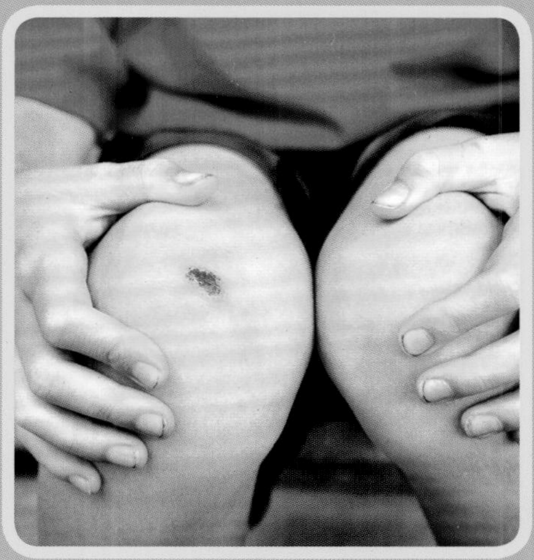

Why do cuts scab up?

The instant you suffer a scrape, cells in your blood rush to the wound and seal it. Eventually, this clot dries and hardens into a crusty protective scab. Resist the urge to pick it.

Why do I get dandruff?

Castaway skin cells atop your scalp collide and cluster in your hair like little snowballs until they finally dislodge in a blizzard of dead epidermis (that's the scientific name for your skin's outer layer).

Why does my belly button get linty?

That dank dent in your belly is like a magnet for dead skin cells and bits of clothing fiber. It all mixes together and becomes a breeding ground for bacteria. Scientist have discovered more than 2,300 species of microbes living in people's navels!

Where does toe jam come from?

Your sweaty gym sock is like a five-star spa for fungus, which squeezes under your toenails and causes a burning itch. Between your toes, bacteria combine with lint to create a smelly, cheesy, absolutely sickening substance called toe jam.

Why do I get wax in my ears?

In this case, gross is good! Your ear canal secretes this waxy stuff to collect and clear out other crud: dust, dirt, and germs. Eventually the wax, along with its nasty cargo, works its way out of your ear canal.

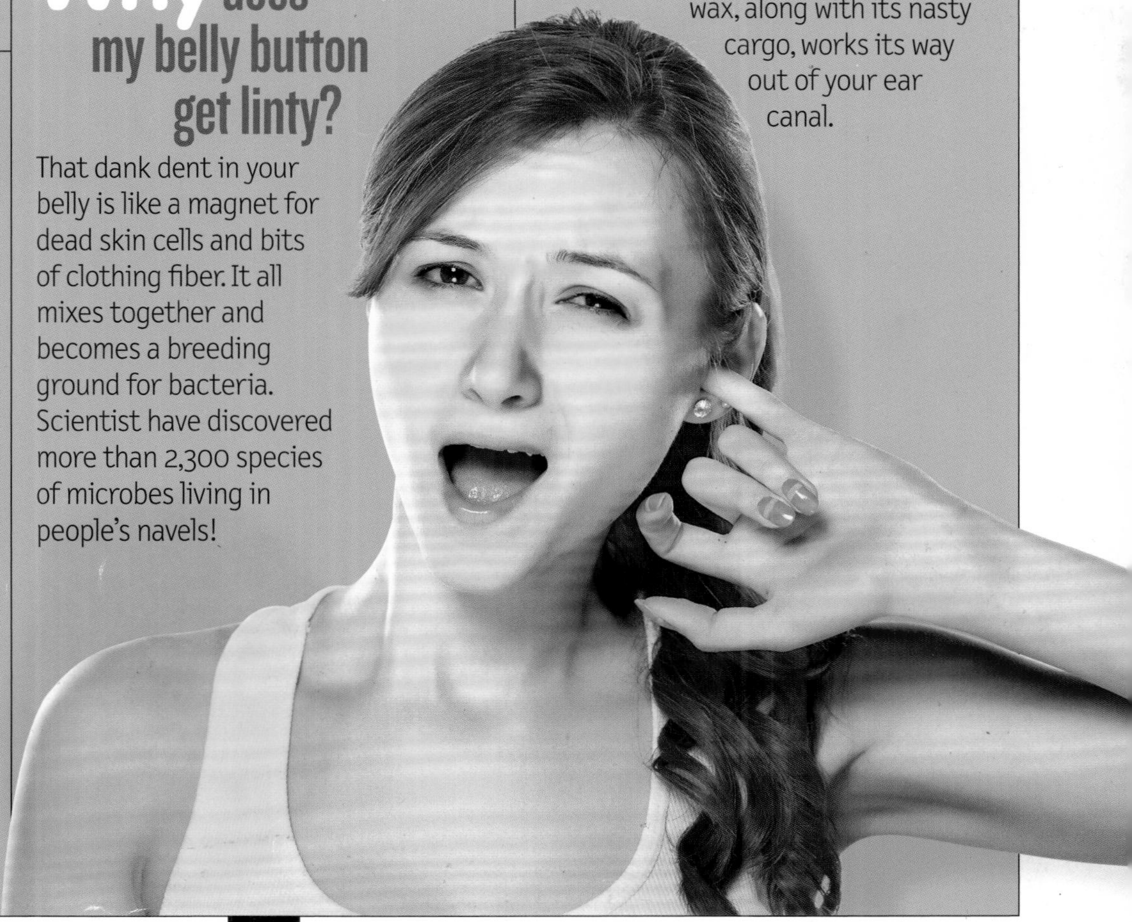

WHY do we get OLD?

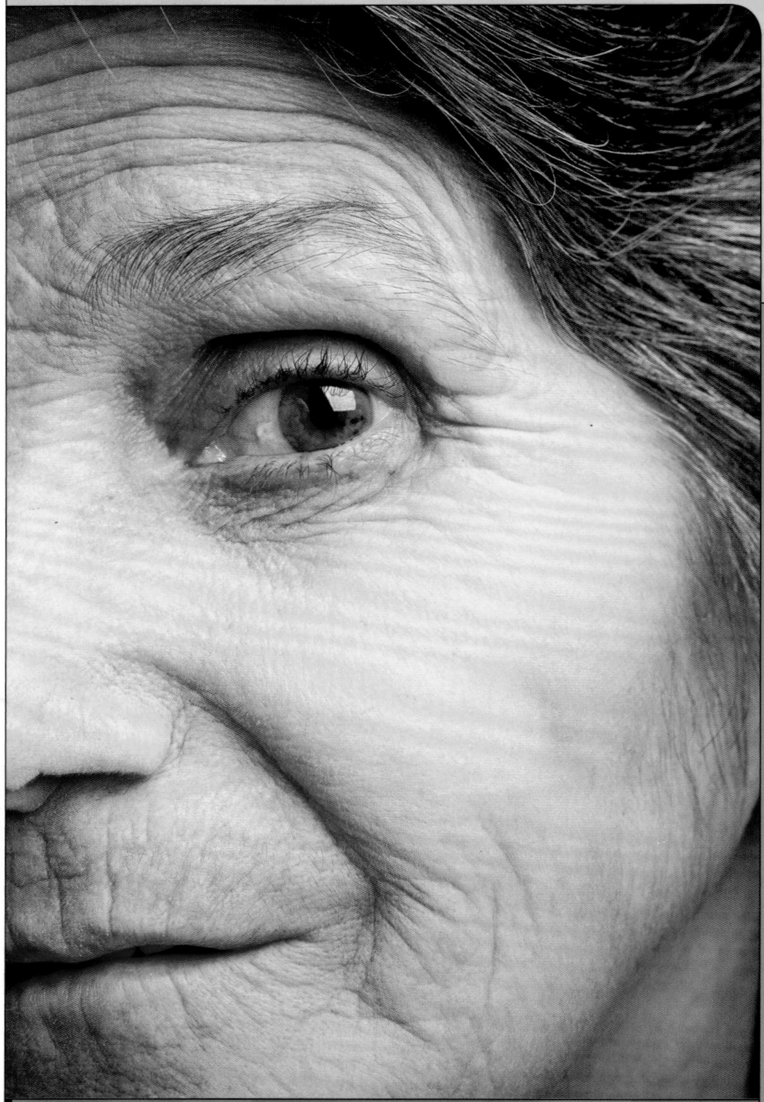

The aging process is a real head-scratcher for scientists. Healthy humans are capable of healing their injuries, recovering from illnesses, and replicating their cells again and again. Why can't this process continue forever? Old age and death are hardly helpful to our species' survival, after all. Scientists have studied nearly every type of animal—from short-lived fruit flies to age-defying flatworms—to unravel this mystery.

According to one theory, our life span is programmed into our DNA, which jump-starts the aging process once we're beyond our reproductive years. (Scientists tinkering with the age-related genes in some worms have been able to dramatically increase their life spans.) Another theory holds that your cells have a sort of expiration date and can only reproduce so many times. Some scientists believe that the longer you live, the more damage your body racks up. Eventually, the "human machine" becomes so bogged down with glitches that it can no longer repair itself properly. Likely, a combination of these theories can explain the aging process.

Our life span is also affected by many factors outside our bodies. How we eat, where we live—even whether we marry—can influence our body's expiration date.

HOW LONG WAS THE AVERAGE LIFE SPAN ...

... IN ANCIENT EGYPT?	40 YEARS
... IN MEDIEVAL TIMES?	45 YEARS
... DURING THE LATE 1800S?	40 YEARS
... TODAY?	80 YEARS

Who WAS THE OLDEST HUMAN?

A French woman named Jeanne Calment lived 122 years and 164 days, making her the world's oldest human at the time of her passing in 1997 (according to Guinness World Records). She credited her routine snacking on chocolate (among other things) for her amazing life span. Meanwhile, a Bolivian man named Carmelo Flores Laura may have surpassed Calment's record. Government documents show that Flores was born in 1890—which would make him older than Calment when she passed away. Flores didn't have his original birth certificate, though, casting doubt on his true age. He died in 2014.

As they get older, why do some people ...

... lose their hair? More than half of all men at some point in their lives will lose their locks to "male-pattern baldness," a genetic condition inherited from either Mom or Dad. High amounts of a particular hormone (or chemical in their body) cause hair follicles on the head to wither and die.

... go gray? Special cells in your follicles—your body's hair-producing factories—produce melanin, the pigment responsible for your hair's color. These cells begin to die as you age, leaving your hair white or gray. As with baldness, the age at which you begin to gray is determined by your genetics. If your parents had gray hair in their mid-30s or 40s, chances are you will, too.

... get wrinkles? Once you reach adulthood, your skin stops growing. It loses its elasticity, taking a little longer to spring back into shape when you laugh or furrow your brow. Wrinkles form as your skin starts to sag in old age. A lifetime of smiling leaves wrinkles alongside your eyes (called "crow's feet").

... suffer from bad eyesight? Our eye muscles weaken as we age—which is why you often see older people with glasses.

... develop a potbelly? Your body is built to store energy as fat, a holdover from an age when securing your next meal wasn't as easy as tossing a burrito in the microwave. As we age, our metabolism—the process that converts food into energy—slows down, meaning we must exercise more frequently to keep flab from forming.

Can we stop the aging process?

Immortality—the ability to live forever—has been a dream since before the days of Ponce de León and his legendary quest for the Fountain of Youth. It turns out that fountain might be right around the corner. In the next 20 to 30 years, doctors could begin injecting patients with microscopic medical robots—called nanobots—that will swim through the bloodstream like a swarm of mechanical bees, replacing old cells and curing diseases. Routine nanobot injections could increase your life span by hundreds of years.

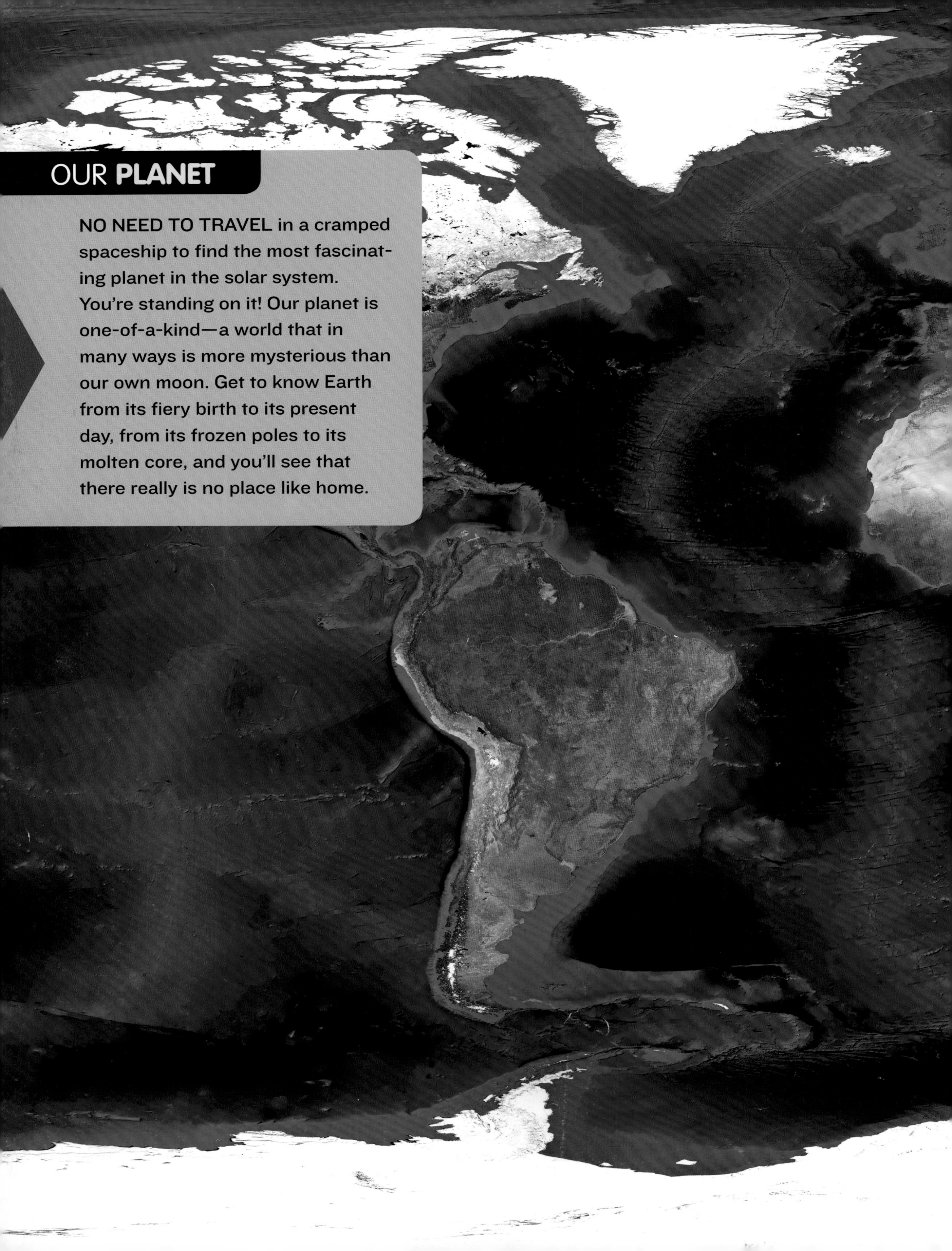

OUR **PLANET**

NO NEED TO TRAVEL in a cramped spaceship to find the most fascinating planet in the solar system. You're standing on it! Our planet is one-of-a-kind—a world that in many ways is more mysterious than our own moon. Get to know Earth from its fiery birth to its present day, from its frozen poles to its molten core, and you'll see that there really is no place like home.

2

WHY ON EARTH?

WHY is Earth SPECIAL?

Earth is a special spot in the solar system for so many reasons—its sprawling continents, its blue seas, its nearly limitless variety of ice-cream flavors. But one earthly thing stands out above the rest: its Earthlings. Ours is the only planet currently known to harbor life. In fact, Earth's unique combination of air, water, and land nurtures life of every sort, from microscopic amoebas to submarine-size blue whales.

What conditions on Earth make it so favorable for life?

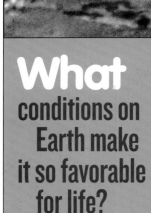

Earth's atmosphere not only provides the right mix of breathable air for animals and plants, but it—combined with an oxygen-rich ozone layer and the planet's electromagnetic field—also acts as a force field against solar radiation and deadly space debris. The solar system's other planets are typically too hot or too cold to supp[illegible]rth is just right. Oceans cover nearly 70 percent of the planet's [illegible] of the water vapor responsible for our weather.

PERSON OF INTEREST

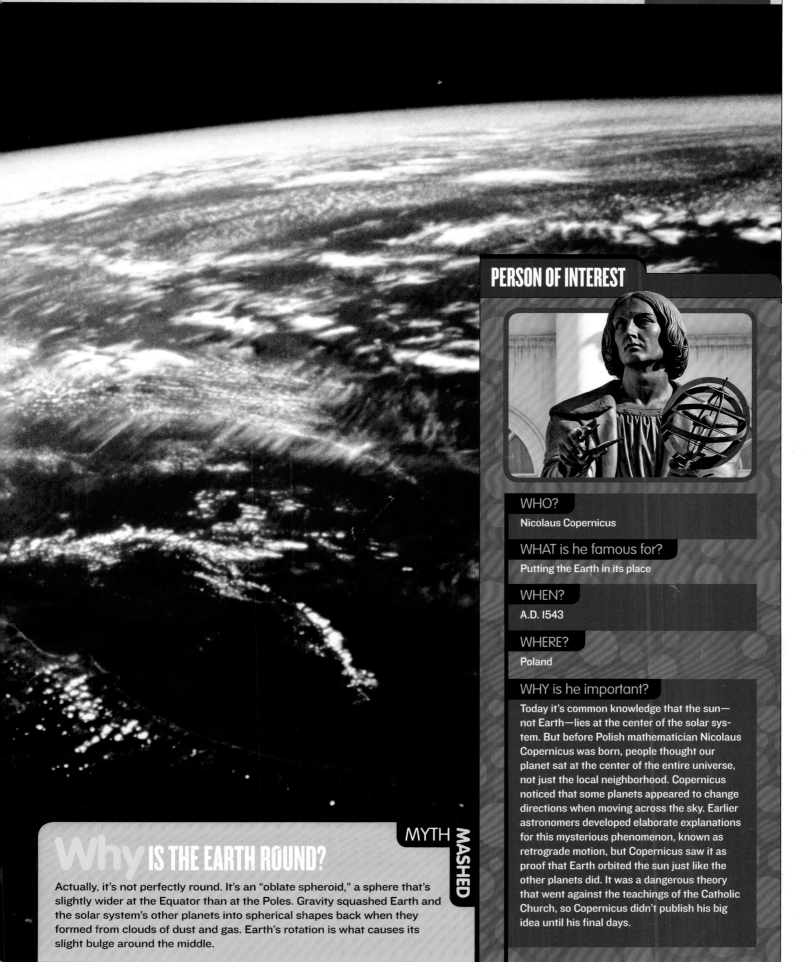

WHO?

Nicolaus Copernicus

WHAT is he famous for?

Putting the Earth in its place

WHEN?

A.D. 1543

WHERE?

Poland

WHY is he important?

Today it's common knowledge that the sun—not Earth—lies at the center of the solar system. But before Polish mathematician Nicolaus Copernicus was born, people thought our planet sat at the center of the entire universe, not just the local neighborhood. Copernicus noticed that some planets appeared to change directions when moving across the sky. Earlier astronomers developed elaborate explanations for this mysterious phenomenon, known as retrograde motion, but Copernicus saw it as proof that Earth orbited the sun just like the other planets did. It was a dangerous theory that went against the teachings of the Catholic Church, so Copernicus didn't publish his big idea until his final days.

MYTH MASHED

Why IS THE EARTH ROUND?

Actually, it's not perfectly round. It's an "oblate spheroid," a sphere that's slightly wider at the Equator than at the Poles. Gravity squashed Earth and the solar system's other planets into spherical shapes back when they formed from clouds of dust and gas. Earth's rotation is what causes its slight bulge around the middle.

WHAT makes the world go AROUND?

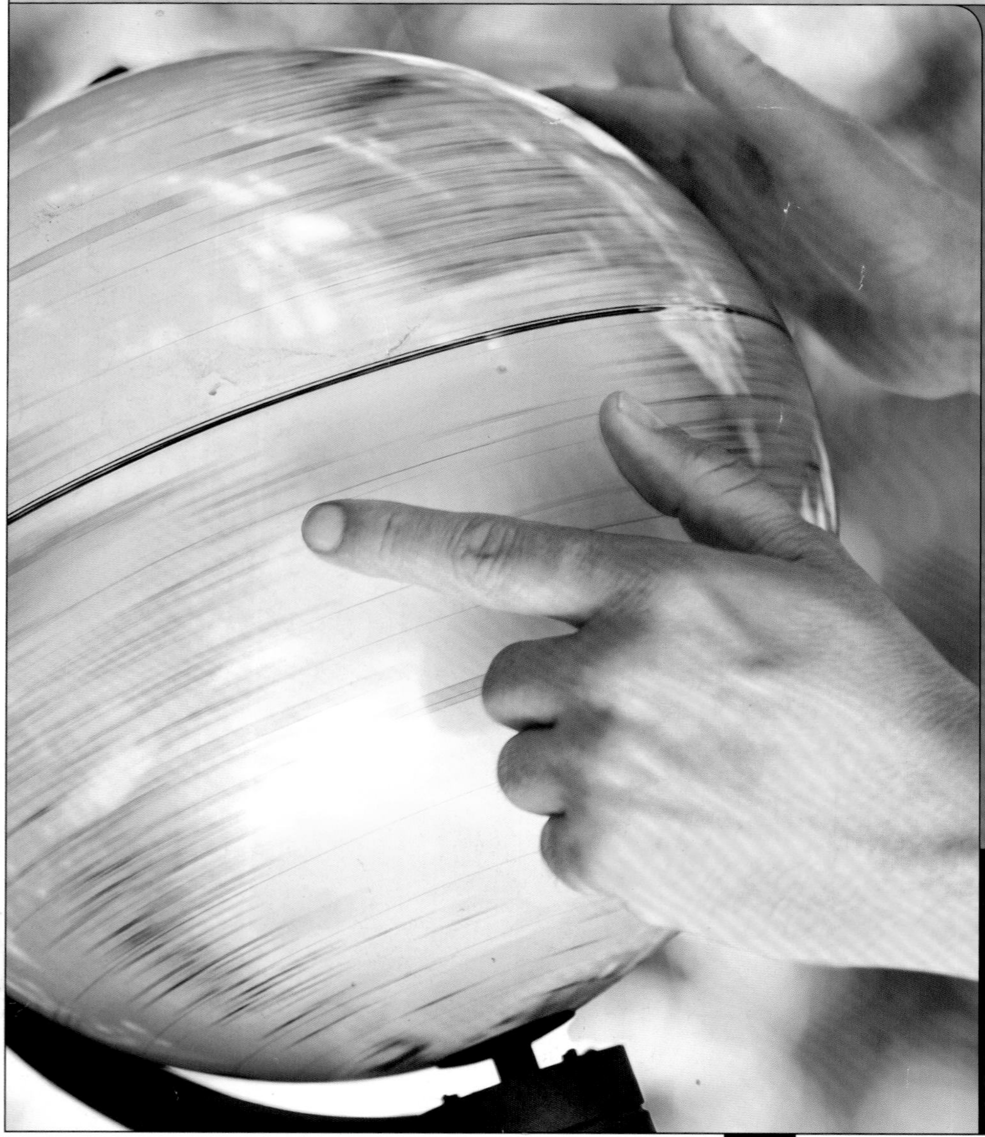

Earth's rotation is a side effect of the formation of our solar system, which started as a massive cloud of gas and dust roughly 4.6 billion years ago. The cloud began to rotate as it scrunched together under its own gravity. The material at the center eventually became the sun, while whirlpools of dust and gas farther out spun faster and faster until they formed into planets. With nothing to stop its spinning motion, Earth retained the rotation from its early days.

SAY WHAT?!

OUR PLANET'S rotation is actually decreasing because of the moon's gravitation pull. Worry not—it will take millions of years for us to notice that our days and nights are just the teeniest bit longer.

How fast does the Earth spin?

Along the Equator—the imaginary line halfway between the North and South Poles—Earth rotates at 1,037 mph (1,670 kph), a speed rivaling that of a fighter jet at full cruise.

Why does the Earth spin fastest at the Equator?

That's where the Earth is widest along its axis, so any point along the Equator has a greater distance to travel during each daily rotation than any point closer to the Poles. Still confused? Think of a merry-go-round. The horses on the outside have a greater distance to travel around the carousel—and thus move faster—than the horses on the inside.

Why don't I feel the Earth spinning?

There are two reasons: gravity and the fact that you're traveling at the same speed as the ground beneath your feet. Just as airplane passengers don't sense the forward motion of the aircraft they're riding in (unless it suddenly speeds up or slows down), we don't notice the rate of Earth's rotation. We're traveling along Earth's surface as it spins and held to the surface by its gravity—along with the atmosphere around us, the bicycles and cars on the road, and the birds in the sky.

SAY WHAT?!

SPACE AGENCIES, like NASA, build their launch facilities closer to the Equator to take advantage of Earth's faster rotation, which gives rockets and shuttles a speed boost into orbit.

What WOULD HAPPEN IF THE EARTH SUDDENLY STOPPED SPINNING?

Buildings would topple. Mountains would crumble. Seas would slosh into your bedroom. If Earth suddenly put on the brakes, everything and everyone on it would suddenly hurl in the direction of the planet's former spin. (People who live closer to the Equator—where Earth's spin is the fastest—would have the roughest ride.) Gravity would keep us from flying into space, but Earth would become a different place—even for those who live far from the Equator. For starters, the worldwide system of time zones (created to adjust local time based on the Earth's rotation) would change drastically. A day would last a year (it would now take 365 days for the sun to return to its original place in the sky). Crops would wither. We'd all need to slather on heavy-duty sunscreen to survive six months of sunlight before bundling up for six months of night. The good news is that this nightmare scenario is a virtual impossibility.

WHY is it SUMMER in Australia when it's WINTER in Europe?

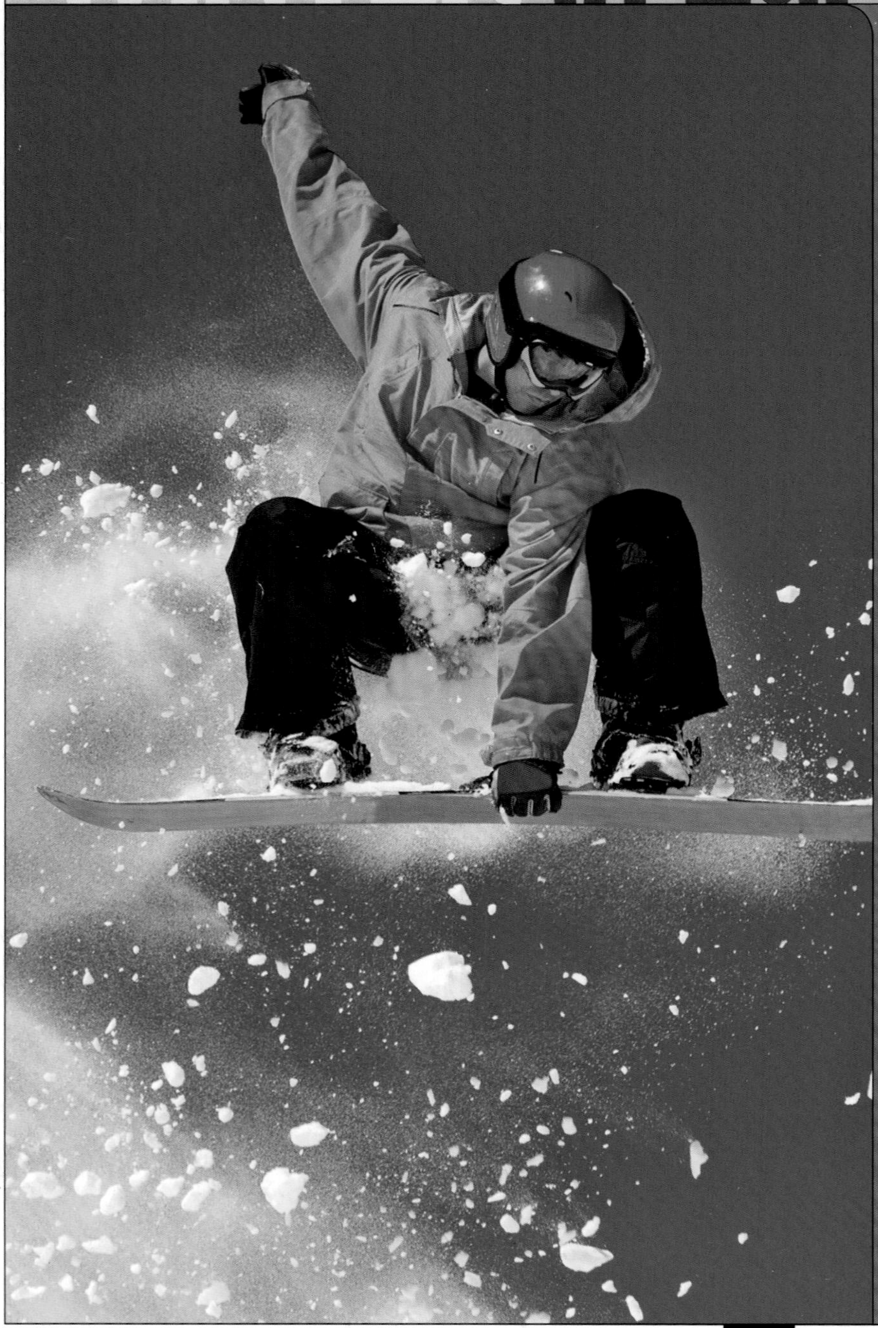

We have four seasons because the Earth doesn't sit up straight: It's tilted on its axis. As it orbits the sun, the planet's slight slouch exposes more or less of the Northern and Southern Hemispheres to the sun, depending on the time of year. When the South Pole is pointed toward the sun, Australia and other countries south of the Equator receive more direct sun exposure, resulting in warm summer temperatures. At the same time, the North Pole is pointed away from the sun, reducing sun exposure and making for chilly winter temperatures. The farther you are from the Equator, the greater this seasonal effect.

Why are days longer in the summer and shorter in the winter?

Again, blame Earth's bad posture. Remember, the North Pole is tilted toward the sun for half the year, while the South Pole tilts toward the sun for the other half. People living in the hemisphere angled toward the sun experience longer days and shorter nights.

MYTH MASHED

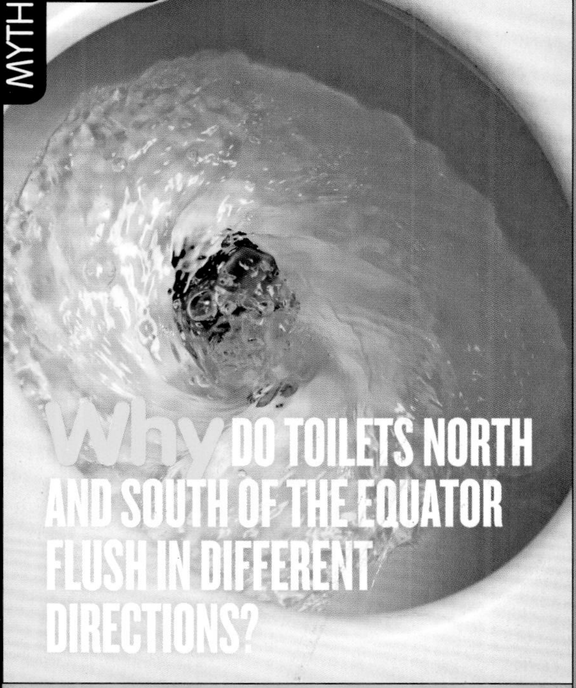

Why DO TOILETS NORTH AND SOUTH OF THE EQUATOR FLUSH IN DIFFERENT DIRECTIONS?

It's a fact confirmed by cartoons and travel shows: Flush a toilet in England and the water swirls counterclockwise; flush one in Australia and it empties clockwise. The reason? The Earth's rotation exerts a spinning force—called the Coriolis effect—on the draining water, and this force works in opposite directions on either side of the Equator. Flush your toilet to see the Coriolis effect in full effect. Neat, huh?

There's just one problem: The Earth's rotation has nothing to do with the direction of draining toilet water. Hidden jets under the rim of the toilet determine which way the water drains, and that direction varies by manufacturer rather than by hemisphere. While the Coriolis effect affects the spin of large-scale phenomena such as hurricanes, the planet's rotation is much too slow to affect your flush.

What would Earth be like if it weren't tilted?

An Earth with a perfect posture would be a little boring. Instead of seasons, the weather would be pretty much the same year-round, affected only by local storms (and the gradual effects of climate change). Regions that see snowy winters and pleasant summers with the tilt would end up locked in an endless autumn. "Winter" and "summer" would be destinations rather than times of the year. You'd have to travel farther north or south of the Equator if you wanted to go snowboarding, while summer would exist only in the tropics. Nearly every day of the year would have 12 hours of daylight and 12 hours of darkness.

DAILY DATA

- The Northern Hemisphere has its LONGEST DAY on June 21 and its SHORTEST on December 21.
- In the Southern Hemisphere, it's the opposite: The LONGEST NIGHT is June 21 and the LONGEST DAY is December 21.
- On March 21 and September 22, the length of day and night is EXACTLY THE SAME (although the length of day and night is nearly always the same along the Equator).
- Because of the planet's tilt, the North Pole and the South Pole experience six months of SUNLIGHT and six months of DARKNESS in their respective summers and winters each year.

WHY am I HERE?

Wow. That's some question. If you're asking for the deeper meaning of life—like, what's the point of our existence on this small ball of rock in a vast universe—then you're better off asking a philosopher. If you're wondering how you personally got here, you'd better have a powwow with Mom and Dad. But if you're asking how you, your dog, that spider in the web outside your window, and all other life came to exist on Earth, well, that's a long story. It all started nearly four billion years ago ...

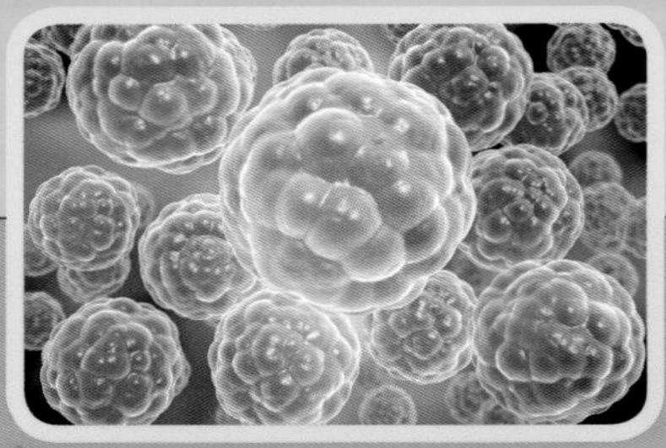

1. 3.8 billion years ago

FIRST SPARKS OF LIFE

Earth wasn't the blue-and-green marble we marvel at today. Liquid water was the hot new thing 3.8 billion years ago, after the planet had finally cooled from the constant bombardment of asteroids that had formed it. Landmasses—or continents—didn't exist yet, and the air was just a fog of toxic vapors: carbon monoxide, carbon dioxide, nitrogen, methane, and cyanide. The planet's surface was dotted with tiny islands in a shallow soup of chemicals: amino acids and fats, the basic components of life. The first life-forms—single-celled microscopic bacteria—formed in this soup, perhaps jolted to life by lightning or meteorite impacts.

2. 2.5 billion years ago

CLEARING THE AIR

Single-celled "cyanobacteria" microbes in the ocean developed the power of "photosynthesis." Later used by plants, this planet-transforming process converts sunlight and carbon dioxide into energy, creating oxygen as a by-product. Oxygen—an important breathable gas for the evolution of a greater variety of life-forms—began to increase in Earth's atmosphere.

3. 1 billion years ago

LIFE LEVELS UP

The first multicellular life-forms appeared in the oceans. A cell is the basic unit of life; multicelled organisms are made of colonies of cells that specialize in different functions. (Your body is made of trillions of cells.)

4. 550 million years ago

LIFE EXPLODES

Life underwent a big boom in diversity—a period known as the Cambrian explosion. Before this time, all life-forms were squishy: boneless, toothless, and without shells. But creatures during the Cambrian explosion—all still limited to the oceans—toughened up to swim, burrow, and hunt. They developed hard parts, such as simple shells, to defend themselves. The ancestors of fish, snails, octopuses, squid, crabs, and bugs appeared in the ocean, along with the first simple vertebrates (animals with a backbone).

5. 430 million years ago

PLANTS TAKE ROOT

Plants transitioned from the water to spread across the land.

6. 370 million years ago

VERTEBRATES HIT THE BEACH

The first amphibians evolved from air-breathing fish and began to crawl on land using fins that work like limbs. They're followed by the earliest reptiles around 70 million years later.

7. 260 million years ago

DINOSAURS DOMINATE

All of Earth's continents—or landmasses—had joined into one supercontinent known as Pangaea. Its dry, hot interior was a paradise for reptiles, which grew in size. The first dinosaur—a plant-eating creature no larger than a kangaroo—showed up on the fossil record 240 million years ago. Dinosaurs exploded in diversity. As Pangaea started to break up around 220 million years ago, dinosaurs spread to every continent on Earth. They reigned for nearly 150 million years.

8. 150 million years ago

EARLY BIRDS

The first birds—which evolved from two-legged meat-eating dinosaurs—took to the skies on feathery wings. With their reptilian tails, arm claws, and sharp teeth, these early birds weren't as pretty as their descendants are today.

9. 60 million years ago

RISE OF THE MAMMALS

The sudden death of the dinosaurs 65 million years ago—likely from an asteroid impact—left a void for smarter, smaller creatures to fill. Enter the mammals. These furry creatures lived underfoot of the dinosaurs for nearly 150 million years, but suddenly the world was theirs. Mammals grew in size and diversified into many of the species we know today: cats, dogs, horses, bats, rats, and tree-dwelling primates (the order of animals that eventually gave rise to gorillas, chimpanzees, and humans).

10. Between 13 and 6 million years ago

DOWN TO EARTH

The common apelike ancestor of humans and chimpanzees (our closest living relative today) climbed down from the trees and eventually evolved to walk on two legs. Not long after, hominids appeared and branched off from the lineage that gave rise to chimps. Hominids include humans and our immediate ancestors (such as *Homo erectus*) and close relatives the Neanderthals.

11. 200,000 years ago

THE BEGINNING OF HUMAN BEINGS

Finally, we arrived on the fossil record (or, rather, our species, *Homo sapiens*, did). The first *Homo sapiens*—which means "thinking humans"—appeared in eastern Africa nearly 200,000 years ago. In tribes of hunters and gatherers, we left the mother continent around 140,000 years later, eventually spreading to every corner of the globe while leaving our less-evolved ancestors *Homo erectus* in the evolutionary dust. Our relatives the Neanderthals died out, possibly because humans hunted them for food or started families with them. Today, humans are the only surviving hominids.

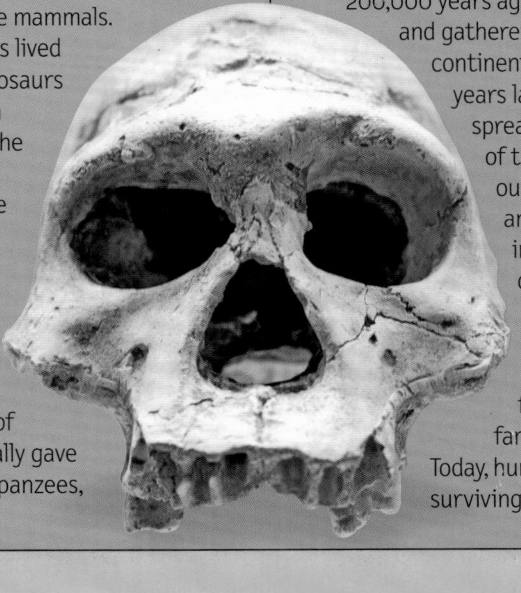

SAY WHAT?!

THE DINOSAURS RULED EARTH for a staggering amount of time compared with humans. The fearsome *Tyrannosaurus rex* (which died out around 65 million years ago) actually lived closer in time to us humans than to the stegosauruses, which thrived 150 million years ago.

WHAT is EVOLUTION?

First proposed by naturalist Charles Darwin in his 1859 book *On the Origin of Species,* the theory of evolution explains how all plants and animals—including humans—slowly change over time to improve their chances of survival. All life-forms are subject to the forces of "natural selection," in which nature favors changes (tougher beaks, sharper teeth, keener eyesight, etc.) that help a species survive and reproduce. These helpful "adaptations" are then passed on to the next generation. Eventually, all these adaptations add up until one species evolves into a new one. If you go back far enough in Earth's history, all life-forms—from great white sharks to cherry trees—evolved from a common ancestor.

If humans evolved from apes, then why do chimpanzees and other apes still exist?

This question is often posed by people who disagree with the theory of evolution, but it ignores one important fact: Humans didn't evolve from modern chimpanzees. We all share a common ancestor, which lived about six million years ago and served as a branching point in the evolutionary tree. The branch that gave rise to humans went in one direction, while the one that led to today's chimpanzees went in another. Also, just because a particular group of animals evolves into a new species doesn't mean the original species has to go extinct. The process of evolution follows a branching path rather than a series of dead ends and new beginnings. New species branch off from the original group all the time.

What ARE THE OLDEST LIVING THINGS ON EARTH?

While many animals outlive humans (giant tortoises live more than 200 years, lobsters and bowhead whales celebrate a hundred birthdays, and the tiny freshwater hydra can live as long as 1,400 years), life spans really start to stretch when you look at other forms of life ...

FIELDS OF MOSS in Antarctica have been around for 2,000 years.

Scientists estimate that a PALMER'S OAK TREE in California, U.S.A., is MORE THAN 13,000 YEARS OLD, meaning it was already old by the time the ancient Egyptians built the pyramids.

Acres of QUAKING ASPEN TREES in Utah, U.S.A., share a root system that has survived for 80,000 YEARS.

But the leader in longevity is a BATCH OF BACTERIA discovered in the frozen ground of Siberia. Scientists estimate it has been growing for HALF A MILLION YEARS, making these microbes Earth's senior citizens.

WHY can't I DIG a hole to the other side of the EARTH?

It seems like it should be a simple task: Dig deeply enough straight down and you should strike sunlight on the other side of the planet. But before you break a sweat while breaking ground, know this: Your hole will lead to a dead end. Why? Behold, the whole hole truth as we examine every obstacle to your shortcut through the soil ...

SORRY, I WAS BUSY DIGGING. YOU SAID SOMETHING MIGHT GET IN MY WAY?

Obstacle 1

Earth's Crust

High or low, wherever you go on the planet's surface, you're traveling on or above the Earth's crust 1. Our planet's outer layer began taking shape 4.5 billion years ago atop the fireball of asteroids, comets, and other space debris that clumped into a gooey lump to form Earth. As the surface cooled and hardened, Earth's crust was formed. It comes in two types:

When you reach down and feel the ground, you're touching continental crust. It ranges from 6 miles (10 km) up to 47 miles (75 km) deep under Mount Everest, Earth's tallest mountain. Continental crust consists of less dense and much older rock than oceanic crust.

Oceanic crust is about 4 miles (7 km) thick at the bottom of the deepest ocean trenches. It's still taking shape in these mid-ocean ridges, where molten rock erupts from cracks in the ocean floor and cools to form new crust.

Neither crust seems particularly thick, right? Tell that to the geologists and mining companies that tried digging through it. Despite using mid-ocean ridges as a starting point for digging operations, they haven't been able to pierce the crust. It's too tough, fiercely hot, and full of hazards, from pockets of molten rock to lakes of boiling sulfur.

Obstacle 2

The Mantle

Even if you manage to dig through the Earth's crust, you've literally only scratched the surface of the planet. Below lies the mantle 2, a layer of semi-molten metals such as iron, magnesium, and aluminum. The heat and pressure here are intense enough to compress carbon into diamonds, the hardest natural material on Earth. The easiest way to reach the mantle is to ride the oceanic crust. (It sinks slowly to the mantle in a process called subduction.) Once it reaches the mantle, oceanic crust melts and returns to the surface as magma in mid-ocean ridges, where it's recycled into new crust. The whole process takes about 200 million years, so you might want to pack a toothbrush.

Obstacle 3

The Outer and Inner Cores

A spherical Mars-size sea of molten iron and nickel swirls 1,800 miles (2,900 km) beneath your feet. It flows around an inner core 3 of iron two-thirds the size of the moon. (This flow of liquid iron around the solid inner core is what creates the Earth's magnetic field.) Temperatures in the inner core exceed 10,000 degrees Fahrenheit (5,600 degrees Celsius)—hotter than the surface of the sun—yet the intense pressure here locks the molten iron into a solid sphere. Good luck digging through that.

Obstacle 4

The Big Squeeze

The deeper you dig into Earth, the deeper your troubles. Gravity pulls trillions and trillions of tons of rocks and metals toward the planet's center, and the weight of all that rough stuff above your head increases as you dig. The pressure in the inner core is 3.5 million times the air pressure you feel on the planet's surface. Your body would suffer serious damage once you hit 27 times the surface pressure.

Obstacle 5

Tug-of-War

If not for the crushing pressure it creates around you, gravity would be your best buddy during the long haul to the center of the Earth. It's all downhill to the Earth's inner core, after all, and you'd actually experience zero gravity at the exact center of the planet (the vast mass of all that molten metal and rock around you pulls you in all directions and cancels gravity's effect). But you've only made it to the halfway point. You must repeat all the backbreaking, physics-defying work that got you here—except now gravity is working against you. It's time to begin the uphill battle to dig your exit tunnel through the opposite half of the planet. That's roughly 3,958 miles (6,370 km) of molten metal and solid rock you'll need to dig through, all of it bouncing off your head as you climb up, up, and up toward the planet's surface.

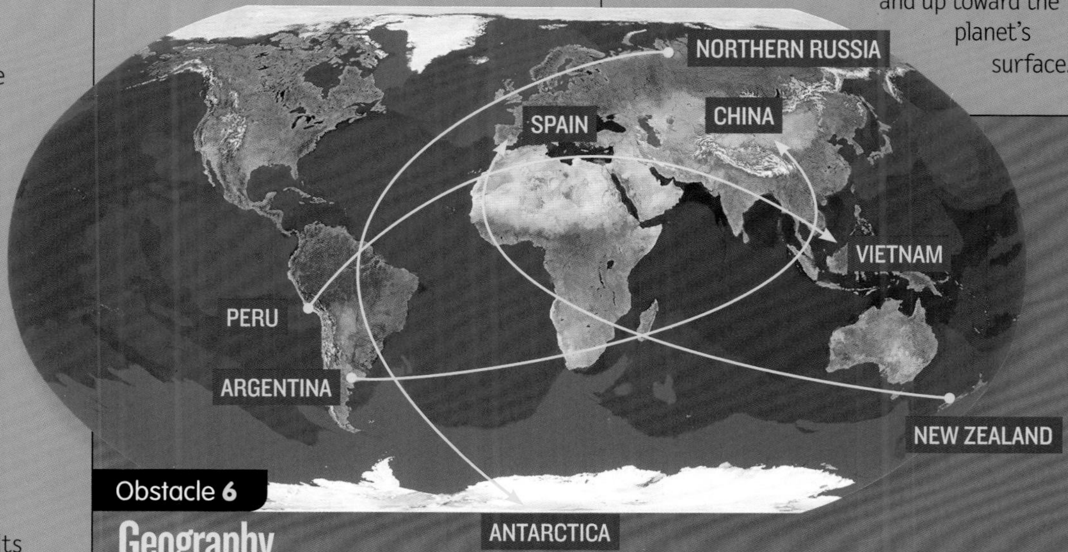

Obstacle 6

Geography

More than 70 percent of the Earth's surface is covered with water, which means you're much more likely to strike seawater than sunlight when you finally reach the other side of the planet. Try to dig a hole to China from the United States and you'd end up all wet under the Indian Ocean. If you're determined to get to the bottom of things through an 8,000-mile (12,875-km) hole in the ground, stick to these start-and-end spots on opposite ends of the globe.

HOW do we know what's in the EARTH'S CENTER (if we can't even dig through the crust)?

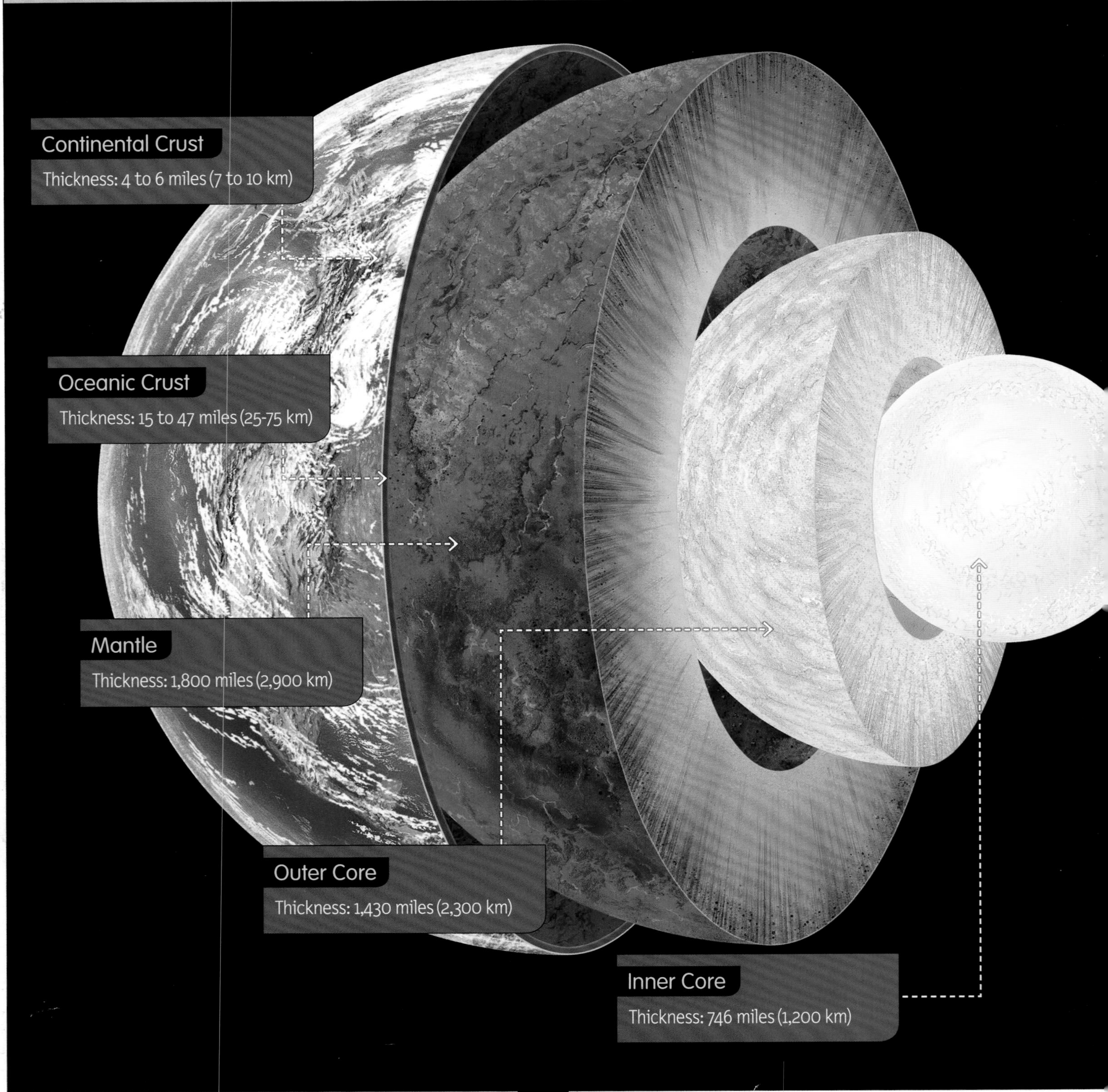

The truth is, we don't know for sure. Geologists can only guess at the planet's ingredients by studying seismic waves created by earthquakes. Bouncing through Earth's interior, these vibrations of energy travel at different speeds through different materials, such as granite, iron and nickel. By measuring the speed of the waves, seismologists can get to the bottom of what lies beneath our feet. We're making new discoveries all the time. In 2014, geologists found what might be a reservoir of water larger than all the planet's oceans combined deep in the Earth's mantle.

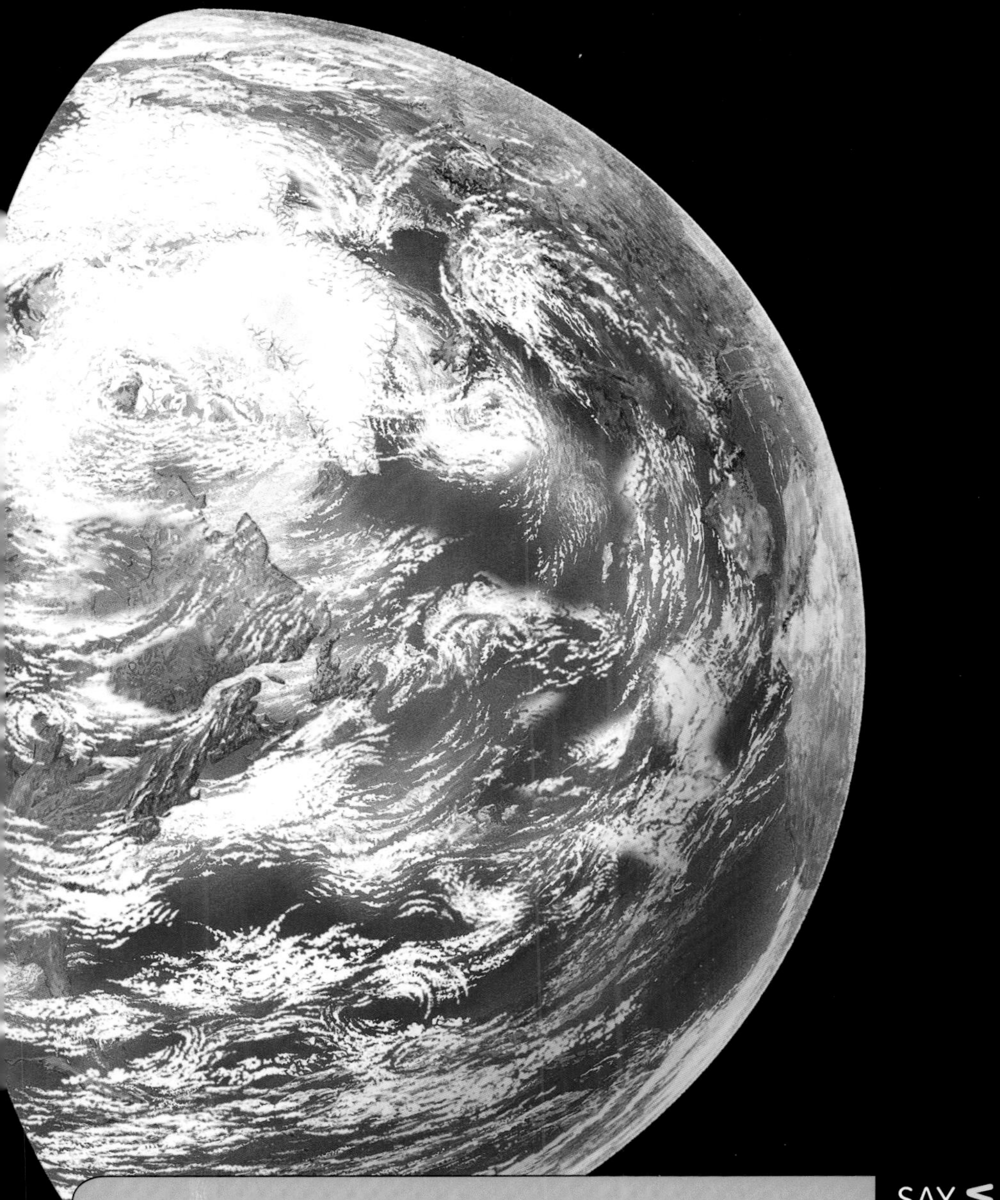

EARTH Ups and Downs

AVERAGE DEPTH TO THE CENTER OF THE EARTH
3,958 miles (6,370 km)

AVERAGE DIAMETER OF THE EARTH
7,917 miles (12,741 km)

EARTH'S WEIGHT
13,170,000,000,000,000,000,000,000 lb (5,974,000,000,000,000,000,000,000 kg)

HIGHEST POINT ON THE SURFACE
Mount Everest, at 29,029 feet (8,848 m)

LOWEST POINT ON THE SURFACE
The Challenger Deep, a canyon nearly 7 miles (11 km) deep at the bottom of the Marianas Trench in the western Pacific Ocean

HIGHEST WATER SLIDE
Verrückt slide at Schlitterbahn Water Park in Kansas City, Kansas, U.S.A. At 168 feet (51 m) high, it's taller than the Statue of Liberty.

DEEPEST HOTEL ROOM
For $800 a night, you can rent the "largest, deepest, darkest, oldest, quietest" hotel room in the world, 220 feet (67 m) below the surface at the Grand Canyon Caverns in Arizona, U.S.A.

SAY WHAT?!

IF YOU WANT TO SEE the deepest hole ever dug—although it's covered by a metal plate—you'll need to travel to the Kola Peninsula in northwest Russia. Here, for more than 20 years, geologists burrowed 7.6 miles (12 km) through layers of rock to unlock the secrets of the Earth's crust. Called, appropriately enough, the Kola Superdeep Borehole, the project ground to a halt in 1992 when the drill hit a pocket of extreme temperatures.

WHY are leaves GREEN?

The green color in leaves and blades of grass comes from a pigment called chlorophyll, which absorbs sunlight during photosynthesis, one of the most important natural processes on Earth. During photosynthesis, plants and trees use sunlight to convert carbon dioxide in the air and water into energy-rich sugars for food. That's why leaves are at their most lush and greenest during the summer months, when the longer sunlight hours kick photosynthesis into overdrive. One bonus product of the process is oxygen, which is essential for life. In other words, most life on Earth is solar powered.

WAIT, most life is solar powered?

But, not all of it? Nope. In the late 1970s, scientists studying the seafloor discovered geysers belching a boiling mineral-rich stew into the crushing depths of the ocean. These "hydrothermal vents" didn't just look like they were from outer space—they were actually teeming with alien life. Here, in the constant darkness, bacteria convert chemicals into sugars in a process called chemosynthesis. Shrimp, crabs, and eyeless tube worms survive by feeding on these bacteria, creating a food chain completely independent of the sun. Astrobiologists—scientists who study the possibility of life on other planets—examine the vents for examples of life that might exist on planets far from the sun. In fact, they wonder if life on Earth began near these geysers rather than on the surface.

Why do leaves change color in the fall?

As the days grow shorter later in the year and temperatures begin to plummet, photosynthesis slows down and produces less food. Chlorophyll in the leaves fades, allowing the foliage to explode in hues ranging from red to yellow.

Why do tumbleweeds tumble?

To set the mood for shootouts at high noon in old cowboy movies, of course. Actually, tumbleweeds tumble to create future generations of tumbling tumbleweeds. The part of the tumbleweed you see blowing end over end in the breeze is actually the aboveground portion of many species of desert plants. When the plant matures and dies, it breaks free from its roots in the ground and tumbles in the breeze, spreading new seeds along the way. When the seeds find suitable soil, they take root and sprout a new tumbleweed.

Why do flowers smell nice?

You're not the only creature that likes to stop and smell the roses. Flowers create a fragrance to attract pollinators: hummingbirds, bees, butterflies, and other winged insects. The pollinators transfer pollen between flowers to create seeds. The sweet smell also warns other animals to search elsewhere for a snack. (Flowers are often toxic.)

Why do cacti have spines instead of leaves?

These prickly plants have evolved to thrive in sunny deserts and sandy soils that would kill your average potted geranium in less than a day. You might think cacti have spines instead of leaves to jab hungry desert animals looking for a cactus snack, but that's only half the story. The spines keep the plant from losing water to the air. They also trap the moisture from morning mist and evening fog. The moisture condenses on the spines (like water drops on a cold soda can), then drips to the ground, where it's soaked up by the roots. In other words, a cactus's spines create the plant's personal rain showers.

Why do some plants eat meat?

All plants soak up energy from the sun and slurp nutrients from the dirt. But hundreds of species have developed an ability to add to their diets in sorrier soils, such as acidic swamps and rocky outcrops. They're called carnivorous plants after their favorite food—fresh meat—which gives them the nutritional boost they need to grow leaves that capture energy from the sun. But humans have nothing to fear from these meat-eating plants. They're deadly only to morsel-size animals, such as flies, mosquitoes, mice, lizards, frogs, and the occasional unlucky bird.

How do plants eat meat?

Evolution has armed carnivorous plants with a wild and wide variety of traps for capturing, killing, and devouring dinner. Consider the pitcher plants, whose leaves are disguised as cups of sweet nectar. Bugs that belly up to the pitcher for a drink tumble inside, where they're trapped by tiny hairs and digested into goo by special enzymes. Some plants have sticky tentacles that work like flypaper to snare insects. The Venus flytrap, the most famous of the carnivorous plants, has leaves lined with interlocking hairs that snap shut when disturbed by insects. At that point, a trapping plant becomes a sort of short-term stomach where the bug is boiled down into nutrients. The leaf hairs are so sensitive they can tell the difference between a bug (which springs the trap) and a raindrop (which does not). So the next time your parents tell you to eat your vegetables, look at the bright side—at least your vegetables aren't eating you!

Why IS THIS TREE THE COLOR OF A RAINBOW?

Bits of the bark of the *Eucalyptus deglupta,* aka the rainbow eucalyptus, fall off at different times of the year to reveal the fresh green bark inside. That bark then turns a rainbow of colors—blue, red, purple, orange—as it ages. You can see this amazing eucalyptus tree on the island of Mindanao in the Philippines.

WHY is the ocean SALTY?

The next time you sputter after accidentally swallowing seawater at the beach, consider this: That bitter liquid around you once washed the land. Each drop of refreshing rainwater contains an itty-bitty bit of carbon dioxide absorbed from the air. That gas gives rain a slightly acidic bite, which washes away rocks and soil when the drops splash against the ground. This process creates salty sodium and chloride ions that follow streams and rivers into the ocean. All those ions add up; roughly 3.5 percent of the seawater's weight is from salt.

Why is it easier to float in the ocean than in a swimming pool?

All that dissolved salt makes seawater more dense (or heavier) than freshwater—and objects float more easily in dense water. Take a dip in the Dead Sea—which is ten times saltier than the ocean—situated between Jordan and Israel and you'll have amazing bobbing abilities.

Why can't I drink seawater?

Consider seawater's awful taste a warning: It contains more salt than your cells and organs can handle. Ocean water is nearly four times saltier than the fluids in your body. Your kidneys need freshwater to flush out excess salt, so every gulp of seawater will just make you thirstier and thirstier. You'll need to take in more freshwater than seawater to avoid dehydration and eventually death.

Why don't fish in the ocean die of thirst?

Marine (or ocean) fish are constantly drinking to keep their bodies hydrated, but not all that water goes to their bellies. Some of the seawater passes over special salt-extracting cells in their gills; the rest is swallowed down. A saltwater fish's gills and kidneys work overtime to process all the salt and flush it back into the ocean. Freshwater fish and sharks, meanwhile, don't need to drink water. Water passing over their gills combined with the chemical makeup of the fluids in their bodies keep them hydrated.

What about marine mammals and seabirds that don't have gills?

Dolphins, seals, whales, sea lions, manatees—these aquatic creatures live in a world of water, but their drinking habits are more in line with those of camels and other animals of the desert. Salty seawater is as toxic to marine mammals as it is to us. When they need a drink, marine mammals grab a bite to eat, sucking the moisture from fish, squid, and other aquatic entrées. Seabirds such as terns and albatrosses, meanwhile, have special glands near their eyes that absorb the salt from seawater and flush it out their beaks.

SILLY QUESTION, SERIOUS ANSWER

What would happen if you piled all the salt in the ocean on land?

You couldn't build a salt shaker big enough to store it all. About 70 percent of the Earth's surface is covered with water, and most of it—97 percent—is salty. If you pulled out all that salt and piled it on land, it would create a layer 500 feet (152 m) deep across the entire land surface of the Earth.

SLOPPY SEAS

Why IS THERE AN ISLAND OF GARBAGE IN THE PACIFIC OCEAN?

Soda bottles tumble into the surf. Garbage cans fall off ships. Grocery bags blow out to sea. About 260 million tons (235.9 mt)of plastic are produced each year worldwide, and as much as 10 percent of it ends up in the ocean. Unlike food and other organic garbage, plastic doesn't dissolve; it just breaks into smaller and smaller pieces that can stick around for centuries. Twine, toothbrushes, discarded toys, to-go bags, and less identifiable pieces of plastic drift around and around in an enormous ocean vortex created by currents, sort of like a slowly flushing toilet that never drains.

Where exactly is this island?

You'll find it 1,000 miles (1,600 km) from shore in the vast expanse of the Pacific Ocean midway between Hawaii and California. Bleach bottles and old garbage bins bob amid fishing nets tangled with rotting sea creatures. Scientists call this swirling mass of trash the Eastern Pacific Garbage Patch. Twice the size of Texas by some estimates, it's the world's largest dump.

Do ships ever crash into this moving island?

No. Much of the Garbage Patch is actually a sort of plastic soup made of confetti-size "microplastics" that float on the surface or hover below the waves. Boats can sail right over it.

So is the patch dangerous?

It is for the locals. Sea turtles, fish, and marine mammals choke on the larger pieces. Scientists fear that the plastic will block sunlight from reaching plankton, tiny organisms that form the basis of the ocean's food chain. If plankton populations plummet, the entire marine ecosystem will suffer.

Why can't we just clean up this mass of trash?

It would take a full year for a ship to skim the microplastics from just one percent of the Garbage Patch. And there's more garbage where that came from. Similar trash vortices swirl near Japan and in the North Atlantic. But it's never too late to cut down on our use of plastic.

WHY is Old Faithful so FAITHFUL?

Tourists flock to see this geyser blow its top— launching superheated water vapor up to 185 feet (56 m) high—every 92 minutes in Yellowstone National Park, Wyoming, U.S.A. Geysers are rare geological features, and Old Faithful is doubly rare for its regularity. Researchers were baffled by the punctuality of its eruptions until recently, when they managed to chart its subterranean plumbing. It turns out that a large chamber beneath Old Faithful fills with steam bubbles boiled by the molten magma below. Those bubbles become trapped in a tube that leads to the geyser's mouth. The tube gradually fills with water, the pressure builds, and—*whoosh*—Old Faithful erupts right on schedule.

Why are the White Cliffs of Dover white?

Tiny creatures are responsible for the color of the cliffs, which stretch for eight miles (13 km) along England's coastline. The cliffs began to form 70 million years ago when a shallow sea covered the region. Microscopic algae called coccolithophores floated in this sea. When they died, their white calcium skeletons sunk to the bottom, forming a white mud that grew thicker over time. When the seas receded, the mud dried into the white, crumbly chalk we see on the cliffs today.

Why is the Grand Canyon so grand?

Carving through 277 miles (446 km) of Arizona, U.S.A., and up to a mile (1.6 km) deep in places, the Grand Canyon exposes millions of years of geological history in layers and layers of colorful rocks. The canyon is proof of the power of water over stone. The raging waters of the Colorado River (along with other forces) carved the canyon over millions of years—a process known as erosion.

Why do diamonds last forever?

Earth's most valuable gemstone is also its hardest natural surface. Only a diamond can scratch another diamond. These rugged rocks are forged 100 miles below your feet, where the molten temperatures and intense pressure of Earth's mantle put the big squeeze on carbon, one of the planet's most common elements (your body is nearly 20 percent carbon). Clusters of carbon atoms mash together over billions of years into a dense and rigid pattern. The end result: diamonds. Eventually, lava pushes veins of these rocks toward the surface, where they look more like pieces of glass than glittering jewels—until a jeweler cuts and polishes them. Scientists figured out how to replicate this process in the 1950s to create itty-bitty artificial diamonds for the tips of cutting tools and industrial drills.

What's the largest diamond?

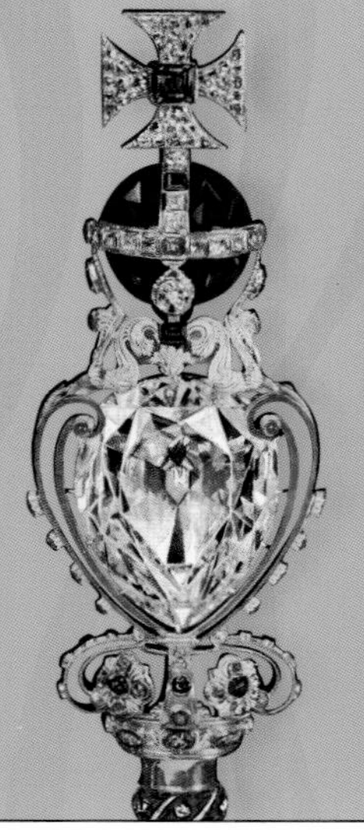

Weighing 1.37 pounds (621 gm) and measuring more than four inches (10 cm) long when it was discovered in 1905, the Cullinan Diamond is the largest diamond ever found. It was cut into nine other diamonds, the largest of which has an estimated value of $400 million.

What's the rarest kind of diamond?

Diamonds form in a variety of colors—from white to black, blue to green, and pink to purple—but the rarest color of all is red. Unlike with other colors (which are caused by chemical impurities), red diamonds result from a rare quirk in the carbon's molecular structure. Red diamonds' rarity makes them extremely valuable.

What's the most cursed diamond?

It's been worn by kings and queens, swiped by jewel thieves, and was once feared lost in a shipwreck, but the Hope Diamond is best known for its history of unhappy owners. King Louis XVI lost his head in the French Revolution. More than a hundred years later, a woman who wore the diamond became convinced it was cursed after her husband, eldest son, and daughter all died. She refused to sell the stone for fear of passing along the curse, and it was later donated to the Smithsonian Institution.

WHY do rainbows appear after a STORM?

That sunshine beaming through your windows might seem completely see-through, but this "white light" is actually composed of many colors—a literal rainbow of them. Astronomer Isaac Newton noticed these colors more than 300 years ago when he held a special piece of glass called a prism to the sunlight. The prism bent the light into its seven component colors, or wavelengths. Raindrops in the sky act like millions of tiny prisms, scattering the sunlight into its seven colors. A rainbow blossoms into living color when you see it from a sunny spot, which is why it looks like rainbows form after a storm.

COLORS OF THE RAINBOW

Why is the sky glowing like this?

Because charged particles cast off from the sun hit the Earth's magnetic field 100 miles (160 km) up, making the air molecules glow green, violet, blue, or red. These curtains of light are called auroras. The best spots to see the aurora borealis (or northern lights) are Alaska, the northwestern regions of Canada, the southern tips of Iceland and Greenland, Norway, and Siberia. The aurora australis of the Southern Hemisphere is trickier to see unless you live in Antarctica.

SAY WHAT?!

ONE RAINBOW NOT ENOUGH for you? When conditions are just right, light is reflected off raindrops a second time to create a rare double rainbow—a second, fainter band of light with its colors reversed. Sometimes, the reflection off lakes and oceans will create a rainbow grand slam: the elusive triple rainbow!

SILLY QUESTION, SERIOUS ANSWER

Why can't I find a pot of gold at the end of a rainbow?

Even if leprechauns were real—and they really did bury their booty at each rainbow's end—you'd never find their treasure. Rainbows aren't fixed to a spot in the sky; they're optical illusions. If you moved toward a rainbow, the angle of the light through the raindrops would shift and the rainbow would stay the same distance from you. So, if leprechauns really are real, they certainly picked the best spot to hide their gold.

WHY are deserts HOT & DRY?

Who said all deserts are hot?

The largest desert in the world is Antarctica, and you definitely won't need shorts and a T-shirt down there. It is true, however, that all deserts are dry (it's their defining characteristic, in fact). Most of the world's hot deserts are located 30° north and 30° south of the Equator in a world-spanning belt of arid (or dry) air. The air here lost all its moisture as it traveled north and south of the Equator, dumping rain over the world's warmer tropical regions along the way. With little rain to nourish vegetation in the dry regions, the soil became sandy and deserts formed.

THE hottest AND coldest PLACES ON EARTH ARE BOTH IN DESERTS...

HOTTEST SPOT

Death Valley in California, U.S.A., holds the official record for Earth's hottest spot: 134 degrees Fahrenheit (56.7 degrees Celsius).

COLDEST SPOT

A ridge on the East Antarctic Plateau in Antarctica measured a blood-freezing minus 133.6 degrees Fahrenheit (minus 92 degrees Celsius).

Why are most deserts hot during the day and cold at night?

With no moisture in the air to provide cloud cover during the day, desert terrain is under the merciless glare of the sun and heats up rapidly. As soon as the sun sets, the heat rises quickly through the dry air, and temperatures plummet.

What causes mirages in the desert?

It's a deadly scenario played out in the desert dunes: A thirsty explorer spies an oasis in the distant sands. He runs toward the refreshing pools, but they recede into the distance, until he eventually collapses from thirst and exhaustion. The desert mirage has claimed another victim! Like rainbows, mirages are optical illusions that an observer can never approach. And also like rainbows, they're caused by a trick of the light. The air near the desert floor is much hotter than the air above it. This change in temperature bends, or refracts, the sunlight, making it appear like a cool pool of reflecting water on the desert floor.

Why is this stone streaking through the desert?

Not much moves in California's Death Valley, a seared landscape of sand dunes and dry mud subjected to daily extremes of heat and cold. But strange things are stirring in a lake bed called the Racetrack. Rocks that tumble to the valley floor have a habit of hiking across the cracked ground, some as far as 1,500 feet (457 m), leaving crooked trails during their travels. Stranger still, no one has actually witnessed the so-called sailing stones in motion. Scientists aren't certain what's animating these inanimate objects. Studies have ruled out earthquakes and gravity (some rocks travel uphill). One theory holds that little donuts of ice form around the stones in the winter, making them float across the flat ground. Other scientists suspect that gusting wind moves the rocks after rains slicken the lake bed.

SAY WHAT?!

NO NEED TO TRAVEL to a hot desert to spot a mirage. Just take a drive. Highway asphalt creates the same shimmering effect as it heats up in the sun.

WHY do EARTHQUAKES happen?

Why can't geologists predict earthquakes?

Earthquakes can happen anywhere and at any time. Although most occur 50 miles (80 km) or less below the Earth's surface, they're just too many—and they happen too randomly—for geologists to predict. Roughly half a million quakes rumble every day!

The ground beneath your feet might feel as solid as a rock, but it's actually moving every minute of every hour of every day. Earth's crust is broken into "plates" that fit together like puzzle pieces. They're always on the march, a phenomenon known as continental drift. (The plates creep about as fast as your fingernails grow.) When the plates scrape against each other, they can slip and create an earthquake. Most earthquakes are harmless because they happen far from populated areas or deep beneath the surface of the land or the ocean, but big ones have far-reaching effects. A powerful earthquake in Alaska, U.S.A., in 1964 sunk boats as far away as Louisiana. Earthquakes can cause landslides, fires, and structural damage to cities and roads. Undersea quakes can unleash powerful tsunamis that slosh over the land.

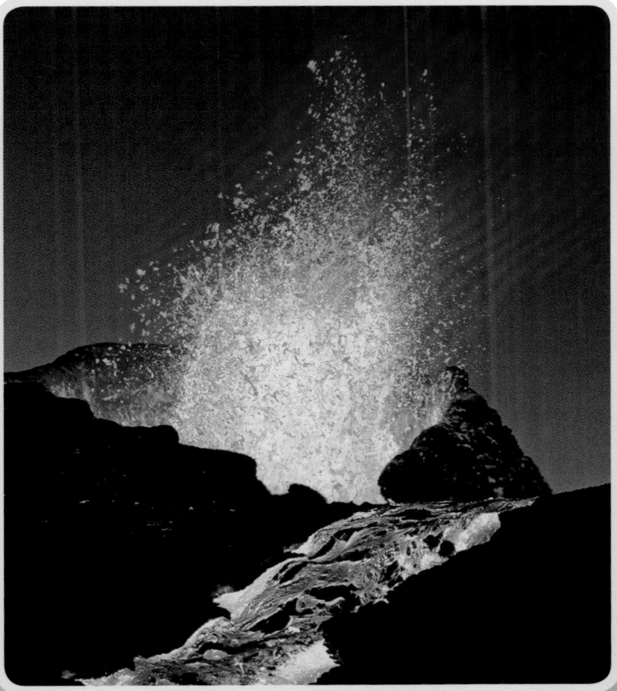

Why do volcanoes blow their tops?

Earth's crust rides on a sea of molten rock called magma, which bubbles to the surface wherever two plates meet. Earthquakes work like pressure valves for this magma (known as lava when it reaches the surface). In "effusive" volcanoes (such as the famous volcanoes of Hawaii, U.S.A.), the lava flows at a steady rate, often forming new mountains and islands. Volcanoes with a lot of gases dissolved in their magma and a high content of a chemical known as silica have "explosive" eruptions in which they literally blow their tops. Potentially much deadlier than effusive eruptions, explosive volcanoes vaporize the landscape in every direction with hot gas and carpet the terrain with choking ash. The explosive eruption of Mount Vesuvius in A.D. 79 destroyed the ancient Roman town of Pompeii, burying it under 13 to 20 feet (4 to 6 m) of hot ash. The geyser-riddled Yellowstone National Park in Wyoming, U.S.A., sits above a "supervolcano" that last blew its top 640,000 years ago.

Why are hurricanes so powerful?

Two reasons: strong winds and storm surge (the crashing of waves inland). So to understand the answer to this question, you first need to know what causes wind and waves. Temperature differences in the atmosphere create changes in air pressure. Wind is the movement of air from areas of high to low atmospheric pressure. Waves, meanwhile, are created by wind blowing over a body of water. Those tube-shaped "barrels" that surfers ride off the north shore of Hawaii? They were created by wind blowing on the ocean's surface thousands of miles away.

Now, hurricanes typically take shape over tropical oceans and coasts, where the warm ocean waters create an area of low pressure in the moist air. Bundles of thunderstorms form, fueled by the warm ocean temps and whipped into a swirling shape by the Earth's rotation and growing wind. What starts as a "tropical depression" becomes a "tropical storm" when the winds reach 39 mph (63 kph). When the winds top 74 mph (119 kph), the storm is officially declared a hurricane.

Hurricane winds can reach 150 mph (241 kph), tearing apart houses and tossing cars. When these massive storms hit land, they bring flooding rain and sometimes spawn tornadoes. Even if a hurricane never makes landfall, its wind can create massive waves three stories high that crash ashore as deadly storm surge.

Why IS THE EARTH GETTING HOTTER?

From frigid ice ages to globe-spanning heat waves, Earth's climate has been subject to natural changes throughout its long history. But in the last century or so, temperatures have risen so quickly and consistently that scientists are now certain the causes aren't natural. Why is it happening? Humans burn fossil fuels (coal, oil, and natural gas) to power their homes, cars, planes, and factories. This creates carbon dioxide, which occurs naturally in the atmosphere (animals exhale carbon dioxide, and plants need it for photosynthesis). A so-called greenhouse gas, carbon dioxide traps heat in the atmosphere. Human activity is adding so much extra carbon dioxide to the atmosphere that it's causing an artificial climate change—a rapid rise in temperatures across the globe. The decade of 2001–2010 was the warmest ever recorded worldwide.

The rise in global temperatures will cause more than some hot summers. Effects of climate change include ...

- The melting of glaciers and ice caps, resulting in catastrophic sea-level rises. Low-lying cities and coastal areas will flood.
- An increase in the instances and unpredictability of "extreme weather," such as hurricanes and tornadoes.
- Longer dry seasons and droughts that will wipe out crops, leading to starvation.

The side effects of climate change will only lessen if humans switch to alternate energy sources (such as solar power), reducing their carbon footprint.

WHAT causes LIGHTNING?

Ever notice how most batteries have little plus symbols (+) on their tops and minus symbols (-) on their bottoms? A storm cloud is like a big fluffy battery—the most powerful battery on Earth. Drops of rain and bits of ice blow and fall within the cloud, bumping against one another to create static electricity. Positively charged particles rise to the cloud's top, while negatively charged particles sink to the lower levels. The difference between the positive and negative particles builds up a current, which arcs through the air as **intra-cloud lightning**, the most common type of lightning.

The much more dangerous **cloud-to-ground lightning** works its way downward from the negatively charged lower levels of a cloud (or, in some cases, from the positively charged tippy-top) through a **stepped leader**, a series of negative charges. The trip down the steps happens faster than the blink of an eye: around 200,000 mph (322,000 kph). Once the stepped leader gets within 150 feet (46 m) or so of the surface, it connects with a positive jolt of electricity that rises through an object on the ground, such as a tree, tower, building, or even you (if you're silly enough to stand outside during a storm). This upward surge is called a **streamer**, and it's the flash of lightning you see with your eyes. When it connects with the leader, it creates a channel to conduct electricity from the earth to the cloud. *Zzzzzt! Krakow!* Lightning can carry up to a billion volts of electricity—about 50,000 times the current of a typical industrial electrical accident.

What are my chances of getting zapped by lightning?

The odds of the average American getting struck are 1 in 5,000. Lightning strikes about 2,000 people worldwide each year, and 9 out of every 10 victims survive with symptoms ranging from memory loss to dizziness to bizarre scars.

Why aren't planes struck by lightning?

They are! Airplanes flying through storm clouds occasionally get struck by intra-cloud lightning, but modern planes are designed to withstand multiple hits and keep on flying.

MYTH MASHED

Why doesn't lightning strike twice?

That old saying is a sham. Bolts strike skyscrapers and other tall buildings twice, thrice, or more. New York City's Empire State Building gets hit about 100 times each year.

What causes thunder?

A bolt of lightning can be five times hotter than the surface of the sun. This superheat wreaks havoc with the surrounding air, creating a shock wave that we hear as thunder.

Q: tips

How TO AVOID THE VOLTAGE

- Seek shelter! The safest place to be in a thunderstorm is inside.
- While inside, don't touch any water faucets or your landline phone (also unplug your computer and other gadgets, which can be damaged by lightning).
- If you're stuck outside, avoid standing under tall trees or towers, which attract lightning. Don't even carry an umbrella!
- Leave the area—seek shelter or climb into a car—as soon as possible.
- If you're swimming, get out of the water as soon as you spy a storm. A lightning zap can zip more than 20 miles (32 km)!

SAY WHAT?!

THINK THE PATTER of raindrops on your roof is a soothing sound? What about the splatter of falling frogs? Residents in a Serbian town scrambled for cover in 2005 when thousands of amphibians plummeted from above. A twister was responsible for the twisted weather. When a tornado passes over a swamp or lake, it sucks up the surface water and anything in it—including frogs and fish. The twister can carry this squishy cargo for several miles until its winds weaken, which results in a hail of aquatic creatures. Deluges of frogs, fish, squid, shells, and worms have been reported since the days of ancient Egypt.

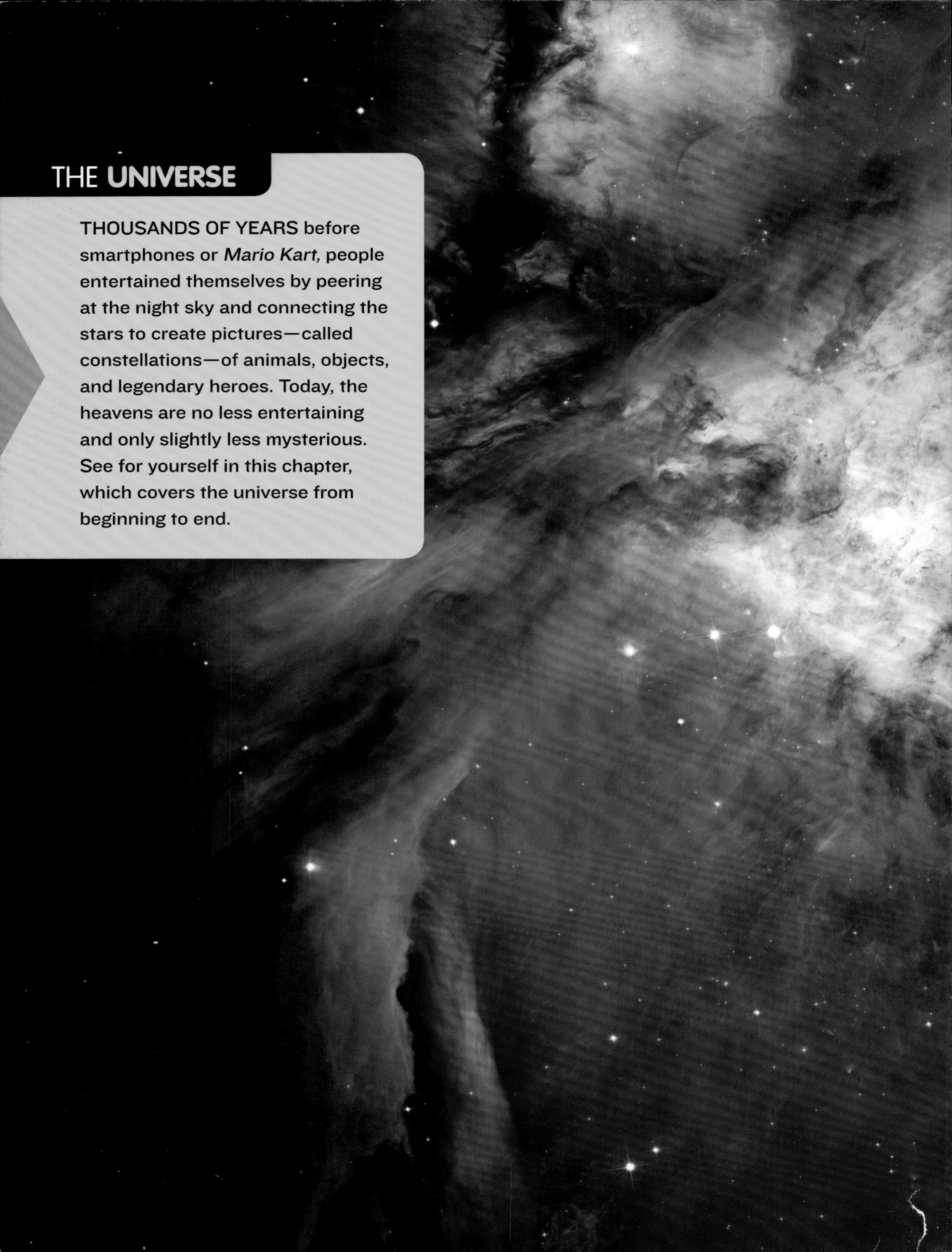

THE **UNIVERSE**

THOUSANDS OF YEARS before smartphones or *Mario Kart,* people entertained themselves by peering at the night sky and connecting the stars to create pictures—called constellations—of animals, objects, and legendary heroes. Today, the heavens are no less entertaining and only slightly less mysterious. See for yourself in this chapter, which covers the universe from beginning to end.

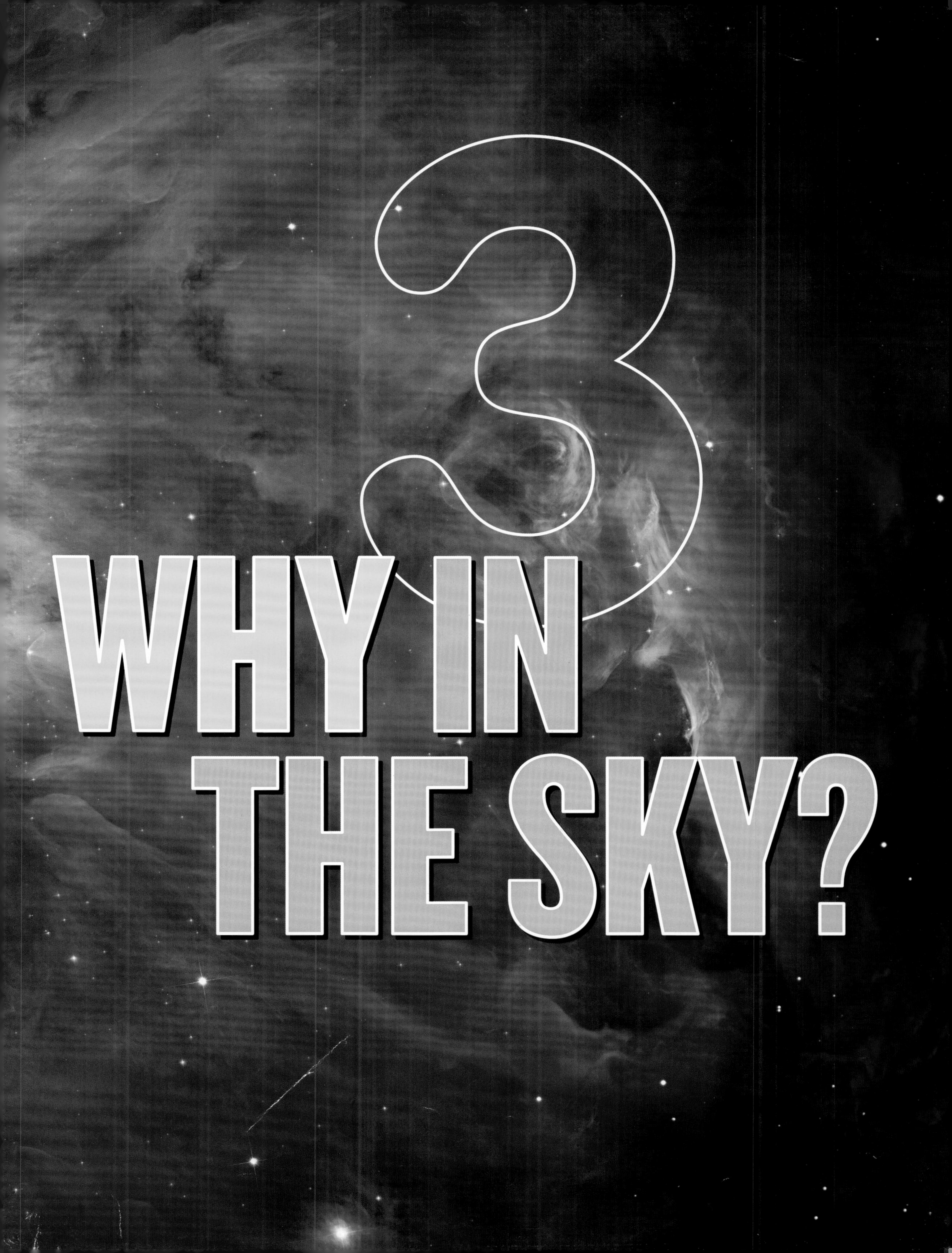

3

WHY IN THE SKY?

WHAT is the BIG BANG?

The "big bang" is the name for the leading theory behind the birth of everything: atoms, light, gravity, gases, stars, planets, galaxies, and even time itself. And while scientists have found plenty of evidence to back up the big bang theory, the name itself isn't entirely accurate. The universe didn't begin with a bang (sound didn't exist yet) or even a mighty explosion (fire and matter didn't exist either). Even light was a relatively late addition to the cosmic chronology. Confused? Here's a guide to how scientists think it all began.

BIG BANG breakdown

IN THE BEGINNING ...

A long time ago, time didn't even exist. Neither did space. And in this nothingness hung a supremely hot spot crammed with all the raw ingredients of the universe scrunched into a point thousands of times smaller than the period at the end of this sentence. Called a "singularity," this spot might even have been smaller than an atom, the basic unit of matter. (But it wasn't an atom, because atoms didn't exist yet.)

A TRILLIONTH OF A TRILLIONTH OF A SECOND LATER ...

Suddenly, the supremely hot, scrunched-up singularity doubles in size, and then doubles again, and then again—at least 90 times—in a process known as inflation. This is the "bang" in the big bang, and it gets bigger. Expanding faster than the speed of light, this growth spurt defies the laws of physics. Everything in the universe explodes into existence, but at this point it's little more than a mess of formless heat.

ONE SECOND LATER

Inflation ends one-millionth of a second after the start of the big bang. The universe's expansion slows and temperatures cool. At just one second old, the newborn universe contains nature's fundamental forces, including the gravity that keeps your feet on the ground and magnetic attraction.

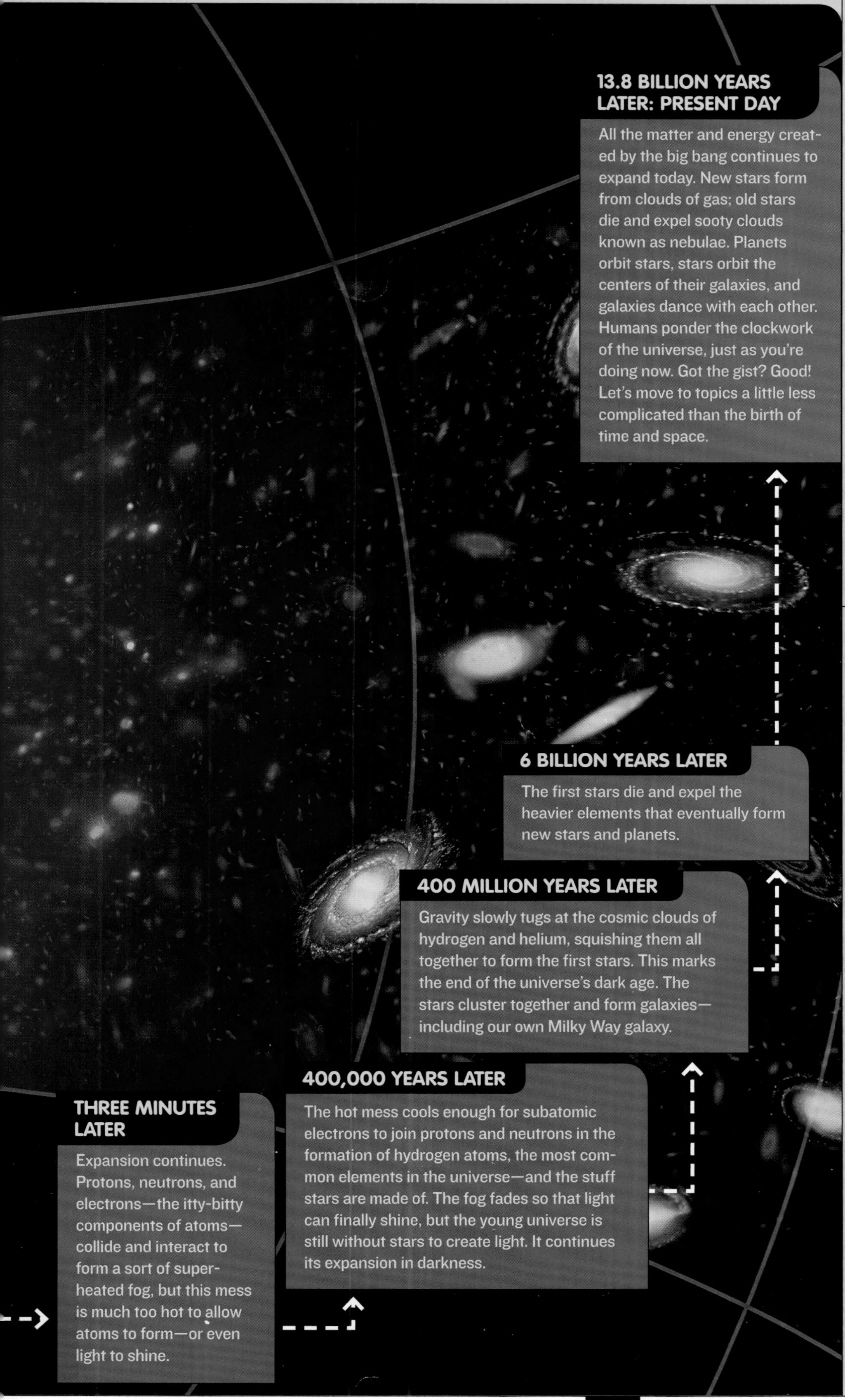

THREE MINUTES LATER

Expansion continues. Protons, neutrons, and electrons—the itty-bitty components of atoms—collide and interact to form a sort of superheated fog, but this mess is much too hot to allow atoms to form—or even light to shine.

400,000 YEARS LATER

The hot mess cools enough for subatomic electrons to join protons and neutrons in the formation of hydrogen atoms, the most common elements in the universe—and the stuff stars are made of. The fog fades so that light can finally shine, but the young universe is still without stars to create light. It continues its expansion in darkness.

400 MILLION YEARS LATER

Gravity slowly tugs at the cosmic clouds of hydrogen and helium, squishing them all together to form the first stars. This marks the end of the universe's dark age. The stars cluster together and form galaxies—including our own Milky Way galaxy.

6 BILLION YEARS LATER

The first stars die and expel the heavier elements that eventually form new stars and planets.

13.8 BILLION YEARS LATER: PRESENT DAY

All the matter and energy created by the big bang continues to expand today. New stars form from clouds of gas; old stars die and expel sooty clouds known as nebulae. Planets orbit stars, stars orbit the centers of their galaxies, and galaxies dance with each other. Humans ponder the clockwork of the universe, just as you're doing now. Got the gist? Good! Let's move to topics a little less complicated than the birth of time and space.

What evidence do astronomers have for the big bang?

Plenty. In fact, they see evidence everywhere they look in the universe. In 1924, astronomer Edwin Hubble noticed that galaxies outside the Milky Way—our home galaxy—were zipping away in all directions, as if they originated from a singularity. Astronomers also see the big bang's "baby pictures" in a cosmic crackle of microwave energy and special ripples in gravity, both evidence of that "inflation" that gave birth to the universe. The amounts of hydrogen, helium, and other elements across the universe all measure up to the big bang model. Astronomers have also failed to find any stars older than 13.8 billion years, the approximate age of the universe.

What existed before the big bang?

The short answer: nothing, nada, zip. But scientists still wonder if something existed before all the nothing. One theory: Our universe is caught in an endless loop of explosions and crunches. Eventually, in billions and billions of years, the iron grip of gravity will slow the growth of the universe, stall it, and then pull everything back toward its center—a process that astrophysicists call the "big crunch." Planets, stars, and galaxies will slowly collapse back into the singularity that started it all, kicking off another big bang and a brand-new universe.

According to another theory, our universe is just one of many, many, many alternate universes just like it in a vast "multiverse." When two of these universes interact at the quantum level (a level smaller than an atom), it kicks off a big bang and the birth of yet another alternate universe. Perhaps in an alternate universe right now, an alternate version of you is reading an alternate version of this book and having his or her alternate mind blown.

WHERE am I?

If you wanted to mail a letter to an alien pen pal in some distant neighborhood of the universe, you'd need to send more than just your street address to receive a reply. Specifically, you'd need to tell your faraway friend that you live on Earth, the third of eight planets (and five "dwarf planets," but we'll get to those in a bit) in the solar system, a star system in the Milky Way. Earth's home galaxy, the Milky Way is a disk-shaped vortex of stars, planets, and clouds of interstellar gas and dust (known as nebulae). The Milky Way is a "barred spiral galaxy," meaning it has several arms and a bar that extend from a bulging core thick with gas, dust, and stars. Everything in the galaxy orbits the core.

Why is our galaxy called the Milky Way?

No, it has nothing to do with a brand of candy bar. Look up at the sky on the darkest, clearest of nights and you'll spot a faint band of stars rising or setting. Ancient stargazers named this patch the "Road of Milk," which eventually became known as the Milky Way. It wasn't until the 20th century that astronomers realized the milky path across the sky was actually the center of our galaxy as seen from Earth.

Can we see the core of the Milky Way from Earth?

Not with our unaided peepers. Clouds of gas and dust block our view of the core. We can see through those clouds with special orbital telescopes that detect heat and other invisible energies.

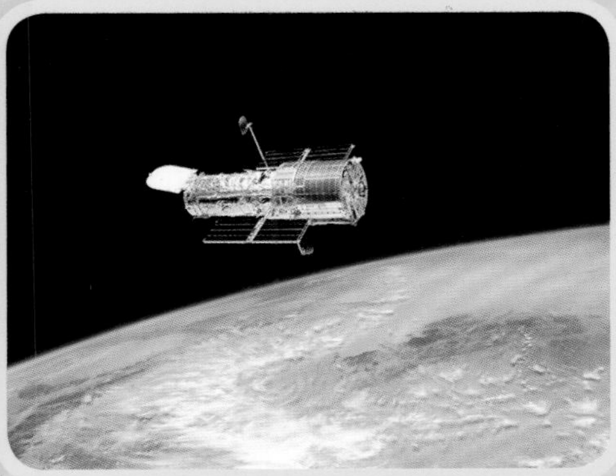

How do we know what the Milky Way looks like?

Actually, we don't know for sure—no more than a bacteria deep inside your belly knows your hair color or shoe size. But unlike bacteria, human astronomers have high-tech sensors and space telescopes. We can measure the distances and densities of star clusters and peer through dense nebulae to the galaxy's core. By comparing these findings with images of distant galaxies, we get a good idea of our home galaxy's structure.

What LIES AT THE VERY CENTER OF THE GALAXY?

Astronomers suspect that a super-massive black hole churns at the core of our galaxy—and perhaps at the cores of all other galaxies in the universe. You'll learn more about these interstellar vacuum cleaners on page 108.

HOW many other GALAXIES are there?

As recently as a hundred years ago, astronomers thought the entire universe was contained in the Milky Way. But then Edwin Hubble figured out how to measure the distances of faraway objects. Suddenly, we learned that many smudges in the night sky weren't within our galaxy at all—they were actually other galaxies outside our own! Today, astronomers suspect that the universe contains about 200 billion other galaxies. Most of them are spiral galaxies like our own.

HOW LONG DOES IT TAKE OUR SOLAR SYSTEM TO ORBIT THE CENTER OF THE GALAXY?

About 230 million years, a "galactic year."

What's our nearest neighboring spiral galaxy?

That would be Andromeda, a spiral galaxy like the Milky Way. Astronomers believe it contains as many as a trillion stars. At 2.5 million light-years away, Andromeda is the farthest thing we can see with the naked eye, but it's getting closer all the time. Someday, the Milky Way and Andromeda galaxies will collide, sharing their star dust and spawning new stars. It's doubtful any humans will see this cosmic collision, which won't happen until four billion years in the future.

How far is Earth from the center of the Milky Way?

About 27,000 light-years. (A light-year is a unit of astronomical measurement for distances between stellar objects; one light-year is how far light travels in a year.)

SAY WHAT?!

IF YOU manage to spot the faint fuzzy dot of the Andromeda galaxy on a clear, moonless night, consider this: The light you're seeing left Andromeda back when humanity's ancestors had just begun to wield simple stone tools about 2.5 million years ago.

How OLD IS...

... the universe?
13.4 billion years old

... the Milky Way?
(our galaxy)
10 billion years old

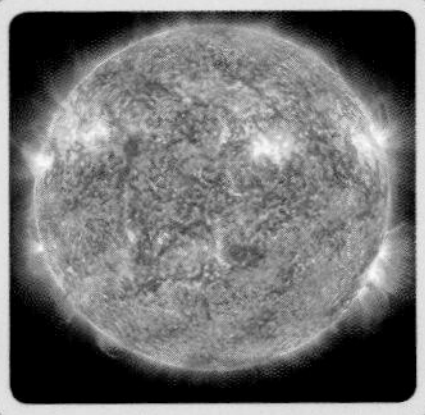

... the sun?
4.6 billion years old

... Earth?
4.6 billion years old

... the moon?
4.5 billion years old

... life on Earth?
3.8 billion years old

... *Homo sapiens?*
(the human species)
200,000 years old

Your Galaxy AT A GLANCE

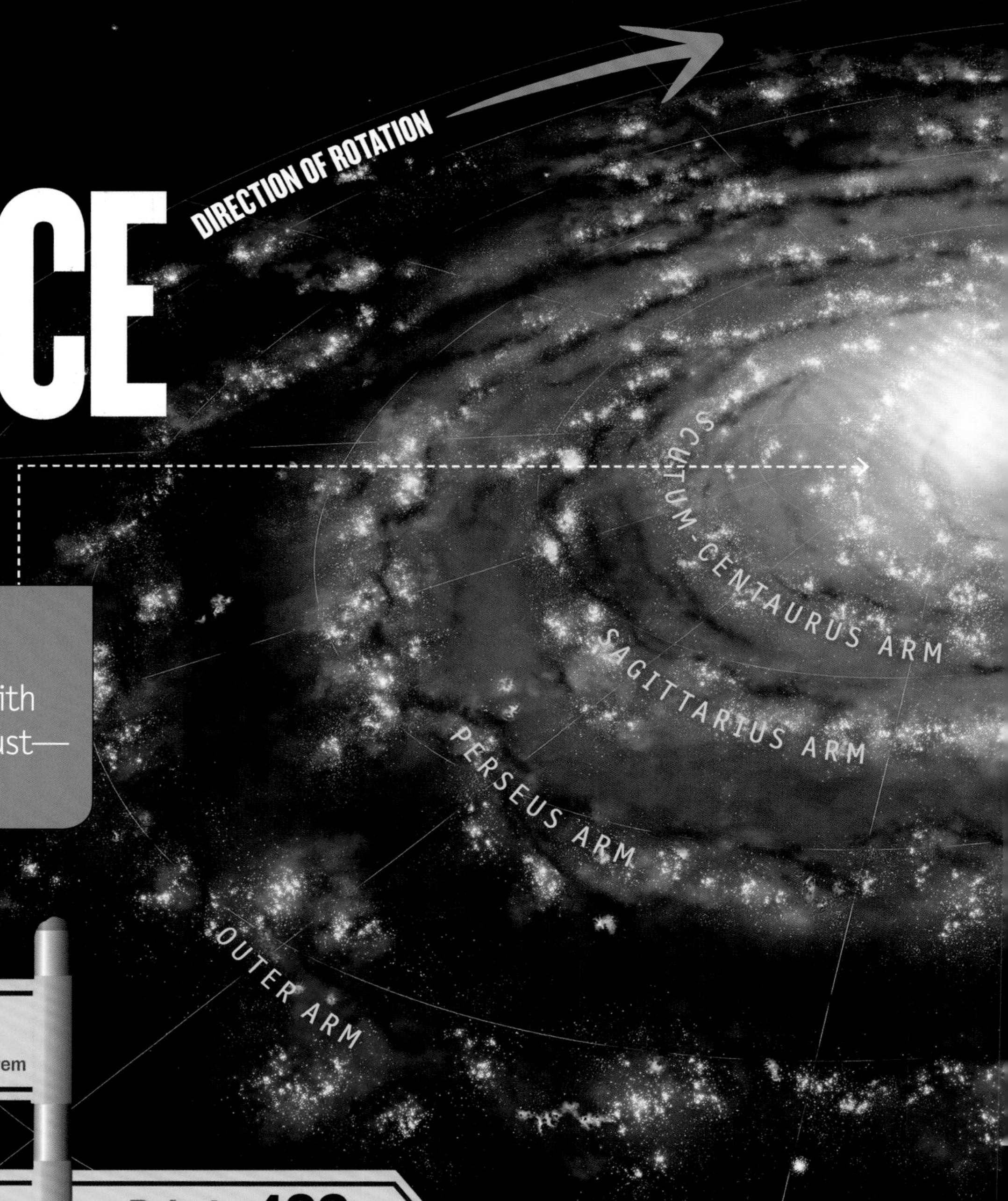

Core

The dense galactic core is filled with older stars and clouds of sooty dust—the leftovers of dying stars.

4.3 LIGHT-YEARS **Alpha Centauri** Closest neighboring star system

8.6 LIGHT-YEARS **Sirius** Brightest star in the sky

Polaris The North Star **433** LIGHT-YEARS

Orion Nebula One of the brightest nebulae **1,345** LIGHT-YEARS

Earth and our solar system lie in the Milky Way's Orion Arm, a smaller spur between two of the galaxy's major arms.

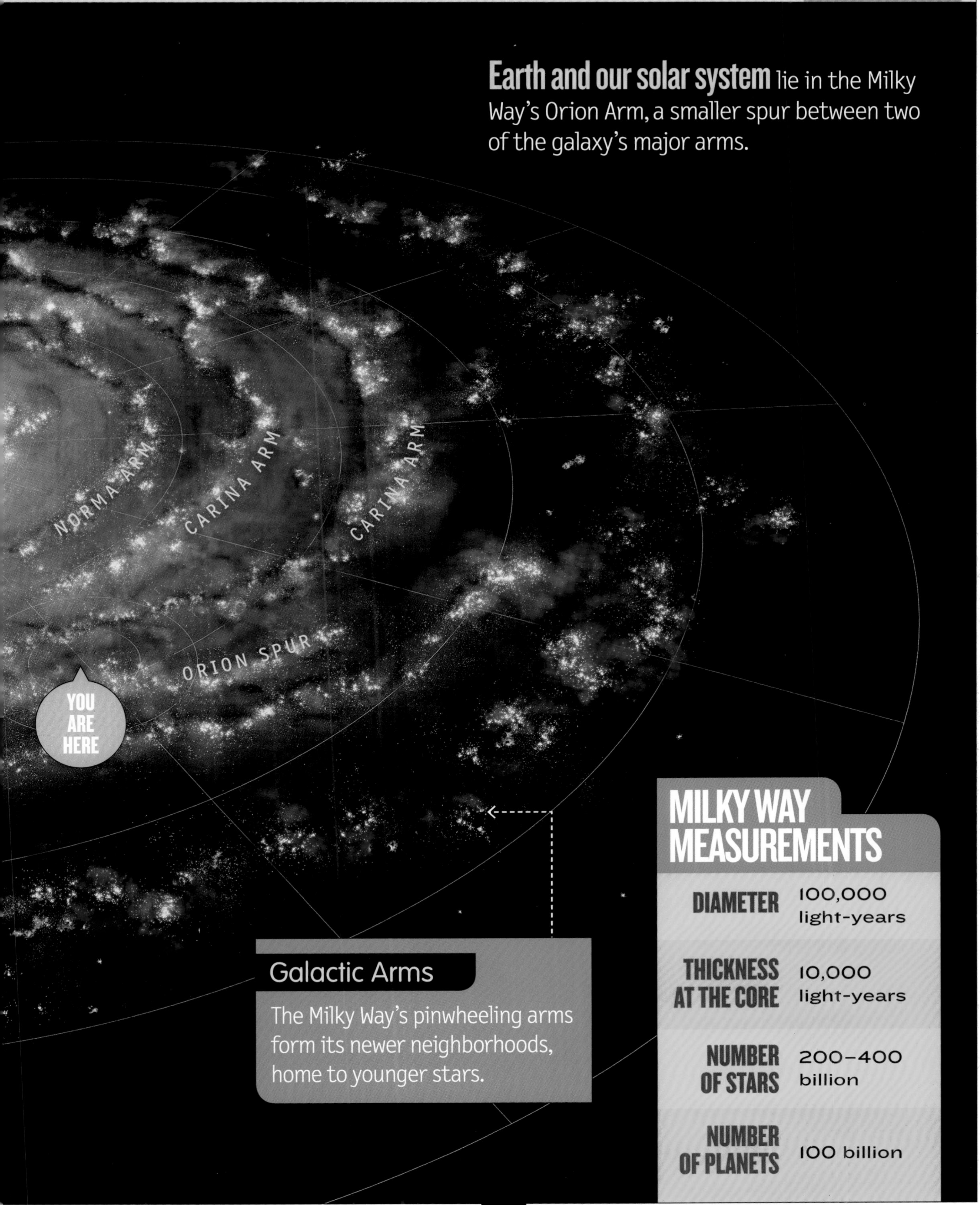

Galactic Arms

The Milky Way's pinwheeling arms form its newer neighborhoods, home to younger stars.

MILKY WAY MEASUREMENTS

DIAMETER	100,000 light-years
THICKNESS AT THE CORE	10,000 light-years
NUMBER OF STARS	200–400 billion
NUMBER OF PLANETS	100 billion

WHY is THE SUN so important?

Think Earth is the most important spot in the solar system? The sun is the real star of the show—literally! The closest star to Earth, it's the source of all our heat and light. Life wouldn't exist without it. It's also the center of our solar system and by far its largest object. Our star's enormous gravitational pull grips the planets, dwarf planets, asteroids, and comets, keeping them from spinning into deep space. Put simply, we wouldn't have a solar system without the sun.

Why is the sun so bright?

It's a big ball of gas accounting for 99.8 percent of the total mass of the solar system. More than a million Earths would fit inside the sun! A process called nuclear fusion converts hydrogen to helium deep in the sun's core, where temperatures hit a balmy 27 million degrees Fahrenheit (15 million degrees Celsius). Fusion creates energy that travels to the sun's surface in a journey that can take 100,000 years.

Why is sunlight good for me?

A sunny day can do more than just raise your spirits—it can make you healthier! Your body converts sunlight into vitamin D, a vital vitamin for stronger bones.

Why does the sun rise and set?

It's not the sun that soars across the sky. The Earth itself is rotating on its axis—one full rotation per day—and that spin makes heavenly bodies appear to rise in the east and set in the west to us Earthlings on the ground.

Will the sun ever burn out?

Yes, the sun's core will run out of hydrogen gas eventually. When that happens, the sun's spent helium will collapse, causing the core to heat up and expand outward—possibly reaching all the way to Earth in a vibrant cloud known as a "red giant." But fear not: That day won't come for at least another five billion years.

Why is sunlight bad for me?

A little bit of sun goes a long way. Sunlight contains invisible ultraviolet (UV) rays that can damage your skin, causing it to burn or wrinkle, and even lead to skin cancers. A colored chemical material in our skin called melanin absorbs UV rays to minimize the damage. Fair-skinned people (whose ancestors came from less sunny places) have less melanin, so they're more susceptible to sunburn and forming harmless spots of melanin known as freckles. People with darker skin (whose ancestors came from sunny places) produce more melanin to combat UV damage. But even high levels of melanin aren't enough to protect skin from wrinkles caused by overexposure to the sun.

Why SHOULDN'T I LOOK AT THE SUN?

The ultraviolet (or UV) light given off by the sun is murder on your eyeballs. (Ever wonder why welders wear helmets? The intense heat of a welding torch generates the same eye-damaging UV light as the sun.) Even the sun's reflection off water, sand, or snow can sunburn our corneas (the clear surface of our eyes), making it feel like the inside of each eyelid is coated with sandpaper. Staring at the sun will damage our retinas, the cells at the rear of the eyes that sense light and color. Recovery from sun damage can take months. In some cases it causes permanent blindness.

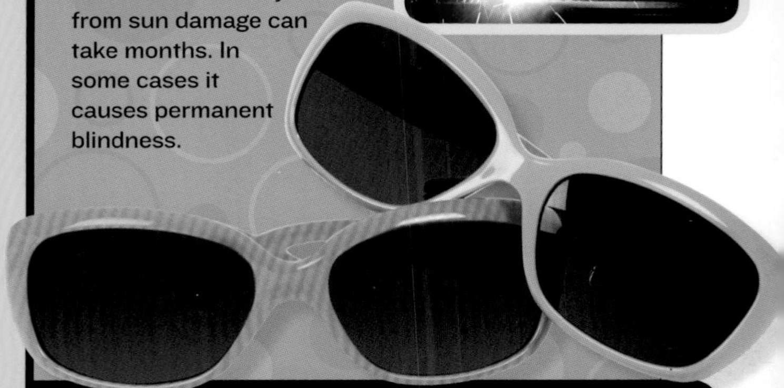

How CAN I AVOID SUN DAMAGE TO MY EYES?

Simple: Never look directly at the sun! Even during a solar eclipse, the sun gives off enough ultraviolet radiation to damage your eyes (watch an eclipse only through a special UV filter). Wear UV-blocking sunglasses while you're on water, snow, or other reflective surfaces.

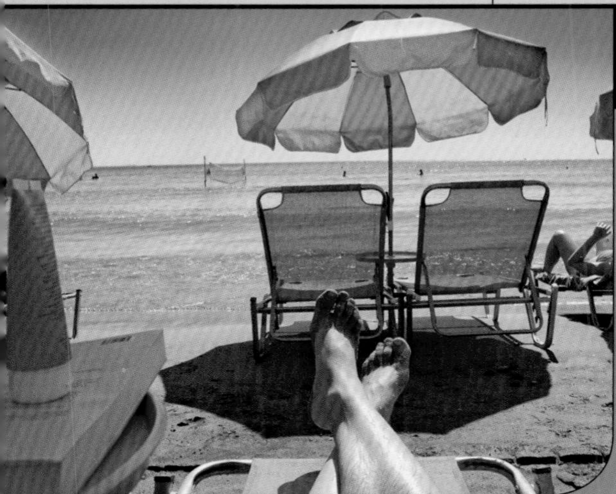

Q: tips

How CAN I PROTECT MY SKIN FROM THE SUN?

- Stick to the shade when the sun is strongest—typically between 10 a.m. and 4 p.m.
- If you can't avoid the rays, cover up. Smear your exposed skin evenly with sunblock and reapply every two hours.
- If you don't like applying sticky sunscreen, wear UV-blocking clothing instead.
- Just because it's cloudy out doesn't mean you're in the clear. Clouds don't block UV rays.
- Take extra precautions in regions closer to the Equator, where the sun is much stronger, or around reflective terrain such as snow, sand, or water.

WHY does the Earth have a MOON?

Our moon is literally a chip off the old block, formed around 4.5 billion years ago when a roving "rogue planet" the size of Mars collided with the infant Earth and knocked a cloud of debris into orbit. That debris scrunched down into the ball of rock, becoming our moon. But it's hardly the only moon in the solar system. Roughly 140 natural satellites (another name for moons) orbit the other seven planets, but ours is the only one known simply as "the moon." It's also the only heavenly body visited by human beings.

Why does the moon have so many craters?

While an atmosphere protects Earth from all but the largest asteroid impacts, the moon's airless surface has come under constant assault over billions of years. The powdery lunar dust is pocked by craters and dented by dark basins people once thought were seas (they're dry, although the moon may contain ice in its deepest crevices).

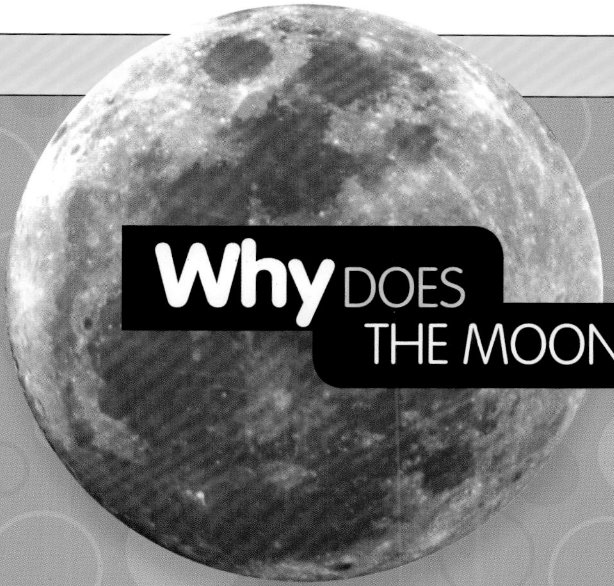

Why DOES THE MOON ...

... SHINE?

Moonlight is actually sunlight reflected off the moon's surface.

... APPEAR ORANGE OR RED?

The atmosphere closer to the horizon is much thicker and scatters the light, giving the moon (and sun) a reddish tint.

... LOOK BIGGER AT TIMES?

The moon will look larger when it's closer to the horizon, where trees, hills, and houses give it some perspective. (During occasional "supermoon" events, the moon looks slightly larger because it's at its closest point to Earth in its oval-shaped orbit.)

What would happen if Earth didn't have the moon?

Life on this planet would be a lot different. Earth's moon has loomed large in our lives since ancient times. Its orbit around Earth inspired our calendar month. Its gravitational pull tugs Earth's oceans (and large lakes) into daily cycles of high and low tide. The moon might even affect how you toss and turn at night (one study showed that people sleep worse during a full moon). In fact, scientists suspect that our satellite's stabilizing effect on Earth's wobble and climates helped life evolve here. Without the moon, there might not have been people here to appreciate it.

Why do we only ever see one side of the moon?

The moon orbits the Earth in such a way that it always shows the same side to us Earthlings. We didn't get our first glimpse of the far side—often mistakenly called the "dark side"—until a probe photographed it in 1959.

Who does the moon belong to?

Although various people have declared the moon as their property—and American astronauts have planted six U.S. flags on its surface—no single person or nation can claim ownership of the moon according to international law.

SILLY QUESTION, SERIOUS ANSWER

Do people really think the moon is made of green cheese?

Not unless they're really easy to fool. Our moon's supposedly cheesy composition originated in a 16th-century expression that no one ever took seriously. That didn't stop NASA from sharing a photo of the moon with an expiration date in one of the craters as an April Fools' joke in 2002.

WHY would I want to VISIT...

Nothing against the world's largest ketchup bottle in Illinois, U.S.A., or the museum of roller skates in nearby Nebraska, but a voyage through the solar system reveals more awe-inspiring attractions than your typical cross-country road trip. See for yourself as we tour the eight main planets in our neighborhood, starting with the rock closest to the sun.

... MERCURY?

DISTANCE FROM THE SUN: 28,583,702 to 43,382,549 miles (46,001,009 to 69,817,445 km)

MINIMUM/MAXIMUM TEMPERATURE: -279/801°F (-173/427°C)

LENGTH OF SPACE JOURNEY FROM EARTH: 4 years

Mercury's crater-pocked surface may contain valuable minerals. It's also the speediest of all the planets, orbiting the sun every 88 days. That means you could celebrate four birthdays for every one back on Earth!

... EARTH?

DISTANCE FROM THE SUN: 91,402,640 to 94,509,460 miles (147,098,291 to 152,098,233 km)

MINIMUM/MAXIMUM TEMPERATURE: -126/136°F (-88/58°C)

Scientists know more about the surface of the moon than they do the depths of the oceans or the composition of Earth's core. Our world still holds plenty of mysteries for the solar system explorer—and you won't even need a bulky space suit to step outside!

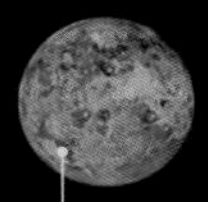

...VENUS?

DISTANCE FROM THE SUN: 66,782,596 to 67,693,905 miles (107,476,170 to 108,942,780 km)

AVERAGE SURFACE TEMPERATURE: 864°F (462°C)

LENGTH OF SPACE JOURNEY FROM EARTH: 6 months

It has been called Earth's twin. The second planet from the sun is roughly the same size and density as Earth, which means the gravity is similar between here and home. Like Earth, Venus also has clouds and wind (although the clouds here are made of sulfuric acid, and the wind exceeds tornado strength—so you'll want to bring more than shorts and a T-shirt).

...MARS?

DISTANCE FROM THE SUN: 128,409,598 to 154,865,853 miles (206,655,215 to 249,232,432 km)

MINIMUM/MAXIMUM TEMPERATURE: -225/70°F (-153/20°C)

LENGTH OF SPACE JOURNEY FROM EARTH: 7 months

Mars is a cold, dead desert world today, but life may have once thrived in ancient seas and riverbeds. The red planet is also home to the solar system's tallest volcano, Olympus Mons, which is nearly three times taller than Mount Everest.

...SATURN?

DISTANCE FROM THE SUN: 838,741,509 to 934,237,322 miles (1,349,823,615 to 1,503,509,229 km)

AVERAGE TEMPERATURE: -288° F (-178° C)

LENGTH OF SPACE JOURNEY FROM EARTH: 3 years

Saturn's awesome rings alone are worth the trip, but *Star Wars* fans might visit the gas giant for another reason: A small crater-pocked moon named Mimas looks just like the Death Star.

...NEPTUNE?

DISTANCE FROM THE SUN: 2,771,162,074 to 2,819,185,846 miles (4,459,753,056 to 4,537,039,826 km)

AVERAGE TEMPERATURE: -353° F (-214° C)

LENGTH OF SPACE JOURNEY FROM EARTH: 12 years

This ice giant is home to the windiest weather in the solar system. Clouds of frozen methane whoosh faster than the speed of sound through storms that would engulf all of Earth.

...JUPITER?

DISTANCE FROM THE SUN: 460,237,112 to 507,040,015 miles (740,679,835 to 816,001,807 km)

AVERAGE TEMPERATURE: -234° F (-148° C)

LENGTH OF SPACE JOURNEY FROM EARTH: 13 months

The largest planet in our solar system—large enough that 1,300 Earths could fit inside of it—rules over a system of its own. Several of Jupiter's nearly 70 moons are worthy of your attention. Mega-moon Ganymede is larger than Mercury and has its own magnetic field. Volcanoes on Io, the most volcanic body in the solar system, spew clouds of yellow sulfur nearly 200 miles (322 km) high.

...URANUS?

DISTANCE FROM THE SUN: 1,699,449,110 to 1,868,039,489 miles (2,734,998,229 to 3,006,318,143 km)

AVERAGE TEMPERATURE: -357° F (-216° C)

LENGTH OF SPACE JOURNEY FROM EARTH: 9 years

One trip to the solar system's coldest planet could pay for itself ten times over. Researchers have found that Uranus's crushing atmosphere can compress methane—an explosive gas—into precious rocks. Clouds in the depths of Uranus's atmosphere might rain diamonds.

WHY are some planets ROCKY while others are balls of GAS?

A planet's makeup depends largely on its place in the solar system. The four "inner planets" formed from the debris that orbited closer to the sun. The "outer planets" developed well beyond the orbit of Mars from gases and ice. The eight planets (and numerous dwarf planets) in our solar system come in three flavors...

TERRESTRIAL PLANETS: These smaller inner planets—which include Mercury, Venus, Earth, and Mars (below)—are made of solid matter: rocks and metals.

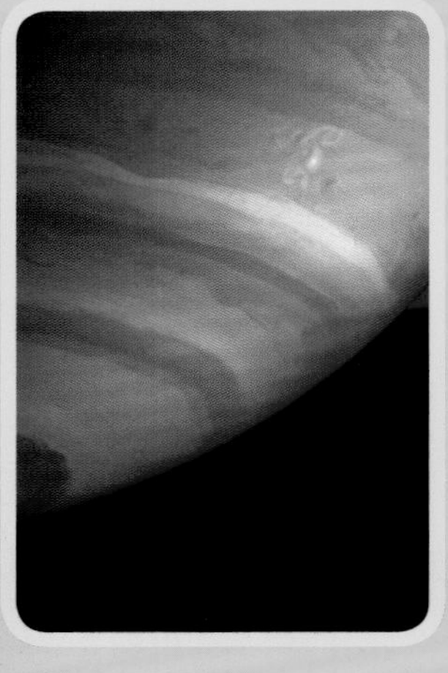

GAS GIANTS: Jupiter and Saturn (above) are titanic balls of hydrogen and helium. Some astronomers consider them failed stars.

ICE GIANTS: The far-flung worlds of Uranus (below) and Neptune are gas giants like Jupiter and Saturn, but astronomers also call them ice giants because their atmosphere is composed mostly of "icy" water, ammonia, and methane.

Why is Venus like Earth's evil twin?

The average temperature here is more than six times hotter than the hottest spot on Earth, making the Venus the most scorching planet in the solar system. It's hot enough here to turn a slab of lead into a molten puddle. Sunset won't bring relief from the heat either. Day or night, from its north pole to its south pole, every day of the year, Venus is locked in a never-ending heat wave. Blame the blanketing atmosphere of carbon dioxide, which is thick enough at the surface to crush a submarine!

Why doesn't Mercury have an atmosphere?

This tiny planet—the smallest in the solar system—is only slightly larger than our moon (and its surface is the spitting image of our moon's, too), so its gravity is too weak to grip a heat-trapping atmosphere.

Why does Jupiter have a big red spot?

Jupiter's rapid spin, its hurricane-force winds, and the chemical composition of its atmosphere create colorful cloud bands that encircle the planet. One of these bands contains a hurricane large enough to span three Earths. This Great Red Spot has been raging for centuries.

Why IS EARTH'S SKY BLUE?

Air molecules in our atmosphere scatter the light, filtering blue out of the spectrum of colors that we can see.

... why is Mars's sky red?

Rusting iron minerals in the rocks and soil blow into the air—occasionally in planetwide dust storms—giving the atmosphere a rusty tint.

... and why does Saturn's sky flash?

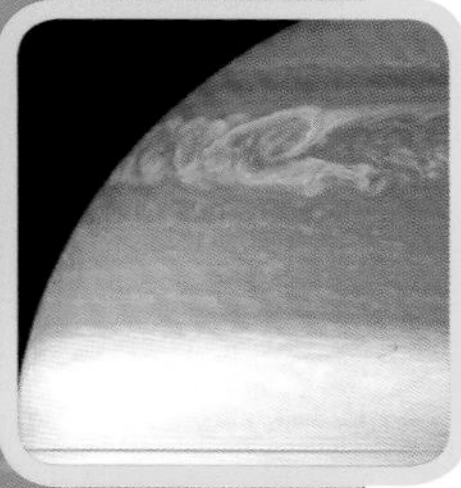

Large ammonia crystals that form in this ice giant's upper atmosphere cause electrical storms the size of the United States and lightning strikes a thousand times more powerful than those on Earth.

Which planets in our solar system have rings?

Four of them: Jupiter, Saturn, Uranus, and Neptune.

Why do they have rings?

Astronomers believe these rings formed from bits of asteroids and comets that were captured by the powerful gravity of these "gas giants." Saturn's rings are the easiest to spot. More than 170,000 miles (270,000 km) wide, dappled with spokes that rotate at different rates, Saturn's awe-inspiring ring system is actually a glittering shower of ice and rock that orbits the planet. And although the rings stretch about three-fourths of the distance between the Earth and the moon, they're incredibly thin—about 30 feet (9 m) wide in places.

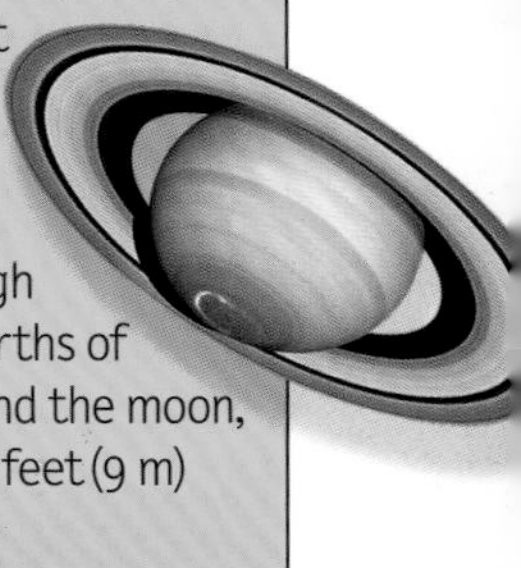

Do ALL THE PLANETS IN THE SOLAR SYSTEM SPIN?

Yes, but at different rates and, in some cases, directions. Venus spins so slowly that its year (roughly 225 Earth days) is shorter than its day (the equivalent of 243 Earth days). It also rotates in the opposite direction: The sun rises in the west and sets in the east! The gas giant Jupiter may be the largest planet in the solar system, but it has the shortest day—just ten hours—because of its rapid rotation.

WHY is PLUTO no longer considered a planet?

The distant cue ball of a frozen world known as Pluto has always been a space oddity (it's smaller than Earth's moon and follows a squashed orbit around the sun that takes 248 years). When astronomers began discovering other heavenly bodies rivaling tiny Pluto in size, they started to rethink their definition of a planet. Pluto no longer made the cut.

So, what exactly is a planet?

Easy question, right? After all, you're standing on one right now! But the scientific definition was fairly loose until recently. Astronomers put their heads together in 2006 and came up with three conditions for planethood: A planet must orbit the sun, it must be large enough that its own gravity molds it into a spherical shape, and it must have an orbit free of other small objects. Unfortunately Pluto failed to meet the third condition. It was downgraded to a "dwarf planet."

Dwarf planet? what's that?

These faraway worlds need to check off only two of the three planet-defining characteristics from the list above: They must orbit the sun and be big enough for their gravity to squish them into a spherical shape. Along with Pluto, astronomers have identified four other dwarf planets. Most of them join Pluto in the Kuiper belt of comets beyond the orbit of Neptune, the eighth planet from the sun. They include 1 **ERIS**, which rivals Pluto in size; egg-shaped 2 **HAUMEA**, one of the fastest-spinning objects in the solar system (its "day" lasts just four hours); mighty 3 **CERES**, the largest of the asteroids at nearly 600 miles (966 km) in diameter; and 4 **MAKEMAKE** (not pictured), which is the most recently discovered and the most awesomely named. The five confirmed dwarf planets—including Pluto—are all smaller than Earth's moon, but some of them have moons themselves.

WHY were ANIMALS sent into space before HUMANS?

The first Earthling to orbit our planet was just two years old and plucked from the streets of Moscow barely more than a week before her historic launch. Her name was Laika. She was a terrier mutt and considered a good dog by everyone who met her. Before the first manned space flights in the 1960s, scientists weren't sure if humans could survive a rocket ride into Earth orbit, where astronauts would experience weightlessness and higher levels of radiation. So they sent test flights crewed by a small zoo's worth of animals: fruit flies, monkeys, mice, and dogs. Laika's 1957 mission paved the way for the first manned spaceflight by Russian cosmonaut Yuri Gagarin four years later.

Why did astronauts land on the moon?

The urge to explore and satisfy scientific curiosity certainly played a role in NASA's multi-mission program to land two astronauts on the moon's stark surface in 1969. But the driving force behind the moon missions—known as the Apollo program—was a so-called space race between the United States and the former Soviet Union, rivals in a global struggle for power. The Soviets had beaten the United States in the race to send the first man into space eight years earlier. The U.S. committed vast amounts of money and scientific brainpower to ensure it would win the race to the moon.

Why do astronauts wear protective suits in space?

Space is a hostile place! (More than 20 astronauts have died doing their jobs.) Outer space lacks air and air pressure, is blasted by radiation, and is either extremely cold or hot depending on whether an astronaut is in the sun or shade. A space suit re-creates all the comforts of home—air, air pressure, temperature control, and even a potty—while the astronaut works in the dangerous void between worlds and stars. The first space suits were modified pressure suits used in the U.S. Navy's high-altitude jet planes.

What would happen if astronauts flew a spaceship deep into a gas giant's atmosphere?

It would be a one-way trip. The ship would sink deeper into clouds of ammonia and water vapor until the intense atmospheric pressure and heat compressed the hydrogen around it into a molten liquid. Science-fiction writers have proposed exploring the gas giants in hot-air balloons high above the crushing depths below.

Space FIRSTS

Who WAS THE FIRST PERSON TO ORBIT THE EARTH?

Soviet cosmonaut Yuri Gagarin on April 12, 1961.

Who WAS THE FIRST PERSON ON THE MOON?

American astronaut Neil Armstrong took "one giant leap for mankind" on July 20, 1969.

What WAS THE FIRST SPACESHIP TO LEAVE THE SOLAR SYSTEM?

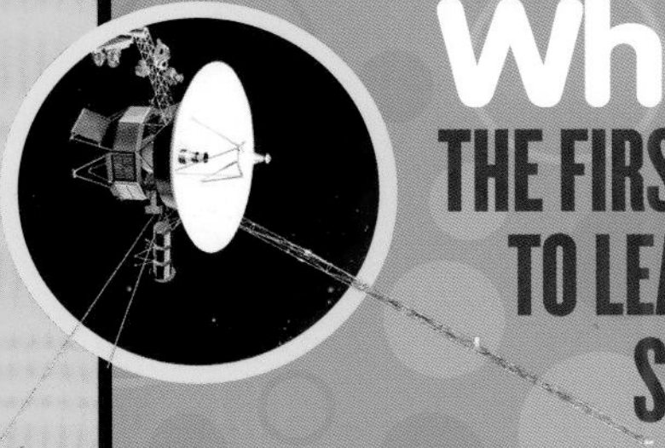

The Voyager 1 probe, which entered interstellar space—the void between stars—in August 2012 after exploring the solar system for 35 years.

What WAS THE FIRST SPACE SELFIE?

American astronaut Buzz Aldrin took this selfie in Earth orbit in 1966.

Who WAS THE FIRST PERSON TO PEE ON THE MOON?

Buzz Aldrin, who took one giant leak for mankind (into a special pee bag built into his space suit) while bounding across the lunar surface in 1969.

HOW fast can our SPACESHIPS travel?

Unlike airplanes, spaceships zipping through the void of space aren't slowed by friction from the atmosphere around them. Using rocket propulsion and the gravity of the sun and planets to sling them across the solar system, our fastest space probes can reach speeds of 150,000 miles an hour (241,000 kph). That might sound fast, but it's only the tiniest fraction of the speed of light and much too slow for travel beyond the planets in our solar system. The first manned flights to Mars will take at least six months. A modern spaceship would take tens of thousands of years to reach Alpha Centauri, the nearest star to our solar system.

How FAST IS THE SPEED OF LIGHT?

Really, really, really fast. As in 186,282 miles a second (299,792 kps).

Can a spaceship travel faster than the speed of light?

Not according to the laws of physics, which treat light speed as a sort of universal speed limit. Albert Einstein observed that even achieving the speed of light would require more energy than exists in the universe.

At light speed, how long would it take to travel to ...

THE MOON? 1.3 seconds.
THE SUN? Eight minutes, 20 seconds.
THE NEAREST STAR SYSTEM OUTSIDE OUR SOLAR SYSTEM? It takes a little more than four years for the light of our nearest neighboring star system—Alpha Centauri—to reach Earth. In other words, Alpha Centauri is more than four light-years away. (Astronomers measure the distance between stellar objects using light-years; one light-year is how far light travels in a year.)

If it takes that long to reach the nearest star, will we ever get to explore the galaxy?

Someday, maybe. Researchers at NASA's Johnson Space Center are looking into ways to beat the universal speed limit with a real-life "warp drive." Just like the propulsion system on the *Enterprise* from *Star Trek,* this engine would bend the universe around the ship—shrinking space in front of the ship and expanding it behind—to propel the crew to places at faster-than-light speed. Using this drive, a trip to Alpha Centauri would take just a couple of weeks rather than thousands of years. Of course, this real-life warp drive is only on the drawing board for now. The researchers are trying to create a mini-model of how this could work, and they've already mocked up a ship, named—you guessed it—the *Enterprise.*

PERSON OF INTEREST

WHO?
Albert Einstein

WHAT is he famous for?
The theory of relativity

WHEN?
1905–1916

WHERE?
Germany

WHY is he important?
Although this wild-haired physicist didn't study the cosmos through a telescope (his tool of choice was mathematics), Einstein laid the foundation for modern physics and our understanding of the relationship between time and space. His observations led him to believe that the laws of physics—and the speed of light—stay the same no matter your location and motion in the universe. He also explained that space and time are not two separate things. They're tied to each other in a concept he called space-time. What's more, Einstein discovered that space and time become distorted (or curved) by strong gravitational fields, such as those given off by large stars or black holes. This, Einstein theorized, can lead to all sorts of wild effects, including time travel.

WHY is up UP and down DOWN?

Thank gravity for every minute you're not flung into space by the Earth's rotation. Gravity is a force of attraction created by every object in the universe. A pebble generates its own gravitational field. So does a basketball. And a battleship. Even you create this attractive force (beyond just your good looks, of course). Gravity is hard to notice on a small scale, but the bigger the object, the greater its gravitational tug. The Earth is a very large object—composed of rocks and molten metals—so its gravity makes everything around it (including the air) "fall" toward the planet's center. That's why down is down for people in both Canada and Australia, even though they're standing on opposite sides of the planet. Earth's gravitational field is strong enough to keep your feet on the ground despite the planet's spin and the gravitational tugs of the moon and the sun (which are strong enough to pull the oceans and cause our tides).

Why do astronauts orbiting Earth experience zero gravity?

Ah, but astronauts do experience gravity! In fact, without gravity, their ships and space stations would slip from orbit on a one-way trip out of the solar system (which, by the way, would also fly apart without gravity). Although Earth's gravitational field is slightly less powerful hundreds of miles above the planet's surface, it's still more than strong enough to pluck passing space rocks or drifting satellites to the surface and hold the moon in orbit.

Why am I heavier on some planets and lighter on others?

Gravity! Remember, a heavenly body's gravitational attraction depends on its size. The larger and more tightly packed with matter an object, the stronger its gravity. And weight is really just a measurement of the force of gravity on an object's mass. Earth is larger than Mars, for example, so our home planet has a greater gravitational tug on all Earthlings and Earth things. That's why everything "weighs" more here. On the smaller asteroids in the asteroid belt, you'd barely notice any gravity at all. One giant leap would launch you into space!

How do spaceships, stations, and satellites stay in orbit?

Maybe a simple experiment in "orbital mechanics" will help. Tie a string to a ball or stick and whirl it around your head. Notice how it travels around you in a circle? Imagine that the object is a spaceship and you are the Earth. The string represents the force of gravity. The same forces are at work when a spaceship orbits the Earth (except gravity, unlike your string, is invisible). If an orbiting ship were to speed up, it would "break" free of gravity and travel into space. If it were to slow down, it would plummet back to the Earth's surface (which is precisely how spaceships return for a safe landing). Ships and space stations maintain orbit by "falling" around the Earth at just the right speed. Because the astronauts are falling at the same speed as the ship around them, they experience the sensation of weightlessness—or free fall. You would experience the same thing if you were in an elevator and the cable snapped suddenly. The elevator would plummet to the ground with you falling inside it at the same speed. You'd float weightlessly inside the elevator until (hopefully) the emergency brakes kicked in and brought your free-falling experience to a slow stop.

What does free fall feel like?

At first, free fall can feel like roaring down a hill in a roller coaster or one of those sudden-drop rides at amusement parks. But these rides are thrilling—and a little scary—because passengers can see the world whiz past them and the ground rush at their feet. Astronauts only see the inside of their spaceships or the distant Earth and stars outside the windows, so they don't have any visual clues that they're falling. To them, free fall feels as if gravity has switched off. The feeling can be disorienting—and a little sickening for some. Two-thirds of the passengers aboard NASA's "Vomit Comet," a plane that flies in slow dives to re-create weightlessness, toss their cookies during flight.

SAY WHAT?!

ASTRONAUTS NOT ONLY have to deal with gravity in space, but they also use it to get where they're going. Traveling from A to B in a spaceship or probe requires complex calculations—literally, rocket science—to "slingshot" from planet to planet (or moon) across the solar system using the gravity of each heavenly body.

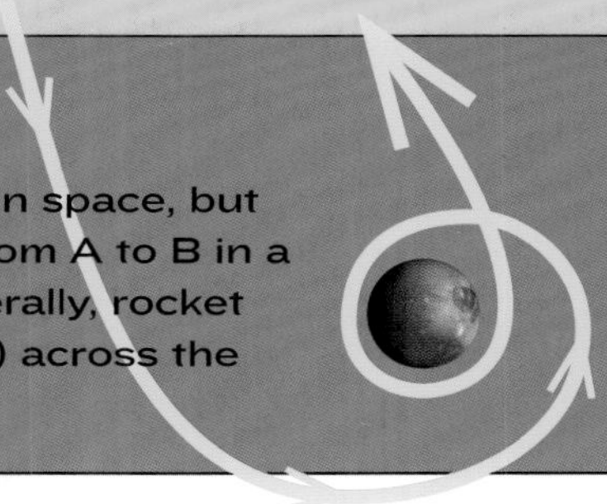

If I WEIGH 100 LB (45 KG) ON EARTH

what would I weigh on ...

... the moon?
17 lb (8 kg)

... Mercury?
38 lb (17 kg)

... Mars?
38 lb (17 kg)

... Venus?
90 lb (41 kg)

... Uranus?
90 lb (41 kg)

... Saturn?
106 lb (48 kg)

... Neptune?
114 lb (52 kg)

... Jupiter?
253 lb (115 kg)

WHY is Earth the only planet with LIFE?

Not so fast, Earthling! Outer space is a big place, and one thing scientists have learned from studying life on Earth is that organisms can thrive in all sorts of harsh environments. Meanwhile, astronomers have discovered nearly 4,000 Earthlike planets beyond our solar system and are spotting more every day. Some of these "exoplanets" orbit their stars in the "Goldilocks zone," a distance that's neither too hot nor too cold to support liquid water and possibly alien life. Who knows? Maybe an alien kid somewhere up there is wondering if you exist.

MYTH MASHED

Why DOES MARS HAVE A FACE ON IT?

When the Viking I orbiter snapped pictures of Mars in 1976, one photo became a hit for its apparent portrayal of a mountainous Martian face resembling an Egyptian pharaoh. Eager to set the record straight on this crowd-pleasing Mars anomaly, NASA used a satellite to re-photograph the region in 1998 and 2001. The high-resolution images revealed a natural geological feature rather than a monument to Martiankind.

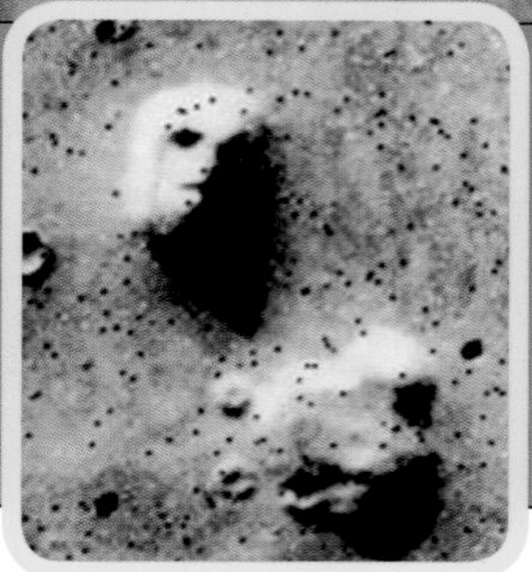

How ARE ASTRONOMERS SEARCHING FOR ALIEN LIFE?

BY DIGGING: Robotic rovers are sampling Martian soils for signs of ancient life.
BY VISITING: Probes are being dispatched to spots across the solar system that might harbor life today.
BY LOOKING: NASA's Earth- and space-based telescopes have been scanning the galaxy for Earthlike exoplanets outside our solar system capable of supporting life.
BY LISTENING: In 1960, scientists began scanning the universe with special telescopes for radio signals from alien civilizations. The project is called SETI, or the Search for Extraterrestrial Intelligence. It hasn't picked up any alien broadcasts yet, but we haven't stopped listening.

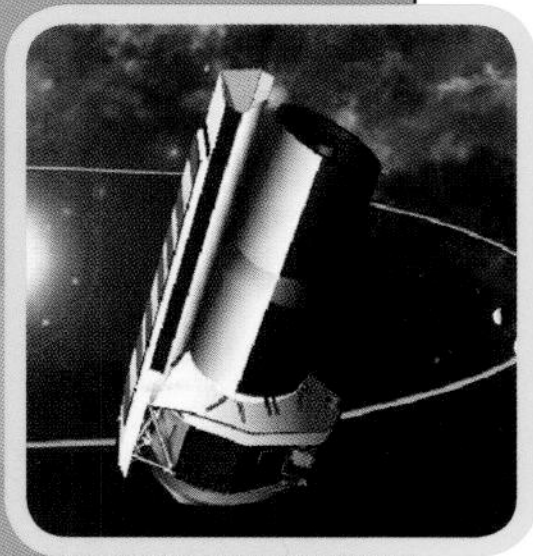

How many exoplanets might support life?

After analyzing the known exoplanets and comparing that data with what they know about the Milky Way, astronomers at Cornell University predict that as many as 100 million worlds in our galaxy could support complex life.

So why haven't we met any aliens yet?

Because space is big. The galaxy might be teeming with life, but the gulfs between stars make visiting our neighbors an impossible mission—at least for now. Remember, it would take thousands of years to travel to the closest star outside our solar system using modern spaceship technology.

Why did people once think Martians lived on Mars?

Astronomers peering at Mars in the 17th, 18th, and 19th centuries saw signs of life everywhere. Seas! Continents! Canals that carried water to Martian farms! But modern telescopes, probes, and NASA landers ruined the fun by revealing our planetary neighbor's dry details: It's just a lifeless ball of red rock. Early astronomers had confused Mars's ancient seas and riverbeds for signs of civilization.

What about the possibility of life closer to home?

Where? Like in London? Ah, you mean in our solar system! Mars was once considered a top candidate for alien life, but so far we haven't found any Martians. (Anything that lived on the red planet is most likely long dead.) Astronomers seeking signs of life are now turning their attention to the solar system's moons instead of its planets.

Which of the solar system's moons might have life?

The frozen surface of Jupiter's moon Europa hides a liquid ocean that might contain alien creatures. Enceladus, one of Saturn's many moons, has a sea the size of Lake Superior under its icy surface. And Titan, Saturn's largest moon, has vast lakes of liquid methane. If life existed here, it would be truly alien.

SILLY QUESTION, SERIOUS ANSWER

Why is the U.S. government hiding evidence of alien life?

Ah, you must be thinking of the "Roswell incident," in which an unidentified craft crashed near the small town of Roswell, New Mexico, U.S.A., in 1947. Conspiracy theorists claim the craft was a flying saucer and that the U.S. military whisked away the wreckage along with the bodies of its alien pilots. The U.S. government released a report on Roswell in the mid-1990s claiming the debris was actually a crashed balloon in its top-secret "Project Mogul," which used high-altitude sensors to monitor for enemy nuclear-missile tests. "Likely story," claim the conspiracy theorists.

WHAT are BLACK HOLES?

Astronomers can't see these mighty munchers of matter, but they spot their effects across the galaxy. Black holes form when stars 20 times larger than our own sun run out of fuel and go "supernova"—or explode. The dying star's core collapses under its own gravity until it scrunches into a singularity—or tightly packed point—smaller than an atom. Despite its tiny size, the singularity still packs a gravitational pull many times stronger than our sun. Like a cosmic whirlpool, the black hole pulls in anything—asteroids, planets, other stars, and even light—that gets too close.

What would happen if you got sucked into a black hole?

Some seriously strange stuff—and none of it good. Everything would go dark as your spaceship approached the black hole's swirling "event horizon," or point of no return. The gravity here is so powerful that even light cannot escape the crushing singularity at the center. Your ship and body would stretch into an impossibly thin and long line, like toothpaste squeezed from its tube. As you approached the speed of light, time would slow and eventually stop, although you wouldn't be alive to notice. Weird, huh? And black holes aren't even the strangest things in the universe. There are darker forces at work ...

What is dark energy?

Until recently, astronomers assumed that gravity was slowing the expansion of the universe that began with the big bang. At the end of the last century, however, they learned a shocking fact: The expansion was actually speeding up. The only way to explain this acceleration is that space is filled with ... something else. Astronomers call this mystery matter "dark energy." They can't see it, but they figure it has to exist everywhere, accounting for roughly 68 percent of the stuff in the universe. (Meanwhile, the atoms that make up planets, stars, your pet goldfish, and everything else account for less than 5 percent of the universe.)

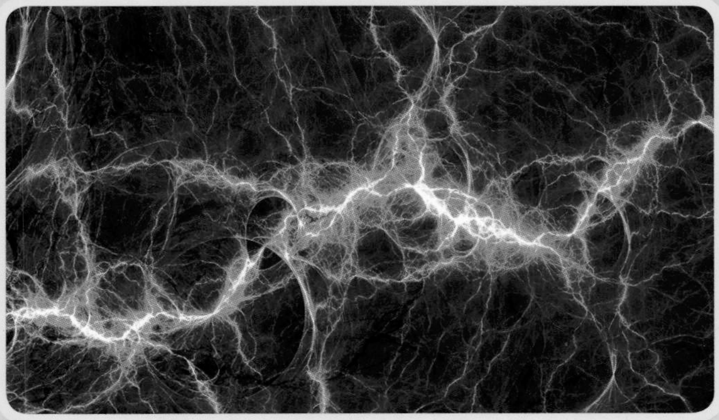

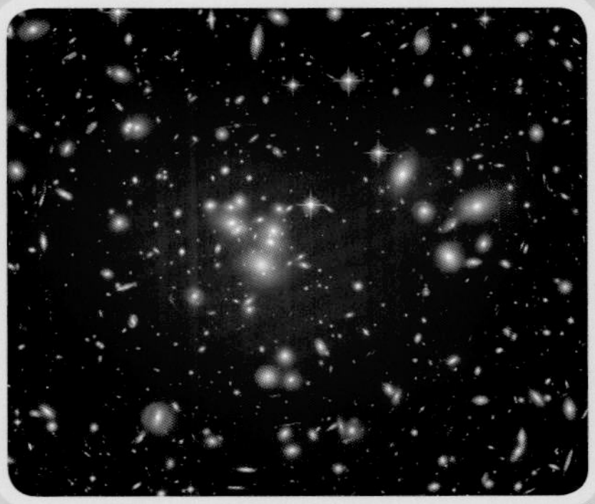

What is dark matter?

The other 27 percent of the universe is made of this stuff, which is easier to detect than dark energy because astronomers can measure its gravitational effect on distant stars. Still, astronomers aren't sure exactly what dark matter is. Two competing—and cutely named—theories attempt to explain dark matter's contents: MACHOs, for Massive Compact Halo Objects such as small stars, and WIMPs, for Weakly Interacting Massive Particles left over from the big bang.

Is time travel possible?

It's not only possible—humans are doing it all the time! Of course, we're all moving forward in time right now (at a rate of one second for every second). And according to laws of physics that are far too complicated to explain here, time slows down as a person speeds up. This effect—known as time dilation—is really noticeable only as you approach the speed of light. Astronauts aboard the International Space Station orbit the Earth at about 18,000 mph (29,000 kph), which is just a tiny fraction of light speed, but they're still moving fast enough to experience time dilation on a measurable scale. Once they return home from a six-month assignment, astronauts are actually .007 seconds behind in time compared with their friends and family on Earth.

SAY WHAT?!

SPEED ISN'T THE ONLY THING that puts the brakes on the relative passage of time. Gravity affects time, too. Remember, all objects in the universe generate a gravitational attraction. The greater the object's mass, the stronger its gravity. And the stronger the gravitational field, the greater its effect on time. So time actually passes slightly slower for a person sitting on the beach versus a climber atop Mount Everest, which is farther from the center of Earth's mass and has a tad less gravity.

PERSON OF INTEREST

WHO?
Stephen Hawking

WHAT is he famous for?
Shedding light on black holes

WHEN?
1960s through today

WHERE?
England

WHY is he important?
Considered the most brilliant scientific mind since Einstein, Stephen Hawking is famous for trying to reverse engineer the workings of the universe through quantum physics—or the study of the universe at its teeniest-weeniest level. He's also an expert on black holes and their bizarre behavior. Based on his observations, Hawking believes that just as the universe began in a cosmic big bang, it will someday end up collapsing into black holes.

WHAT is an ASTEROID?

Asteroids are chunks of rock that orbit the sun and wander around the solar system. They're the rubble left over from the solar system's formation roughly 4.6 billion years ago. An asteroid is made of the same stuff under your feet—rock, bits of metal, maybe some carbon.

Where do they come from?

Scientists estimate that millions of these pint-size planetoids orbit the sun in the asteroid belt, a stretch of space between the orbits of Mars and Jupiter. Some scientists believe the asteroid belt is from the rubble of a planet that never formed.

How do they end up in our neck of the solar system?

Asteroids are fine when they stay where they belong, orbiting the sun in the asteroid belt. But occasionally Jupiter's gravity tugs one of the larger asteroids loose and sends it hurling in our direction.

How big are these roving rocks?

The largest asteroid, Ceres, is nearly 600 miles (966 km) across. Others range in size down to 20 feet (6 m) wide. Some asteroids are large enough to have their own moons. Many are more like piles of rubble moving through space—squadrons of small rocks held together by their own gravitational attraction.

Why should we keep an eye out for asteroids?

Because they've smashed into every planet in the solar system, including Earth, and one good hit could mean game over for life here. Asteroids travel at tens of thousands of miles an hour—speeds that transfer into destructive energy when they collide with a planet, moon, or each other. An asteroid 450 feet (137 m) across could destroy an entire city. More than a thousand people were injured in 2013 when an asteroid just 62 feet (19 m) wide exploded high in the atmosphere above Chelyabinsk, Russia. An asteroid impact 65 million years ago may have wiped out the dinosaurs.

When will the next big asteroid strike Earth?

Nobody knows, but don't lose any sleep over the thought of a space rock landing in your living room. Several monitoring projects—such as Spacewatch and the Minor Planet Center—use powerful telescopes to scan the skies and track the courses of any "near-Earth objects," including asteroids that might drift too close to home. NASA has identified 90 percent of all the near-Earth objects large enough to cause catastrophic damage if they struck our planet. So far, we're in the clear.

What's THE DIFFERENCE BETWEEN ...

... an asteroid?

Asteroids are roving rocks found in the asteroid belt between Mars and Jupiter.

... a meteor?

Also known as shooting stars, meteors are pieces of rocks or ice that enter the Earth's atmosphere. As much as 22,000,000 pounds (10,000,000 kg) of meteors burn harmlessly in the atmosphere each day.

... a meteorite?

Any piece of space debris that survives the fiery entry into Earth's atmosphere is known as a meteorite once it touches down.

Why would we want to visit the asteroid belt?

There's gold (and other precious metals) in those rocks! In fact, a company called Planetary Resources plans to send robot miners to the asteroid belt.

MYTH MASHED

Isn't IT TOO DANGEROUS TO VISIT THE ASTEROID BELT?

Although movies portray asteroid belts as spaceship-smashing jumbles of rock, our solar system's real asteroid belt isn't nearly so treacherous. The average distance between rocks is nearly a million miles (1.6 million km), which would give spaceship pilots plenty of wiggle room.

WHAT is a COMET?

Like asteroids, comets are leftovers from the formation of our solar system, but they're made of different stuff. Each is an irregular ball of icy slush, frozen gases, and dark minerals just a few miles or kilometers wide. Like planets, some comets orbit the sun on a predictable schedule. Halley's comet, the most famous of these weird wanderers, drops by Earth every 76 years or so (it's not due for its next visit until July 2061).

Where do comets come from?

Comets originate far out in the solar system—some from the Kuiper belt of icy bodies beyond the orbit of Neptune, and others from a more distant region known as the Oort Cloud.

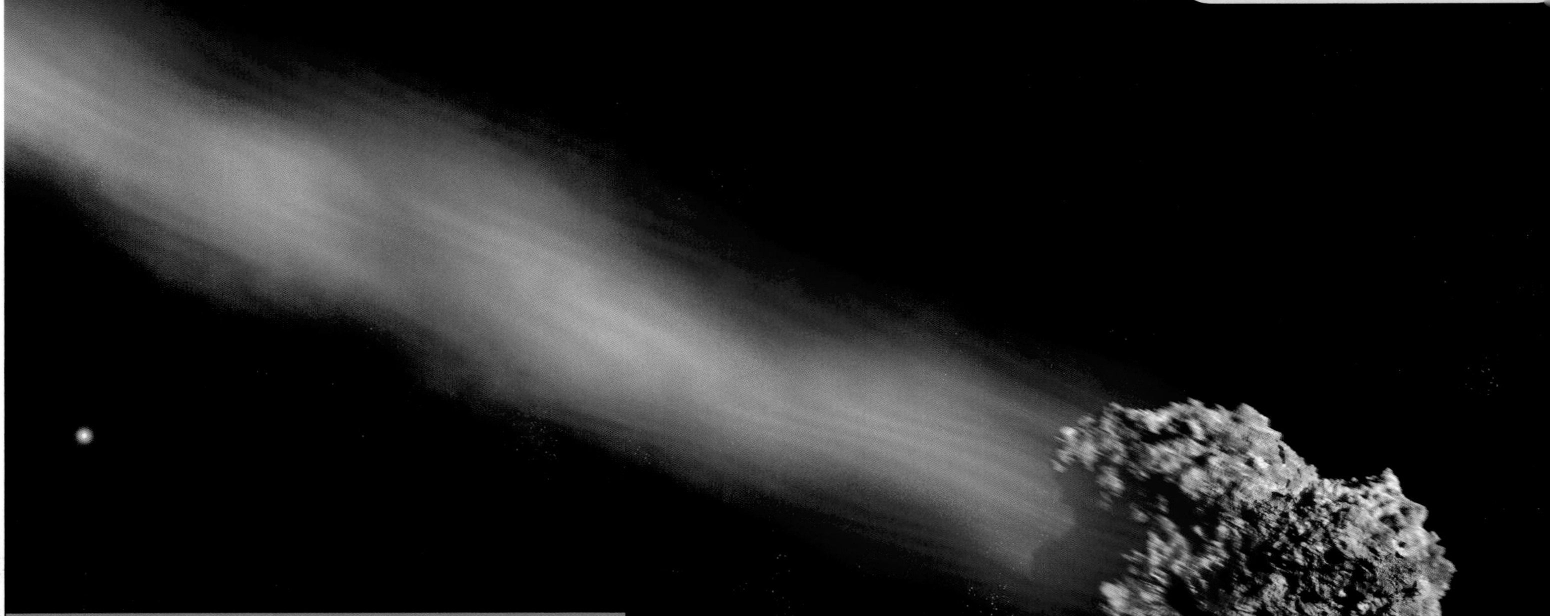

SAY WHAT?!

TO HELP FIGURE OUT how to stop dangerous asteroids, NASA is planning to capture one. Its Asteroid Redirect Mission may attempt to nab an asteroid in a space probe's "capture bag" and release the roving rock into lunar orbit. NASA hopes to begin landing astronauts on its captured asteroid by the mid-2020s.

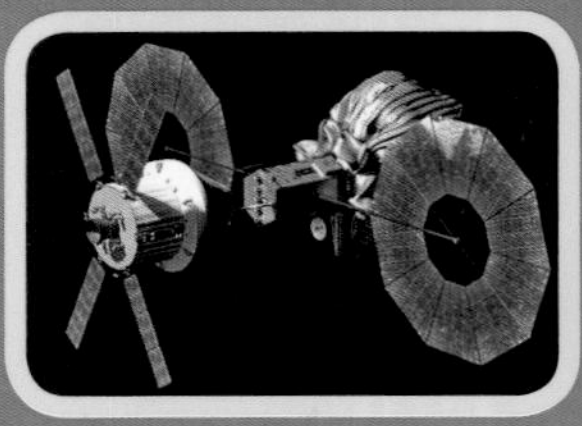

Unwelcome VISITORS

Until relatively recently in human history, the appearance of comets was thought to symbolize doom and upheaval. For instance ...

Caesar's Comet

This onetime visitor was heralded by the Romans to mark the assassination of Julius Caesar in 44 B.C. Today, astronomers debate whether the comet actually existed.

Halley's Comet

Our most famous visitor's regular appearances were blamed for the overthrow of an English king in 1066 and the later outbreak of the "Black Death" plague. The Catholic Church declared Halley an agent of evil in 1456, but that didn't stop the comet from coming.

Shoemaker-Levy 9

Discovered in modern times, this heavenly body demonstrated the destructive power of comets when it broke apart and slammed into the gas giant Jupiter in 1994, creating dark marks up to twice the size of Earth in the planet's atmosphere.

What happens when comets head in our direction?

As a comet nears the sun, ice and dust boil from its icy center—called a nucleus—to form an atmosphere known as a coma. Sunlight "blows" gas and dust from this coma to create spectacular tails. Some tails reach 100 million miles (160 million km) long and can be seen from Earth. Like asteroids, comets occasionally collide with planets and have the potential to cause massive destruction.

How could we defend Earth from a large asteroid or comet?

In 2013, NASA announced its "Grand Challenge" to locate any nasty asteroids heading our way and prevent their impact. Rock-stopping options include ...

NUKING IT: Attack the asteroid with a nuclear missile, smashing it into space dust.

RAMMING IT: Launch a rocket directly into the asteroid to break it in half or divert its course.

BLASTING IT: Target the asteroid with a space-based laser to vaporize it before it gets too close

REDIRECTING IT: Mount rocket engines to the asteroid's surface to change its course so it misses Earth.

HISTORY

IMAGINE IF YOU COULD zip across the centuries in a time machine. Where—er, actually, when—would you start? A mummy's tomb in ancient Egypt? A knights' tournament at a medieval castle? Strap in as we visit these ancient venues and many others in a chapter that rewinds time and solves some of history's mysteries.

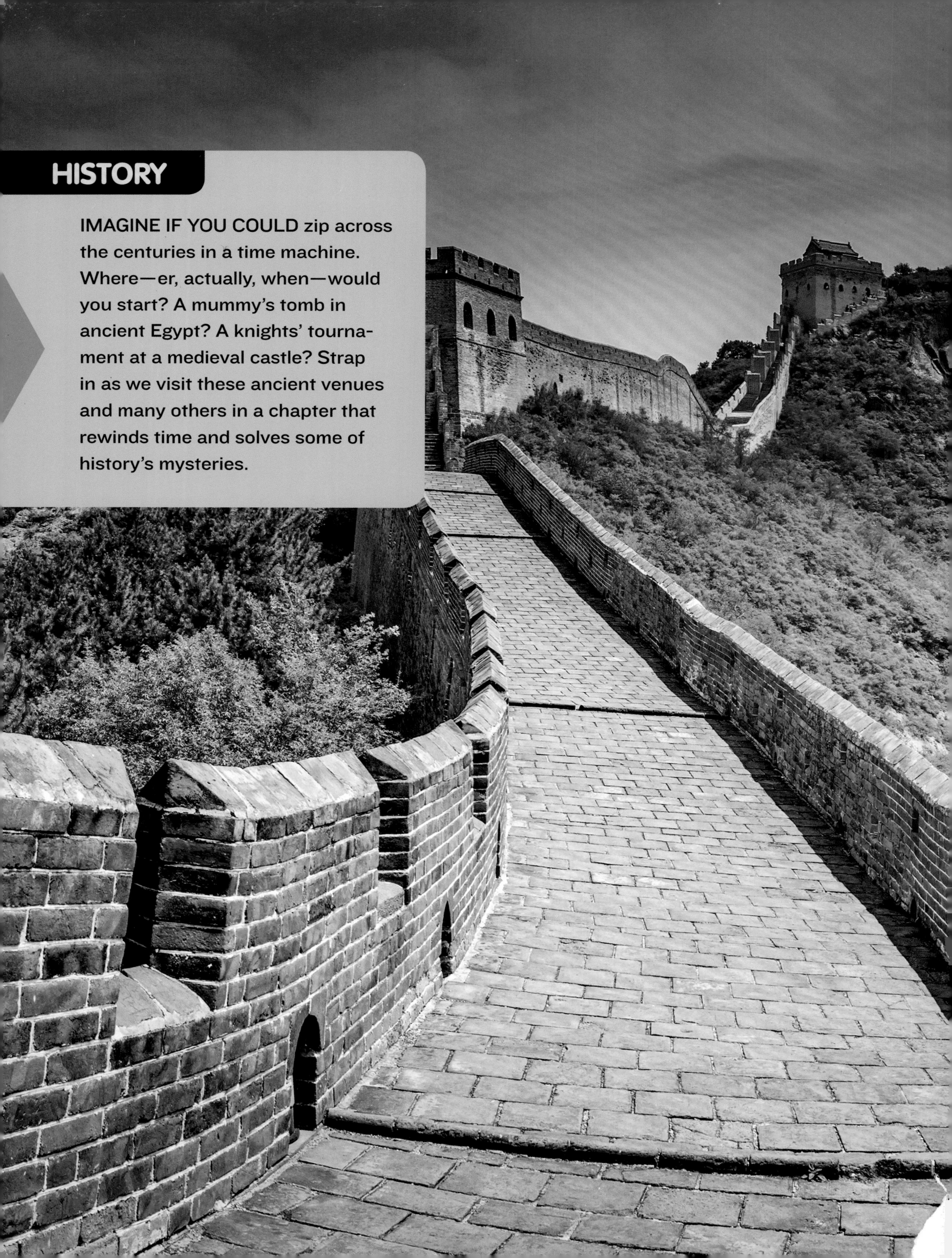

4
WHY, WHERE & WHEN

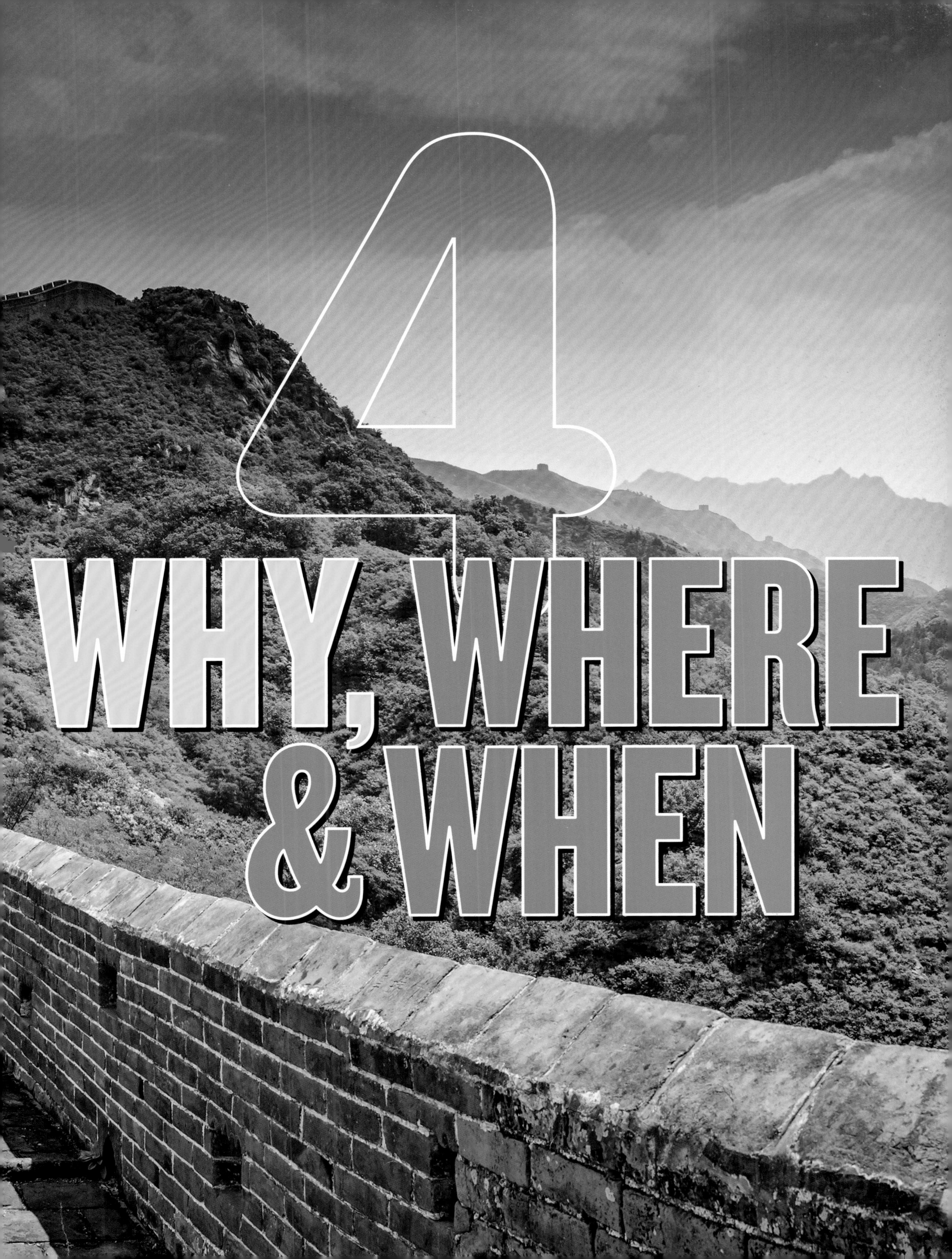

WHY did ancient humans PAINT cave walls?

Ice Age beasts and geometric designs, hunting parties and herds of horses—the painted imagery of our ancestors took many shapes and styles. As far back as 41,000 years ago, working in the dim light of oil lamps, humans (and possibly our Neanderthal relatives) expressed themselves in caverns across the world with etchings and paintings. But while archaeologists know how Stone Age artists turned cave walls into canvasses—by using chisels, charcoal, berries, and even bat poop as paint applied with straw brushes or blown through hollow bones—no one knows for certain why they did it.

In an age before the written word, cave artists probably painted as a form of communication: to teach other members of their group about animals in the region and how to hunt them. Some archaeologists believe cave art may have served as a sort of magic. By painting animals and hunting scenes on the walls of sacred caverns, or special caves used for ceremonies rather than as shelter, ancient artists may have hoped to bring success on the next hunt.

Captivating CAVE PAINTINGS

Cueva de las Manos
(Cave of the Hands)

WHERE is it?

Santa Cruz, Argentina

WHEN was it painted?

13,000 years ago

Profiles of human hands, perhaps created in some sort of coming-of-age ritual, join images of birds and beasts on the walls of this cave system in the Patagonian wilderness at the tip of South America. Most of the hands are lefties, leading archaeologists to believe the ancient artists created their stencils by blowing paint through hollow bones held in their right hands.

Lascaux Cave

WHERE is it?

Southwestern France

WHEN was it painted?

20,000 years ago

Crammed with more masterpieces than any art museum, this cave complex in the French countryside offers a window into the wild world of our Stone Age ancestors. The cavern walls are awash with stunning etchings of horses, bison, birds, humans, and bulls—one of which is 17 feet (5 m) long. Imagine having a poster the size of a minivan on your bedroom wall!

Altamira Cave

WHERE is it?

Northern Spain

WHEN was it painted?

15,000 years ago

Using charcoal and the curves of the cave walls to create 3-D effects, ancient artists painted bison, horses, deer, and other animals that looked so realistic, archaeologists thought they were forgeries when the caves were discovered in the late 1800s. They didn't believe Stone Age artists had the intellectual capacity for such creativity. They were wrong.

WHY are there different LANGUAGES?

Researchers can only guess when humans first began forming sounds into words to communicate thoughts (there certainly weren't any books to record the invention of language). Ancestors of the human species possessed the mouth and throat parts necessary to pronounce words nearly two million years ago, but they likely didn't have much to talk about until they started creating complex tools and building fires more than a million years later. The first system of words might have described tools and fire-making techniques. "Carl blow on fire, fire grow big," Carl the *Homo erectus*—our immediate evolutionary ancestor—may have explained to his campfire pals 500,000 years ago.

No doubt the earliest members of our species—*Homo sapiens*—added to the conversation when they appeared around 200,000 years ago. But as they started leaving Africa to explore Asia, Europe, and eventually the rest of the world around 60,000 years ago, our human ancestors began to develop more complicated tools—and probably words to describe them—within their own tribes. Their vocabularies grew and split off from the languages spoken by more far-flung groups. The farther these pockets of humanity moved from southwestern Africa—the point of origin for both *Homo sapiens* and language—the more their languages changed. And that's why we have nearly 7,000 languages spoken around the world today.

What are the five most commonly spoken languages in the world?

And how do you say hello in them?

- #5 **ARABIC** "Salaam" (sah-LOM)
- #4 **HINDI** "Namaste" (nah-MA-stay)
- #3 **ENGLISH** "Hello" (hell-OH)
- #2 **SPANISH** "Hola" (OH-lah)
- #1 **CHINESE** "nǐ hǎo" (nee-how)

Why did the U.S. military deploy Native American code talkers in World War II?

Although it's crucial in battle, communication is worthless—even dangerous—if it's intercepted by the enemy. Even messages created by complex "encryption machines," which convert plain words into secret codes, can be hacked given enough time. Native Americans, however, speak complex languages that are virtually unknown outside their tribes. Since the First World War, they've used their unique linguistic abilities in the U.S. military's signal corps as "code talkers," translating sensitive communications into their language and transmitting them much faster than any machine. Even if enemies learned to decode Cherokee, Comanche, Navajo, Choctaw, or any of the other code-talker languages, they would still need to figure out the secret terms for words that didn't exist in those languages. The Navajo word for "iron fish," for instance, was used to describe submarines. A tank became "turtle" in Comanche.

The code talkers' mission was so top secret they weren't even allowed to share details with their loved ones. Their existence was finally made public in 1968 (23 years after the close of the war), but it took several decades before they were recognized for their crucial role in winning World War II.

MYTH MASHED

Why DO ESKIMOS HAVE A HUNDRED DIFFERENT WORDS FOR SNOW?

This question has a flaw from the get-go. Eskimos—a broad term for people native to frigid subarctic regions in the United States, Canada, Greenland, and Russia—don't speak a single language. They actually speak five of them, none of which has a hundred words for snow. The myth of their ice-obsessed vocabulary comes from the way their languages work. Eskimos create larger words (and full sentences) out of smaller "root" words. Their languages have only a few root terms for snow, but to those small terms they add other words to create long one-word descriptions of the snow's conditions and uses ("the snow is icy and dangerous," for instance, or "this wet snow is excellent for making a snowman"). The structure of Eskimo languages makes it seem like they have hundreds of words for everything, not just snow.

SAY WHAT?!

THE FRENCH ARMY DISCOVERED a sort of "universal translator"—at least for ancient Egypt's written language—in 1799. Uncovered near the Egyptian village of Rosetta, this slab of granite was engraved with a royal announcement from 196 B.C. written in both Greek and hieroglyphics, an ancient Egyptian script composed of pictures that represented sounds, words, or concepts. Scholars who knew Greek set to work translating the Egyptian words, and by 1822 a French genius named Jean-François Champollion had cracked the code. Suddenly, archaeologists could make sense of the symbols scattered across Egypt. Tombs, temples, and monuments became open books.

WHY were pyramids so POPULAR in the ancient world?

The ancient Egyptians took pyramid construction to new heights along the Nile River in northeastern Africa 5,000 years ago, but they weren't the only civilization to build massive pyramid-shaped monuments (or even to mummify their dearly departed, which other ancient cultures also practiced). Pyramids were the most structurally sound buildings that could be constructed out of stone—as long as a civilization had sufficient rocks to quarry and the manpower to move them. Cultures all over the world built pyramids throughout history. They came in different forms and functions, as you can see on this page.

How big is the biggest pyramid?

Egyptians built more than a hundred pyramid tombs, but the biggest is the Great Pyramid at Giza. Nearly half as tall as the Empire State Building when finished, the Great Pyramid was built from 2.3 million limestone blocks assembled by a workforce of 20,000 laborers and craftsmen over two decades of construction. It held the title of world's tallest building for nearly 4,000 years.

THE ROSTER OF rocking rock CONSTRUCTION

Temple of Kukulkan

WHERE is it? Tinum, Mexico
WHEN was it built? Around A.D. 1000
HOW big is it? 98 feet (30 m)
WHY was it built? As a temple for sacrificial rituals to a Mayan snake god.

Pyramid of Cestius

WHERE is it? Rome, Italy
WHEN was it built? Around 12 B.C.
HOW big is it? 125 feet (38 m) tall
WHY was it built? As a tomb for Roman magistrate Gaius Cestius.

Ziggurat of Ur

WHERE is it? Ur, Iraq
WHEN was it built? 21st century B.C.
HOW big is it? 210 feet (64 m) tall
WHY was it built? As a shrine for the Sumerian moon god.

Pyramid of the Sun

WHERE is it? Teotihuacán, Mexico
WHEN was it built? A.D. 100
HOW big is it? 234 feet (71 m)
WHY was it built? Unknown, but likely as a temple for an Aztec god.

Why did the ancient Egyptians build pyramids?

These mountain-size monuments were built as tombs for ancient Egypt's kings, or pharaohs. Ancient Egyptians believed their pharaohs were living gods who deserved towering tombs as a stepping-stone to the heavens. Burial chambers within the pyramids were packed with all the treasures a pharaoh might need in the afterlife.

Were the pyramids built by slaves?

No. They were built by Egyptian farmers drafted into a national labor force called the corvée, which handled the heavy lifting on pyramid construction sites. They were fed, clothed, and housed, and received medical care when they got hurt on the job. Ancient graffiti hints that these men and women took pride in building a "house of eternal life" for their god-king. And unlike slaves, corvée workers could go home when the work season ended. Still, pyramid building was hardly an easy gig. Archaeologists digging up a worker cemetery found bodies with busted bones and diseases related to a lifetime of heavy lifting.

How did the ancient Egyptians build pyramids?

The hard way. Before the invention of pulleys or iron tools, Egyptian work crews relied on strong muscles and even stronger ropes. The blocks were quarried on-site or shipped down the Nile River from across the kingdom. Gangs of workers loaded the blocks on wooden sledges and hauled them across sand moistened with water, which made the sledges slide more easily. The blocks were then hauled up long mud ramps at the rate of one block every two minutes.

SAY WHAT?!

THE BLOCKS USED to build the Great Pyramid weigh roughly 2.5 tons (2.27 t) each and were piled so tightly together that not even a razor blade fits between them.

WHY did ancient Egyptians MUMMIFY their dead?

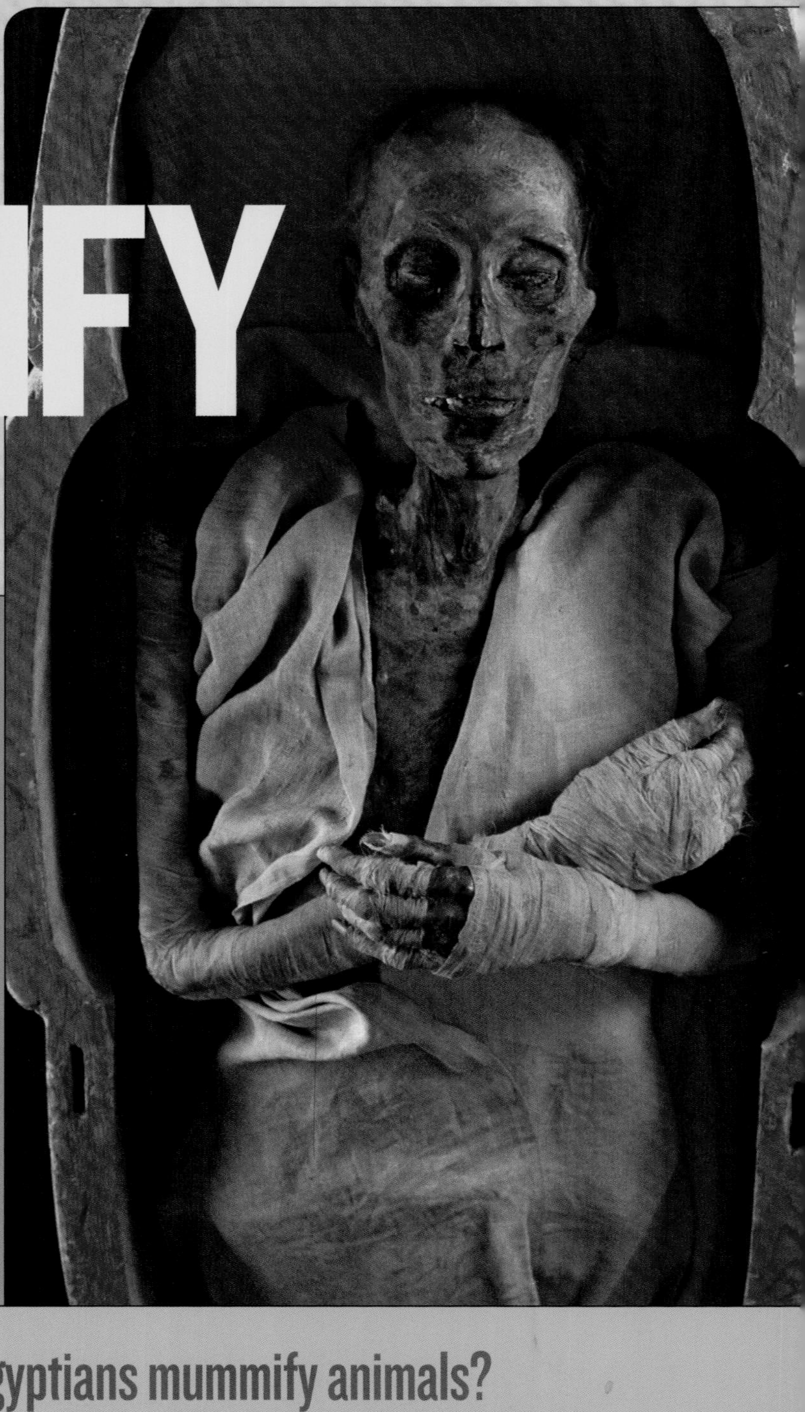

To the people of ancient Egypt, death was only the beginning. Egyptian kings (called pharaohs) were thought to become gods when they passed away. Ordinary Egyptians believed they would spend eternity with their ancestors in a perfect version of Egypt. But gaining entry into the afterlife wasn't as easy as tumbling off a pyramid. The Egyptians believed the spirits of their dearly departed wouldn't have a happy afterlife without access to their former bodies, so priests perfected the process of mummification to keep corpses from rotting away.

Why did ancient Egyptians mummify animals?

Archaeologists combing Egypt have excavated an entire zoo's worth of preserved animals: cats, dogs, donkeys, lions, rams, and shrews. Ancient Egyptians made these mummies for many reasons. Beloved pets were embalmed and entombed with their owners so that they might reunite in the afterlife. Sometimes, only the meat was mummified, to serve as an eternal jerky snack. Crocodiles, ibises, and other animals linked to specific gods were mummified by the millions. Although some mummies ended up in museums, the majority of human and animal mummies were burned as torches, used as fertilizer, or even ground up for medicine!

Why were ancient tombs packed with treasures and treats?

To the ancient Egyptians, who viewed death as the start of a great journey, passing into the afterlife unprepared was unsettling. That's why family and friends stocked the tombs with everything they'd need in the hereafter. Graves of poor Egyptians were packed with just the basics: food, cosmetics, and a few trinkets. The burial chambers of kings overflowed with priceless treasures and works of art.

Why were ancient Egypt's tombs cursed?

Tomb walls in ancient Egypt were inscribed with spells to frighten away grave robbers. "To all who enter to make evil against this tomb," read one inscription, "may the crocodile be against them on water and the snakes and scorpions be against them on land." Indeed, tragedy tracked the discovery of King Tut's grave by archaeologist Howard Carter in 1922. When the sponsor of the Tut expedition, Lord Carnarvon, died less than a year after the tomb was opened, reporters pounced on the idea that he'd fallen victim to a mummy's curse. It wasn't crocs or scorpions that did in Lord Carnarvon, however. He died from an infected mosquito bite. Despite the threat of curses (along with confusing dead-end corridors and decoy treasure rooms), most royal tombs were raided and robbed in ancient times—sometimes by the very workers who built them and knew their layouts.

Was King Tut murdered?

King Tutankhamun, aka King Tut, wasn't the first boy king to rule ancient Egypt, but he is the most famous, thanks to the discovery of his tomb and its trove of treasures in 1922. The most valuable artifact was Tut's mummy, nested inside the many coffins and boxlike shrines to protect his spirit for eternity. Unfortunately, Egyptologists a century ago weren't as gentle with mummies as they are today. They cut Tut into pieces to pry his body from the sticky sacred oils that coated the inside of his coffin. Such rough handling inflicted injuries on the 3,300-year-old mummy that made it tough to tell what caused Tut's demise.

Some suspected he was murdered. But modern technologies like 3-D scanning revealed that the all-powerful king was actually in poor health. He suffered from a bone disease that made walking a chore. Bouts of malaria left him shaky and weak. None of the tests pointed to foul play as the cause of Tut's death. Instead, the likely culprit is a broken leg revealed by x-rays. Perhaps the frail pharaoh tumbled from one of the chariots found in his tomb. With his immune system already weakened by malaria, Tut could have easily died from an infection in the busted bone.

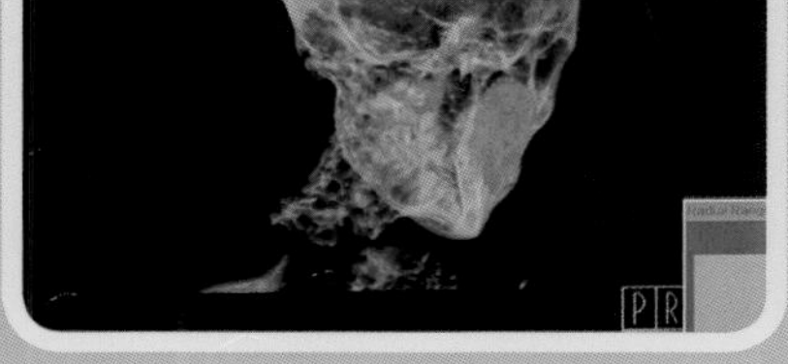

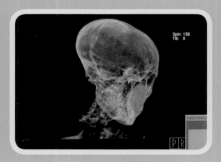

How did ancient Egyptians make mummies?

Here's the 4,000-year-old formula in four grisly steps ...

Step 1

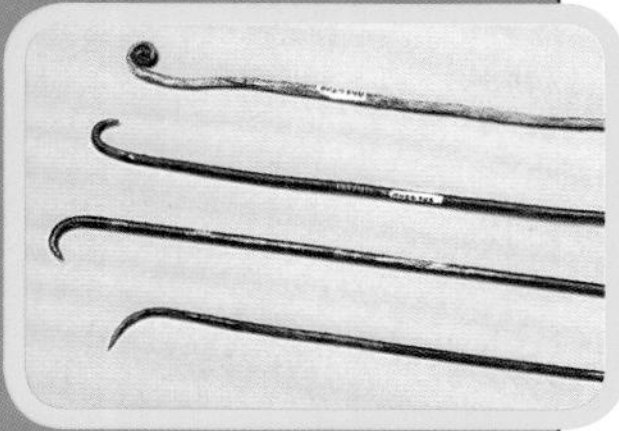

A priest poked a special hook up the dearly departed's nose to yank out the brains (which were considered useless).

Step 2

The liver, stomach, intestines, and lungs were all removed, cleaned, preserved, and sealed in special "canopic jars" carved to look like the gods who guard these organs. The heart—considered crucial equipment for the perilous journey through the underworld—was kept in place.

Step 3

Priests packed the body inside and out with a special salt to sop up the moisture. After the body dried for 40 days, it was stuffed with rags and plants so it didn't look like a deflated balloon.

Step 4

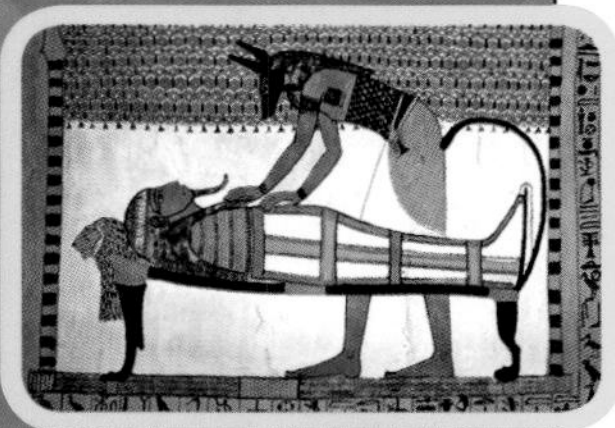

Priests rubbed the corpse's skin with oils and resins to soften it. Layers of linen, treated with the same oils, were wrapped around the mummy, giving it the famous bandaged look seen in movies. Finally, the priests tucked amulets into the wrappings and uttered spells to activate their protective powers.

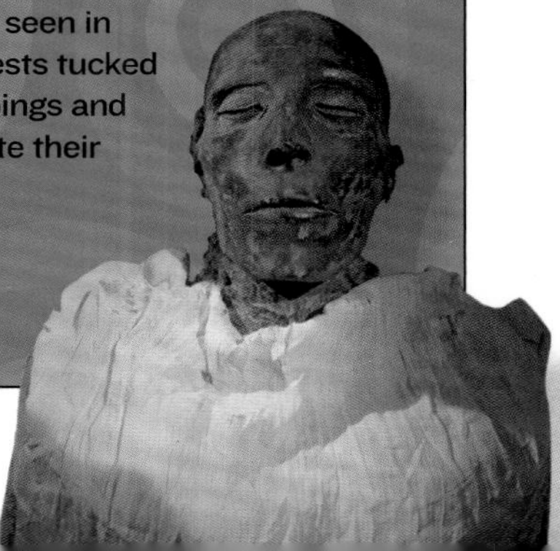

WHY do they say MONEY makes the world go around?

Because it buys just about everything we need to survive: food, homes, gas for our cars, electricity, heat, water, and cookies-and-cream milk shakes (okay, that last one isn't exactly a necessity, but you get the idea). People invest money in stocks, bank savings plans, property, and their education to eventually make more money.

How did people buy things before money?

They didn't buy—they bartered! Tens of thousands of years ago, when humans began establishing villages and farms rather than following herds of animals, they traded for what they needed: animal furs for vegetables, plant seeds for fish, arrowheads for farming tools, grain and candle wax for goats and cows.

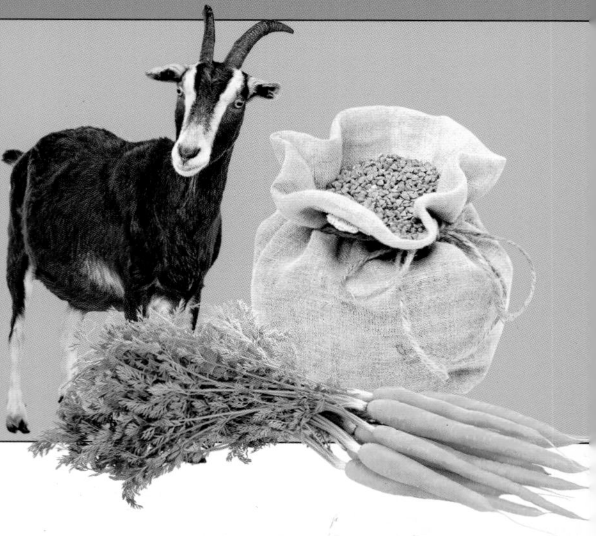

When did people start using money?

Around the year 1200 B.C., people in China started using mollusk shells called cowries to trade for goods. Cowries became the world's first form of currency, and they were adopted by civilizations across the world and used until the middle of the 20th century.

When did people start using coins?

The first chunks of change you'd recognize as coins—round lumps of precious metals impressed with images of gods and rulers—appeared around 700 B.C. in Lydia, in modern-day Turkey.

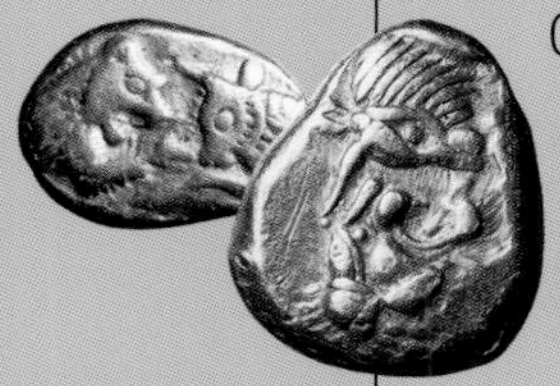

What about cash?

Paper currency—also known as notes or bills—didn't appear until the ninth century in China, but it eventually became so common that it lost its value. Consequently, paper currency fell out of use for hundreds of years until it reappeared in 17th-century Europe.

What gives today's money its value?

Nothing—or at least nothing we can reach out and touch. Today's currency is worth something only because we believe it's worth something. Its value is influenced by a number of factors, such as the cost of borrowing money and the rise or fall of the stock market. As a result, your cash might be worth a little more or less tomorrow. It wasn't always this way. The currency of some countries in Europe and the United States was once based on the value of gold. But this "gold standard" was abandoned nearly 90 years ago.

Why DO THE PRICES OF TOYS, CANDY, CARS, AND EVERYTHING ELSE RISE OVER TIME?

That fast-food burger your grandparents bought in 1964 for 15 cents costs six times as much today, but not because it's six times tastier or contains traces of gold in the mustard. Blame "inflation," a gradual increase in prices over the years. It's caused by many factors: a rise in demand for a particular good that suddenly becomes rare, an increase in cash in the money supply, a boom in the economy's health, a sudden shortage of a commodity (such as oil, chocolate, sugar, or cotton), and so on. Compare the (not-adjusted-for-inflation) prices from the past with the average prices of today and you'll see inflation at work. (Just keep in mind that incomes also tend to rise over time; workers today earn more than they did when burgers cost three nickels.)

Prices on the Rise

NEW CAR	1908:	**$825**
	Now:	**$32,300**
GALLON OF GASOLINE	1919:	**$0.25**
	Now:	**$3.69**
CANDY BAR	1929:	**$0.05**
	Now:	**$0.99**
BANANA SPLIT	1955:	**$0.39**
	Now:	**$5.49**
BARBIE DOLL	1959:	**$3.00**
	Now:	**$10.99**
GI JOE FIGURE	1964:	**$1.95**
	Now:	**$6.98**
MOVIE TICKET	1973:	**$1.76**
	Now:	**$8.38**
VIDEO GAME CONSOLE	1985:	**$299**
	Now:	**$299**

WHY DOES MY $20 BILL

... a funny feel to it?

Currency is printed on a special type of paper made from cotton and linen, which is why your bills don't become blobs of papery mush when they're accidentally run through the wash. That unique paper (combined with the intense pressure of the printing presses) gives genuine money its thin, crisp, unique feel, which is nearly impossible to replicate.

... a vertical strip in it when I hold it to the light?

To make it more difficult to counterfeit (make a copy and try to pass it off as the real thing), this skinny thread is implanted vertically and imprinted with the tiny words "USA TWENTY." (It also glows green under ultraviolet light.)

HAVE ...

... a tiny 20 on the bottom right corner?

The small 20 on the bill's front shifts from green to copper. It's printed with color-shifting ink that's hard for counterfeiters to copy—even with high-definition printers.

... a fainter portrait of President Andrew Jackson to the right of his main image?

This second image of Jackson is barely visible to the right of his main image when you hold your bill up to the light. This special type of hidden image is called a watermark—another anti-counterfeiting feature.

Which OF THESE OBJECTS WAS ONCE USED AS CURRENCY?

Salt

Giant stones

Strings of beads

Knives

Spices

Squirrel pelts

Cocoa beans

Seeds

Answer: Actually, all these items were used as currency at various points in history throughout the world.

WHY did powerful people build CASTLES?

They built them for a lot of reasons. Warlords in ninth-century France constructed the first castles—little more than wooden forts surrounding their homes—to protect their families and the local farmers from pillaging Vikings. From the 11th through the 14th centuries (part of a period known as the Middle Ages, or the medieval era), kings built castles to show off their power and wealth. It was a time when land was more precious than gold, and kings rewarded their most loyal supporters by granting them pieces of the realm and noble titles. These "lords" and "ladies" then built castles and hired their own supporters, such as knights for defense and peasants to farm the lands outside the castle (a system of government known as feudalism). No matter who you were in this feudal society, the castle loomed large in your life.

How much did a castle cost to build?

Castles weren't cheap! The massive castle Caernarfon in Wales cost an estimated $50 million in today's dollars to construct.

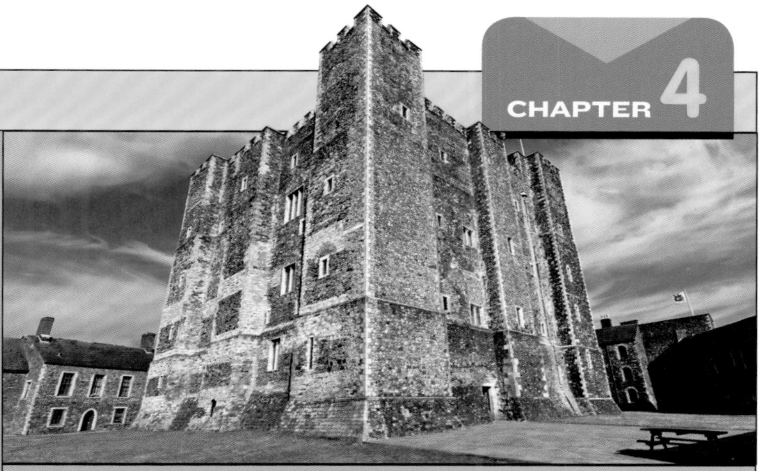

How were castles built?

Stone keeps, moats, and castle walls were major construction projects, involving thousands of workers and taking years—even decades—to complete. Workers quarried stone and hauled it to the building site in boats or horse-drawn wagons. Freemasons shaped the stones into square blocks that roughmasons laid to build the walls. Blacksmiths fixed the tools. Carpenters created scaffolding. Diggers dug the moat and well. Lime-burners created the mortar that held the stone together. A medieval castle-building site looked like a modern construction zone. Workers wielded familiar tools: hammers, chisels, mortar trowels, and saws. They used winches and hoists to lift heavy loads. The difference, of course, is that all these tools and lifting machines were people-powered. All of these workers had to be paid, making castle building an expensive business. Thousands of local peasants, meanwhile, might be forced to handle heavy labor for no pay. It's no surprise that many peasants hated castles.

Why did kings and lords attack castles?

Castle sieges were common in the Middle Ages. Any English lord who built a castle without the king's permission risked having it taken away or destroyed. And an ambitious lord couldn't conquer new territory unless he took control of each castle along the way. Otherwise, his army faced constant harassment from soldiers stationed in each of the enemy's castles. And many castles were worth the risk and expense of a siege because they sat in strategic locations—alongside vital river routes or near important cities. Dover Castle, overlooking the English Channel, was considered the key to England's defense. If it fell, the rest of England would be easy pickings.

How WERE CASTLES CONQUERED?

All sieges started the same way: The attacking army would surround a castle, making sure no one inside could escape and no one outside could sneak in food. With their blockade in place, the besiegers could try these options:

Negotiation

Once it had a castle surrounded, a siege army would send its messenger to request the surrender of the besieged. Sometimes, a castle's lord or constable would promise to give up if friendly reinforcements didn't arrive within a month. The surrendering castle guards would be allowed to leave peacefully, although the lord and lady might be held for ransom.

Deception

The history of siege warfare is filled with tales of castles lost to cunning tricks rather than after long, bloody battles. Attackers might bribe castle guards to lower the drawbridge, for instance. Sometimes, besiegers would send men-at-arms disguised as merchants to the castle gates. When the starving defenders rushed out to buy supplies, the attacking army would charge in.

Starvation

Castles were pricey pieces of property—as long as they weren't reduced to rubble—so besiegers preferred to capture them with their walls and towers intact. If they could blockade a castle long enough, its defenders would eventually eat all their food and be forced to surrender—or starve.

Excavation

Besiegers could send special miners called sappers to dig tunnels beneath the castle walls and cause them to collapse. Castle defenders often placed pots of water around the walls to detect the vibrations of enemy mining operations. If they suspected a tunnel was in the works, they'd dig their own countermine and fight the sappers in ferocious underground battles.

Destruction

When these tactics failed, attackers had no choice but to build siege engines: devices designed to batter the castle and its defenders. Catapults hurled stones that smashed walls and the people hiding behind them. Attackers placed long ladders and rolled tall towers alongside the castle to storm the walls. The castle's garrison of knights and soldiers, meanwhile, mounted a furious defense, raining arrows and boiling water on the attackers and shoving siege ladders away from the walls. By the time the castle fell, both sides would have suffered heavy losses.

WHY did people become KNIGHTS?

The road to knighthood was long and rough, but the journey was often worth the trouble. Successful knights found fortune and glory. But knights also had the most dangerous jobs of all the castle's characters. These professional warriors were charged with protecting the lord's land from invaders, leading the castle's men-at-arms during sieges, and fighting on behalf of the church. Between battles, they competed in deadly games called tournaments to sharpen their skills.

In exchange for outstanding military service, knights were granted their own land—along with peasants to farm it—and noble titles. The mightiest knights rose to rival lords in power and property. Sir Ulrich von Liechtenstein, one of the 13th century's most famous knights, owned three castles.

Not just anyone could become a knight. Armor, weapons, and warhorses cost more than a typical peasant might earn in a lifetime, so knights often hailed from noble families. They started their training early in life—at the age most kids today begin first grade.

How did someone become a knight in the Middle Ages?

Step 1: Serve as a Page

A boy destined for knighthood left home when he was seven to become a page in a great lord's castle, where he worked as a servant for the lord, learned courtly manners, and received a basic education from the castle priest. Life wasn't all chores and studying. The page wrestled with other pages and wielded practice weapons. Pages even rode piggyback to master the balance skills needed to fight from horseback.

Step 2: Squire for a Knight

Once he turned 14, a page became a squire for a knight. He learned about armor by cleaning his master's suit and helping him dress for battle. He practiced fighting with swords, shields, and other medieval weaponry. Most important of all, he learned to attack from the saddle of a huge warhorse—the type of mounted combat knights were famous for. Sometimes, squires followed their knights to war and fought in real battles.

Step 3: Get "Knighted"

By the time he turned 21, a squire was tough enough, skilled enough, and gentlemanly enough for knighthood. All that was left was his dubbing ceremony. After taking a bath and praying through the night, he knelt before his lord or the knight who trained him. This man then delivered a punch to the squire's cheek—in some cases with enough force to knock the would-be knight to the ground—to help him remember his oath. This blow later evolved into a friendlier sword tap on the shoulders. The newly dubbed knight was given the title "Sir" before his name and could seek service at a lord's castle.

WHY did PIRATES fly the skull & crossbones?

The *Pirates of the Caribbean* movies portray buccaneer crews as likable bands of high-seas misfits, but real-life "freebooters" were ruthless thieves who relied on their cutthroat reputation to frighten ships into surrendering without a fight (after all, a ship plundered in one piece was worth more than a cannon-blasted wreck). No one knows who flew the first pirate flag, also known as the "Jolly Roger." It was most likely a simple red or black strip of cloth hoisted above the ship's tallest mast to send a message to merchant ships: "Surrender or we'll sink you." Pirates during the golden age of piracy (from the late 1600s to the early 1700s) decorated their flags with images of skeletons, swords, skulls and crossbones, drops of blood, and other scary symbols to instill as much fear as possible, turning their flags into weapons that messed with the merchant sailors' minds.

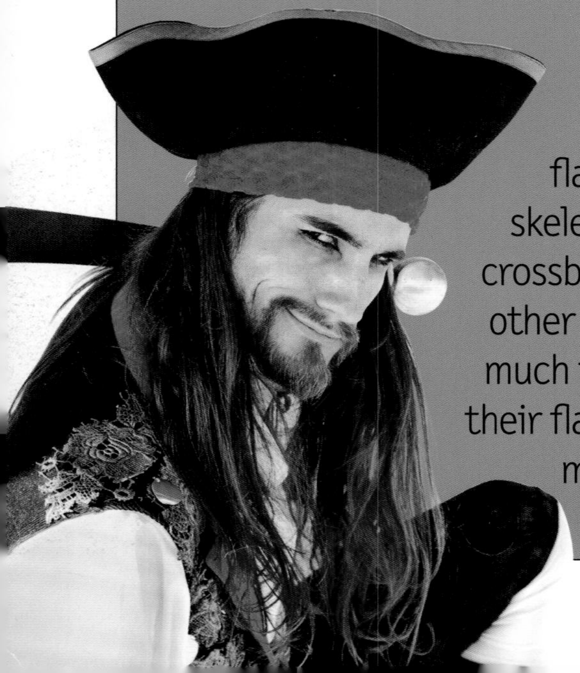

Four FAMOUS PIRATE FLAGS

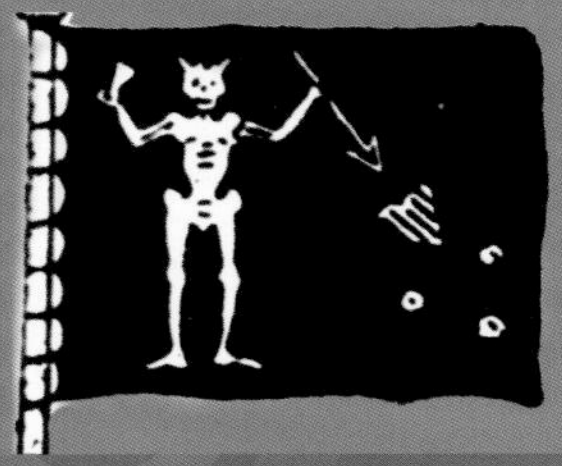

BLACKBEARD: The notorious Edward Teach, aka Blackbeard, let his reputation speak for itself when he ran up his Jolly Roger: "Resist and you will bleed."

BARTHOLOMEW ROBERTS: Above the flagship of his pirate fleet, the dreaded "Black Bart" flew a flag depicting him standing on the heads of his enemies.

SAMUEL BELLAMY: Flying the skull and crossbones—a universal symbol of poison, disease, and death—"Black Sam" plundered more than 50 ships to become the wealthiest pirate of the 18th century.

JOHN "CALICO JACK" RACKHAM: Cutlasses replaced the traditional crossed bones on the flag of this sharp-dressing real-life version of Captain Jack Sparrow.

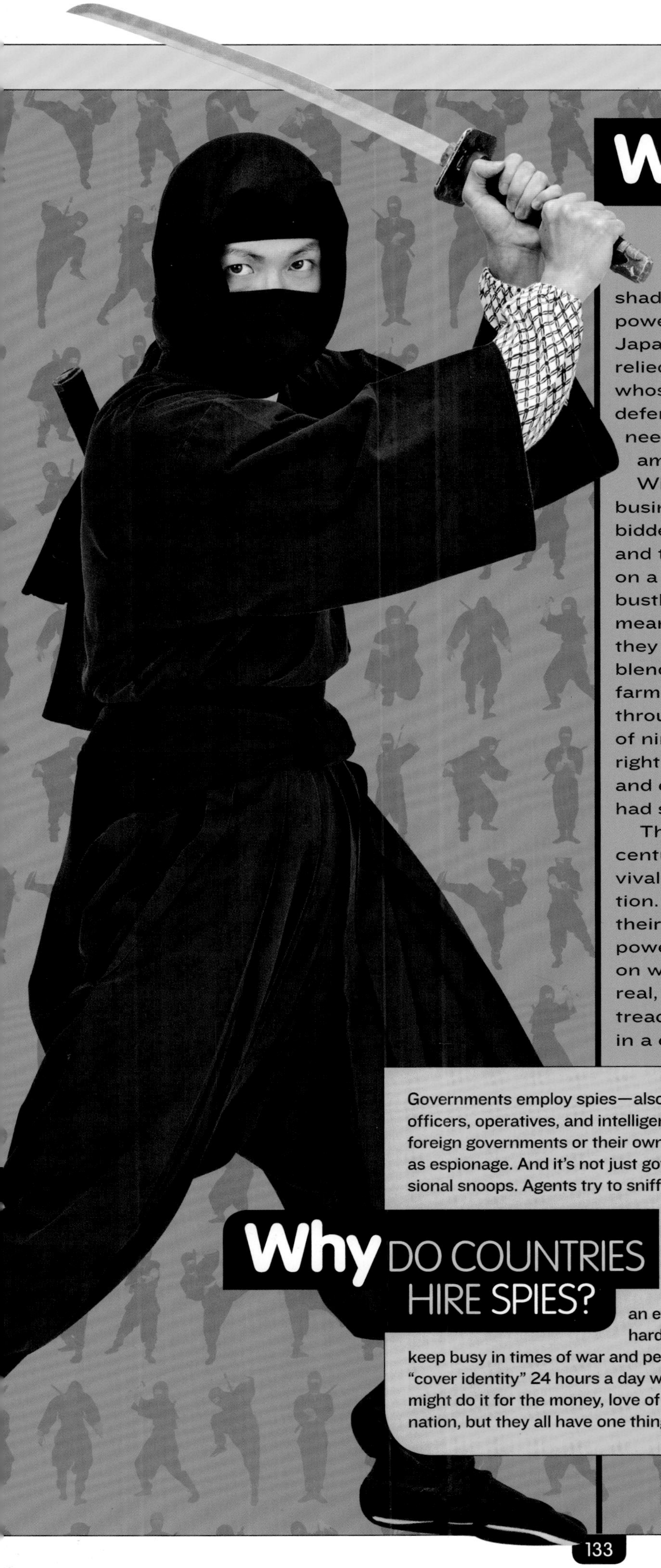

Why WERE NINJA WARRIORS SO SNEAKY?

These black-clad warriors emerged from the shadows in the 16th century, when hundreds of power-hungry warlords squabbled over control of Japan. During this violent "feudal" era, warlords relied on their armies of samurai—noble warriors whose code of battle forbade sneaky tactics—to defend their lands and attack rivals. But when they needed to spy on, assassinate, or create confusion among rivals, the warlords hired ninjas.

With no code of honor to put a damper on their business, ninjas hired themselves out to the highest bidder. A ninja might work for a warlord one year, and then spy on that same warlord the next. A ninja on a mission needed to blend in anywhere, from a bustling village to a castle rooftop at midnight. That meant he or she was a master of disguise. When they weren't wearing their traditional full-body suit to blend in with the shadows, ninjas would dress as farmers, merchants, or musicians to slip unnoticed through the countryside. In one famous siege, a team of ninjas dressed as the castle's guards and marched right through the front gate, set fire to the fortress, and escaped as the inhabitants bickered over who had started the flames.

The roots of the ninja stretch back to the eighth century—to secretive mountain clans trained in survival, self-defense, stealth, and the art of assassination. These warriors were feared and despised for their sneaky tactics and supposed supernatural powers. According to legend, a ninja could fly, walk on water, and vanish. Two of these powers were real, sort of. (Ninjas wore special wooden shoes to tread on water and explosive powders to disappear in a cloud of smoke.)

Why DO COUNTRIES HIRE SPIES?

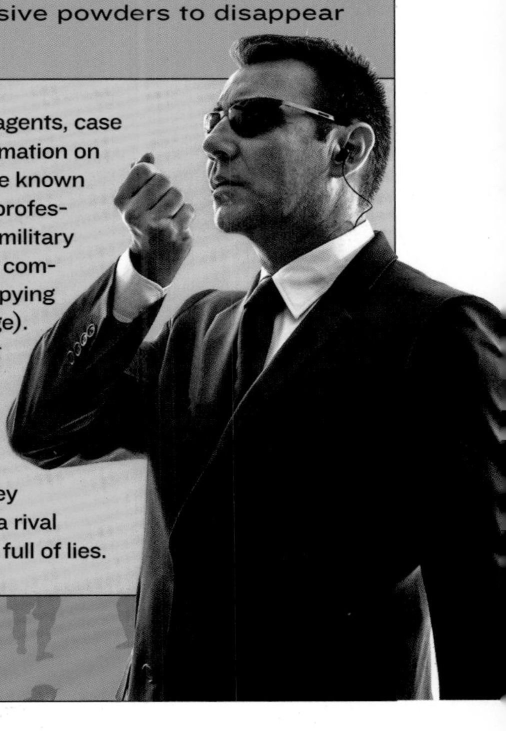

Governments employ spies—also known as spooks, secret agents, case officers, operatives, and intelligence assets—to gather information on foreign governments or their own people in secret, a practice known as espionage. And it's not just governments that hire these professional snoops. Agents try to sniff out secret information for military organizations and private companies (a special sort of spying called corporate espionage). It's not a new job (ancient Egypt hired spies to keep an eye on its enemies), and it's hardly part-time work. Spies keep busy in times of war and peace, working under a "cover identity" 24 hours a day when they're in the field. They might do it for the money, love of their country, or hatred of a rival nation, but they all have one thing in common: A spy's life is full of lies.

WHY did GLADIATORS fight to the death?

As many as 50,000 spectators gathered in Rome's Coliseum in the second century A.D. to witness gory spectacles: reenactments of famous battles, live hunts for exotic animals (released from cages kept in an elaborate basement under the sandy floor), and bloody battles between trained warriors. These gladiators were the professional athletes of their day. But although they were celebrities, most gladiators were slaves or prisoners-of-war forced into fighting for the bloodthirsty crowd's amusement. Rome's emperors hosted these expensive events—which were often free to the public—to make the citizens happy and thus easier to govern.

Why did the ancient Maya and Aztec play brutal ball games?

As far back as 1400 B.C., people in Mexico and Central America suited up in painted deerskins and elaborate headdresses and sprinted across ball courts covered with stone to volley a primitive rubber ball with their hips, knees, shins, elbows, and heads. Many of the ball courts remain today, some with stone rings that may have acted as goals, but the rules to these games have been lost to history. Weighing as much as nine pounds (4 kg), the solid-rubber balls left players bruised and bloody. Games sometimes resulted in broken bones and even death as players dove to the stone court to keep the ball from touching the ground. The ancient athletes played for religious reasons. The games were thought to represent the battle of good against evil. Some games may have ended in sacrificial rituals to appease the gods. A modern version of the ball games—called ulama—is still played today.

Why did knights enter jousting tournaments?

Hosted in special arenas, called lists, within castle walls or in nearby fields, the joust was one of the most thrilling forms of entertainment in the Middle Ages. Two mounted knights in gleaming armor spurred their warhorses at each other in a ferocious charge. Just before the moment of impact, they leveled their 12-foot (3.6-m) lances and—crash!—the weapons splintered against shield and helm. (A knight scored points in a joust by shattering his lance against his opponent's shield or helm—or knocking him off his horse.)

The joust was part of a larger event called the tournament, which evolved from military training into a spectacle for lords, ladies, and peasants alike. Despite strict rules, tournaments were dangerous games; many knights were permanently injured or killed in jousts. King Henry II of France died in a joust when a lance pierced his visor. But success in the tournament outweighed the risks for knights, who played for keeps. A victor won the loser's armor and horse, which could be ransomed for a small fortune. The tournament champion might win the favor of a lady in the stands.

Why do people look so unhappy in old photographs?

Peruse photos from the late 19th century and you'll notice that every person portrayed—from Civil War generals to Wild West cowboys—looks extremely serious, or even downright mad. It's as if early photographers never asked their subjects to say "cheese." You might chalk up all the frowning faces to bad teeth or the inconveniences of early camera technology (long exposure times meant subjects had to sit still for up to a minute), but the truth is more complicated: Smiling was considered bad form. From the days of portrait painting, it was thought that only rude, poor, stupid, or silly people exposed their teeth in formal settings. The tradition continued with portrait photography, which is why everyone in old photos looks like they just got bad news. "A photograph is a most important document," said American author Mark Twain, "and there is nothing [worse] to go down to posterity than a silly, foolish smile caught and fixed forever."

Why did people once settle grudges with deadly duels?

Today, anyone with a beef might hire a lawyer to settle a disagreement in court or simply argue in online message boards and let public opinion decide the victor. But from the Middle Ages up to the early 20th century, men from the upper crust of European and American society relied on one-on-one combat to seek "satisfaction" for even minor slights to their reputations. And so went the "duel," a deadly deal struck between two men (duelists were nearly always men) to resolve a dispute by calmly standing face-to-face, drawing pistols (or swords), and attacking each other.

Although not all duels were to the death, thousands of men—including famous politicians and military commanders—perished from injuries received in these ghastly grudge matches. Abraham Lincoln escaped a sword duel by apologizing to a local politician he had offended in a newspaper story. Even after duels were outlawed, deaths were still common and victors were often pardoned—as long as they followed the rules. Duelists adhered to a strict code of conduct (known as the code duello, a document typically kept inside every gentleman's pistol case). To break the rules meant bringing shame on your name, which many considered a fate worse than death.

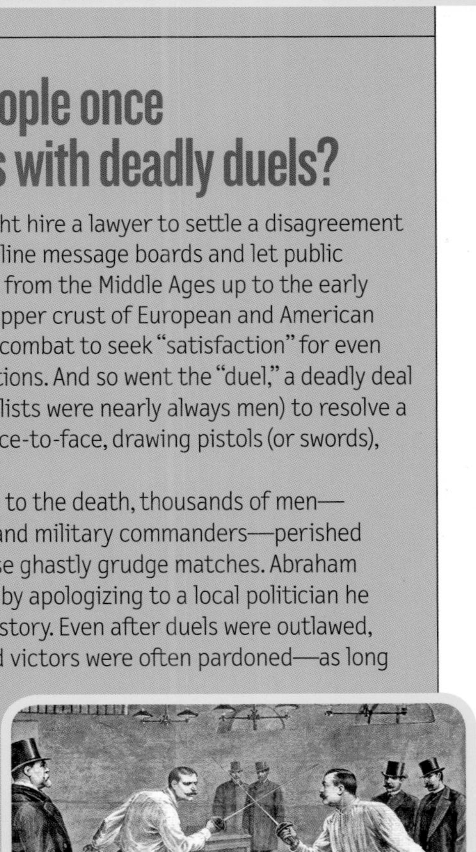

WHY did Salem, Massachusetts, have a WITCHCRAFT trial?

Centuries before they were portrayed as heroes in the Harry Potter books, witches were considered public enemy number one. Church officials in 15th-century Europe linked the practice of witchcraft to the devil, claiming that all witches drew their power from evil. According to folklore and books written at the time, witches could ruin crops, curdle the milk of livestock, blot out the stars, control the weather, and curse their neighbors. Anyone suffering a run of rotten luck could blame it on a witch. Suspected witches were rounded up, tortured into confessing any number of crimes, and then burned alive at the stake. By the 1700s, as many as 60,000 suspected witches had been tried and executed in Europe.

Fear of witches spread across northern Europe and even to the new colonies in North America. One of the most famous witch trials took place in Salem Village (now Danvers, Massachusetts, U.S.A.) in the 1690s. It started when a group of young girls began suffering from bizarre fits. They blamed a West Indian slave named Tituba for teaching them witchcraft, and soon the list of suspected witches grew to include other villagers, including men and a six-year-old child. The panic that followed cost the lives of 20 people. Scholars suspect the girls who started the ordeal were simply looking for attention. Another possibility: A fungus in the town's food supply may have caused hallucinations of bewitchment.

Why WERE PEOPLE ONCE ACCUSED OF WITCHCRAFT?

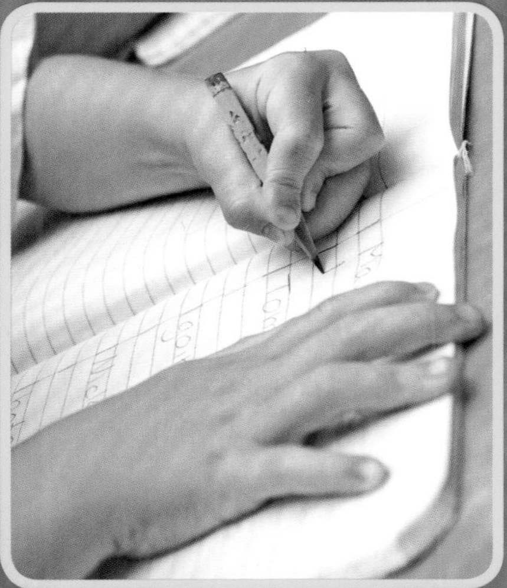

They were left-handed.

In the age of witch hunts, southpaws lived under constant suspicion. Left-handedness was seen as an insult to the natural order of things and a sign of evil. In fact, the term "sinister" comes from the Latin word for "left."

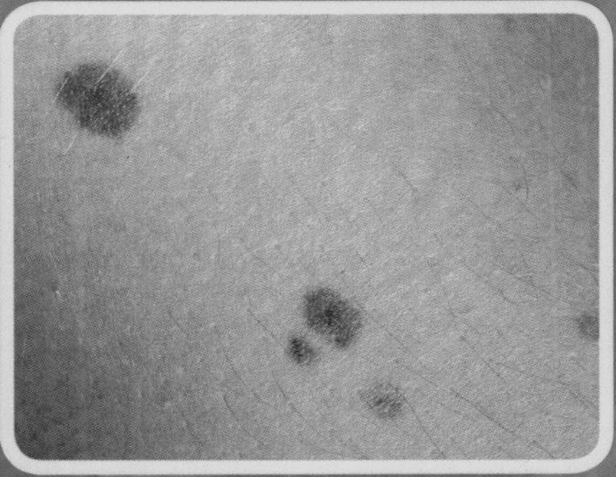

They bore the witch's mark.

Witches were thought to soar on broomsticks to "Sabbaths," rowdy sorcery conventions held deep in the forest. At these sinister shindigs, the devil would initiate novice spellcasters by scarring them with his horns. His "witch's mark" could take the shape of animals—perhaps a cat or toad—or look like a birthmark. Accused witches underwent head-to-toe inspections for such markings.

They floated instead of sank when dunked.

One test for a suspected sorcerer was to tie him or her to a chair and toss it into a river. Genuine witches—supposedly immune to the holy power of baptism in water—would bob to the surface. Thus proven guilty, they were usually executed. Those innocent of witchcraft would sink instead of float. They often drowned, making this test a lose-lose proposition.

They were at least 40 years old.

Folks in their 40s are considered middle-aged today, but few people reached such a ripe old age in the 14th and 15th centuries. Those who did were suspected of cozying up with evil forces to achieve a freakishly long life.

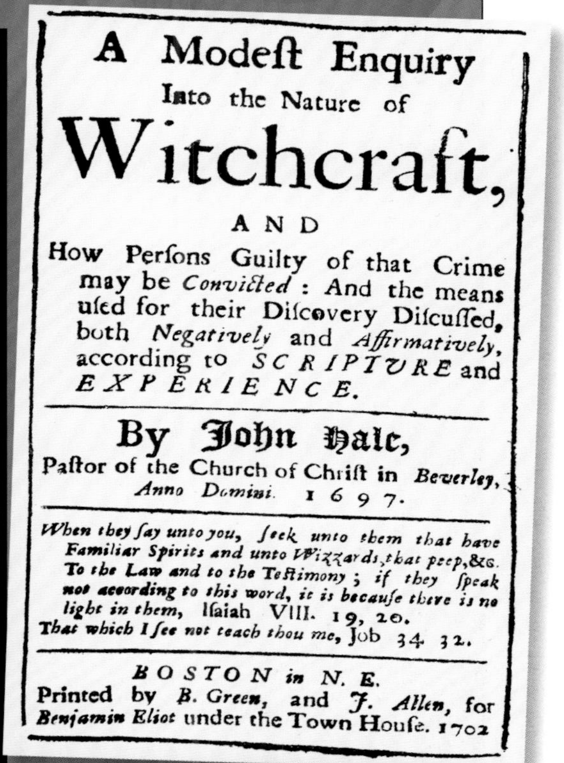

A Modeſt Enquiry
Into the Nature of
Witchcraft,
AND
How Perſons Guilty of that Crime may be *Convicted*: And the means uſed for their Diſcovery Diſcuſſed, both *Negatively* and *Affirmatively*, according to *SCRIPTURE* and *EXPERIENCE*.

By John Hale,
Paſtor of the Church of Chriſt in *Beverley*,
Anno Domini. 1697.

When they ſay unto you, ſeek unto them that have Familiar Spirits and unto Wizzards, that peep, &c. To the Law and to the Teſtimony; if they ſpeak not according to this word, it is becauſe there is no light in them, Iſaiah VIII. 19, 20.
That which I ſee not teach thou me, Job 34. 32.

BOSTON in N. E.
Printed by *B. Green*, and *J. Allen*, for *Benjamin Eliot* under the Town Houſe. 1702

They had a falling-out.

At the height of the witch panics, people were encouraged to report suspected witches to religious officials and witch hunters. That gave anyone with a grievance the opportunity to get even. They could accuse enemies of witchcraft!

Fearless explorers who PUSHED the BOUNDARIES

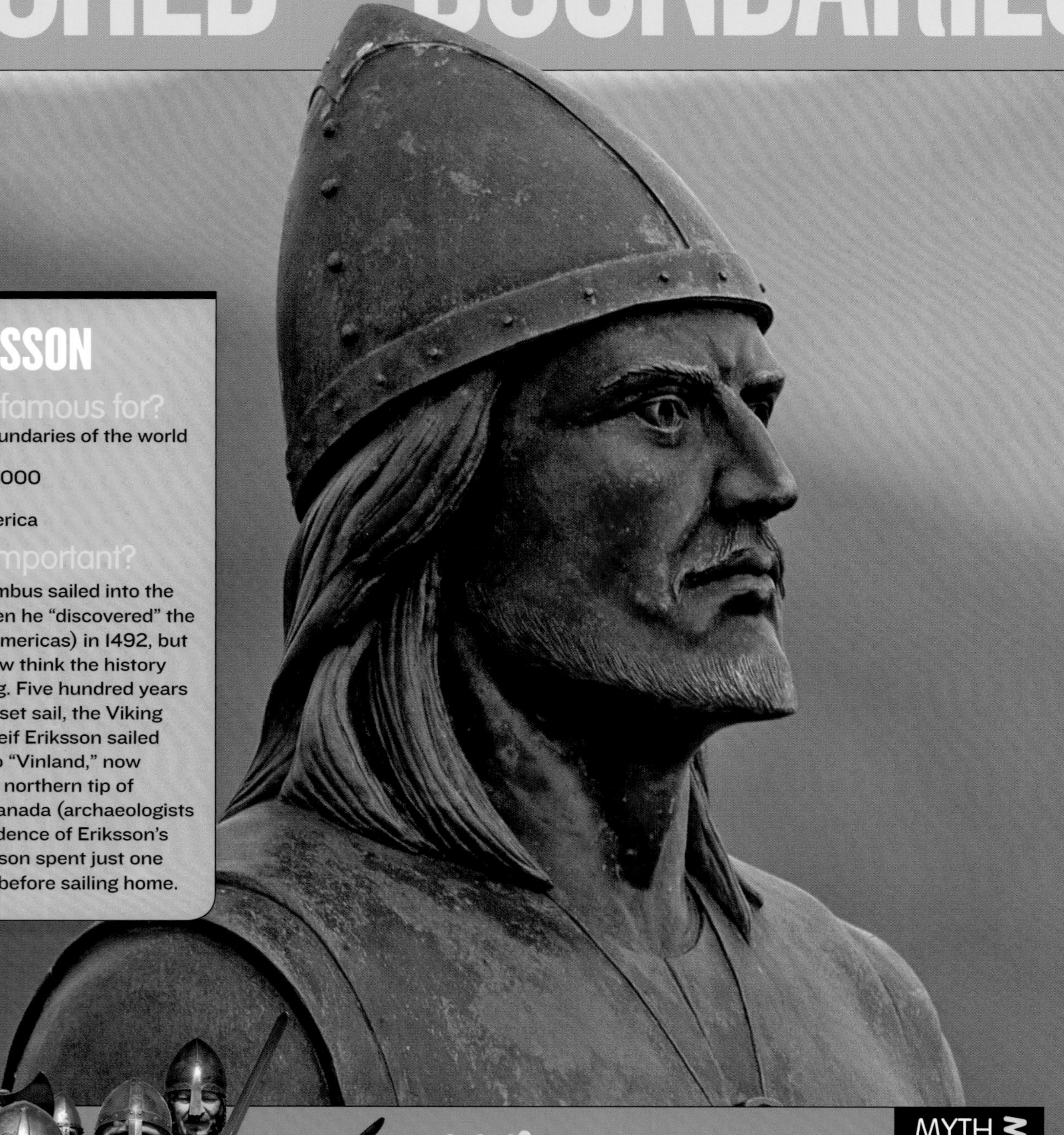

LEIF ERIKSSON

What is he famous for?
Expanding the boundaries of the world

When? A.D. 1000

Where? America

Why is he important?
Christopher Columbus sailed into the history books when he "discovered" the New World (the Americas) in 1492, but archaeologists now think the history books got it wrong. Five hundred years before Columbus set sail, the Viking explorer named Leif Eriksson sailed from Greenland to "Vinland," now believed to be the northern tip of Newfoundland, Canada (archaeologists in 1960 found evidence of Eriksson's settlement). Eriksson spent just one winter in Vinland before sailing home.

MYTH MASHED

Why did Vikings wear horned helmets?

Don't believe everything you see in movies and at Halloween parties. Although Vikings are shown as fearsome horn-helmeted raiders in popular culture, archaeological evidence paints a more clearheaded picture. The Norse warriors wore simple iron helmets or no helmets at all.

SIR ISAAC NEWTON

What is he famous for?
Expanding the boundaries of the universe

When? 1687

Where? England

Why is he important?

One of history's most influential minds, this English scientist, mathematician, and philosopher literally wrote the book on physics. His three laws of motion explain how every object in the universe affects the movement of every other object. He helped invent the mathematical study of calculus (now you know who to thank when you take that tricky course). But Newton is most famous for sitting in a garden and spotting an apple falling from a tree—an observation that inspired his law that explains how all objects in the universe attract each other with a force relative to their size and distance from each other. In other words, gravity.

MARTIN LUTHER KING, JR.

What is he famous for?
Expanding the boundaries of civil rights

When? 1950s

Where? America

Why is he important?

When Rosa Parks, an African-American woman, was arrested in 1955 for not giving up her bus seat to a white passenger in Montgomery, Alabama, U.S.A., Martin Luther King, Jr.—a pastor—began his crusade to end discrimination against African Americans. King relied on peaceful demonstrations and marches, the most famous of which was his 250,000-strong March on Washington in 1963, where he delivered one of the most famous speeches in history. A year later, the U.S. Congress passed the Civil Rights Act, which outlawed discrimination and racial segregation in schools and at the workplace.

WHY is the Golden Gate Bridge ORANGE?

Since it opened in 1937, this architectural wonder spanning San Francisco Bay in California, U.S.A., has always been "International Orange," a color chosen because it's easy to spot by passing ships and blends nicely with the land on both sides of the bridge. The name "Golden Gate" was never meant to describe the famous suspension bridge's color. It's the name of the strait that marks the entrance to the San Francisco Bay from the Pacific Ocean.

SAY WHAT?!

TO MAKE THE SPAN even easier to spot by passing ships, the U.S. Navy wanted the Golden Gate Bridge painted like a bumblebee, with black and yellow stripes.

Why is the Statue of Liberty green?

Covered in thin copper plates, the Statue of Liberty (a gift from France) was originally a dull brown when it arrived in New York Harbor in 1885. But unlike most things, the statue actually got prettier with age. Over the next 30 years, she slowly took on the greenish tinge you see today. The salty air from the harbor reacted with the copper to create a thin layer of salt called a patina. Lady Liberty's green sheen is a good thing: The patina actually protects the statue from rusting.

Why is the Leaning Tower of Pisa leaning?

It's a familiar photo snapped by sightseers in the Italian city of Pisa: The subject stands in the foreground pretending to prop up a curiously crooked eight-story tower in the background. The Tower of Pisa's extreme lean has been around a lot longer than the art of silly tourist photography. The tower, meant to function as a bell tower, started to sway soon after construction on it started more than 800 years ago. Its foundation was set on soil too soft to support its weight. The tower began to lean as soon as its builders completed the second floor in 1178. Construction continued off and on for the next 192 years, but attempts to straighten the tower only made it worse. By the time the tower was completed in 1370, its lean had increased to 1.6 degrees. Its slow topple continued over the centuries, until it eventually reached 5.5 degrees.

Will the Leaning Tower of Pisa eventually tumble over?

It's stable for now, thanks to some modern architectural mojo. Engineers have shored up the foundation, installed counterweights and cables, and removed soil from the nonleaning side—fixes that reduced the lean by about 1.5 degrees. The tower is still 13 feet (4 m) off its center, but stable, meaning the Leaning Tower of Pisa won't become the Tumbled Tower of Pisa for at least 300 years.

Why is Venice built on water?

Life was no fairy tale in fifth-century Italy. When waves of invaders threatened the countryside and cities in the northeastern part of the country, the locals needed a safe place to lie low. A marshy lagoon between the mouths of two rivers made a good refuge from the barbarians. The Roman refugees spread their settlement across the lagoon's 118 islands, connecting them with wooden bridges and commuting in the canals between them. In the centuries since, Venice developed into a thriving city and a wonder of the world. Today, the city faces a new threat—rising sea levels due to climate change.

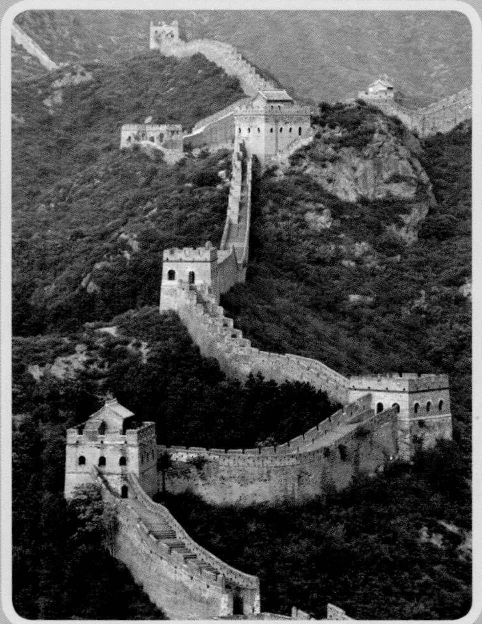

Why was the Great Wall of China built?

The largest man-made structure at the time of its completion in the 17th century, China's Great Wall spans 5,500 miles (8,850 km) across northern China, from the Korean border west into the Gobi desert. It actually started out as a series of smaller walls built by Chinese warlords in the seventh century B.C. to defend their individual lands. As China became a united empire, the walls were joined and fortified over the next 2,000 years to repel enemies, particularly the Mongolian and Manchu armies. Built from countless bricks and stones and guarded by watchtowers, the Great Wall is an engineering marvel of the ancient world.

MYTH MASHED

Why IS THE GREAT WALL OF CHINA THE ONLY MAN-MADE OBJECT YOU CAN SEE FROM SPACE?

There are two things wrong with this question. One, you can't spot the Great Wall from Earth orbit with the naked eye (the wall tends to blend in with the mountainous landscape). And, two, astronauts can see all sorts of other man-made objects—roads, cities, dams, and even the Great Pyramids—from their spaceship portholes.

TECHNOLOGY

TOUCH SCREENS, JET PLANES, laptops, video games—machines that might've seemed miraculous a century ago are considered humdrum today. But have you ever considered what makes this technology tick? In this chapter, you'll wonder at the workings of your favorite gadgets and look under the hoods of some essential machinery. Surprise: Everyday tech is even more amazing than you might think.

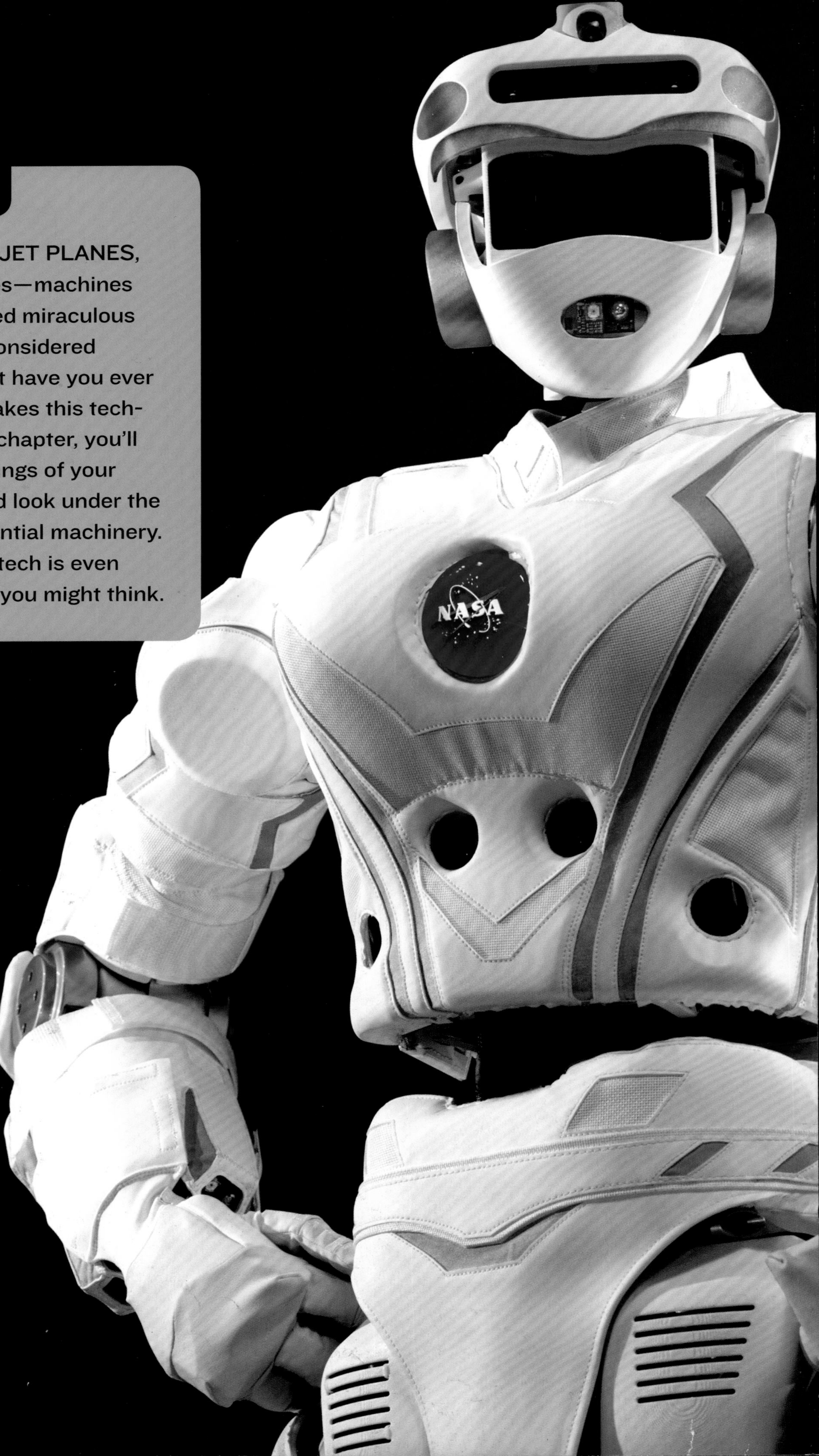

5

WHY-FI

WHY was the INTERNET invented?

The strands of today's Internet stretch back to the early 1960s, when computer scientists began brainstorming a system for researchers, educators, and government agencies to share information through their computers. Officials in the United States government saw the value of a network of linked computers that would continue to operate even if bits of it were blasted in a war. The U.S. Department of Defense funded research into an early network known as the ARPANET, which, over time and through many upgrades, evolved into the modern Internet and the World Wide Web (the system of linked pages that most people browse on the Internet). What started as a link between four computers has grown into a network of at least 75 million servers.

Who owns the Internet?

Nobody—not a single person, company, or government. The Internet is a network of millions of interconnected computers and servers spread across the globe. A nonprofit international group called the Internet Society does watch over the global network, establishing protocols (a system of rules for sharing data) and promoting its evolution and access to everybody.

Why do Internet addresses start with "http://www"?

HTTP, which stands for "hypertext transfer protocol," is the language of rules that controls how your browser navigates the network of linked pages known as the World Wide Web (which is where the "www" comes from). When you enter a website name into your browser's address bar (or click on a link within a page), protocols contact the site's hosting server and fetch the requested Web page, which then pops up on your computer screen.

Is THE WORLD WIDE WEB REALLY AVAILABLE WORLDWIDE?

Technically, yes, but many countries—such as Iran, the People's Republic of China, Syria, and North Korea—block or filter access to the Internet or punish citizens who post information that's deemed critical to the government.

HOW does a SEARCH ENGINE work?

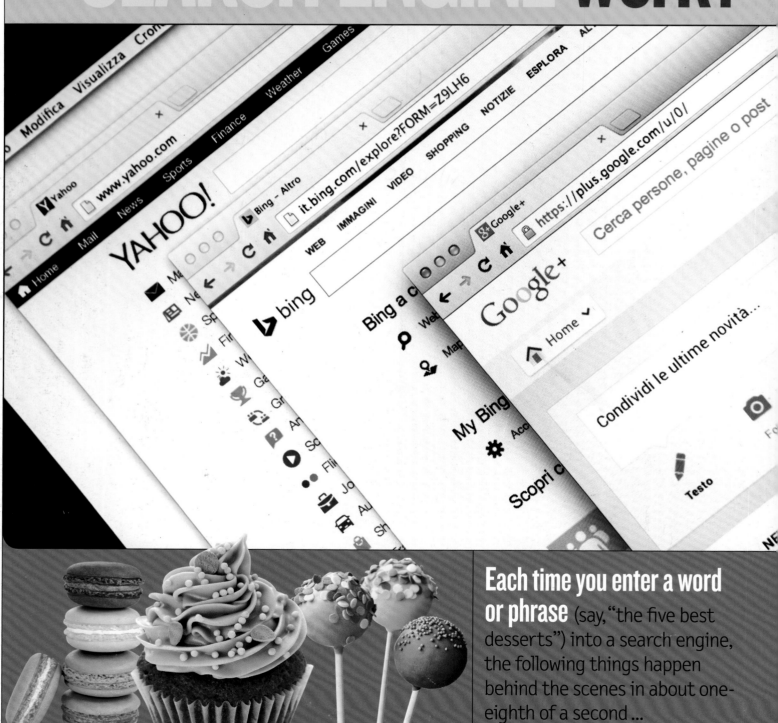

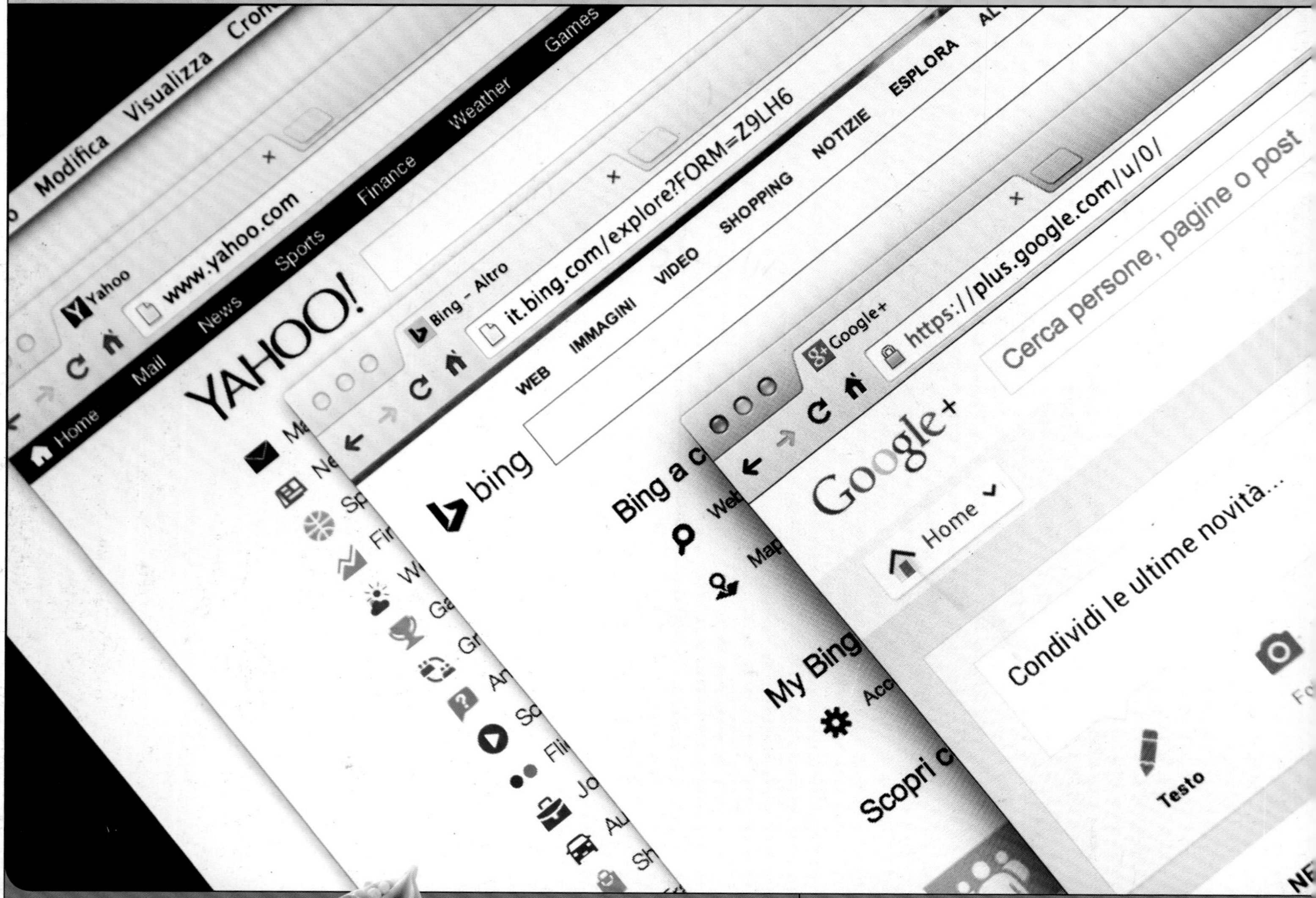

Each time you enter a word or phrase (say, "the five best desserts") into a search engine, the following things happen behind the scenes in about one-eighth of a second ...

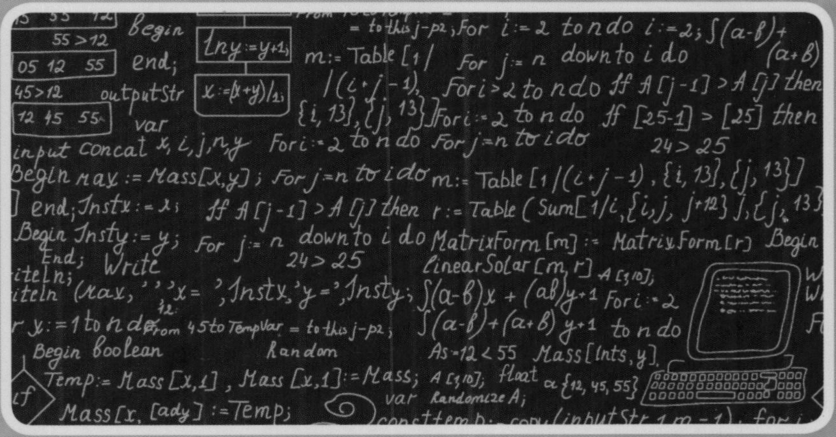

Step 1: Search

The search engine uses algorithms (mathematical formulas) to determine exactly what you're hunting for, adding in synonyms ("tastiest treats"), anticipating your terms before you've even finished typing, and offering corrections in case you've made a mistake (did you mean "best deserts" instead of "best desserts"?).

Step 2: Sort

Your request is sent to the search engine's servers. Here, the company that owns the search engine maintains a massive index of all the words, photos, videos, songs, and other data strewn across the World Wide Web. This information—enough to fill hundreds of millions of gigabytes—is continuously collected and updated by programs called "spiders" that crawl across the Web and sift through its information.

Step 3: Collect

From its index, the search engine gathers every Web page with content that matches your search term. Results are filtered based on hundreds of factors, including the pages' age, the number of people who've visited the pages, their estimated reliability, and more.

Step 4: Voilà!

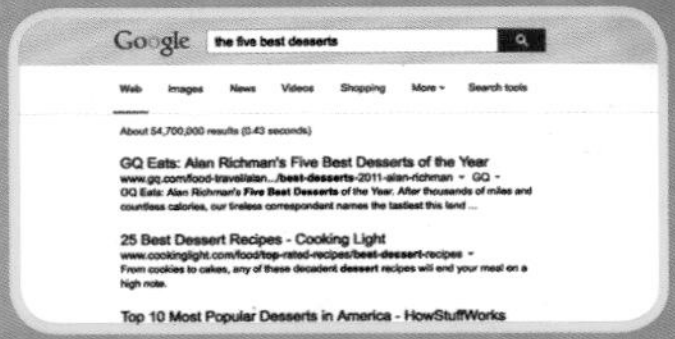

The results are ranked as links in your Web browser, with the most relevant Web pages at the top of the list.

How BIG IS THE WORLD WIDE WEB?

According to Google, the World Wide Web is made of more than 60 trillion individual pages—more pages than the number of neurons in your brain.

Do SEARCH ENGINES REALLY SEARCH THE ENTIRE INTERNET?

No. The Internet encompasses much more than just the World Wide Web, the linked pages people typically surf and the portion plumbed by search engines. File-sharing sites, corporate data banks, government "intranets," workplace servers, and other private sites are strictly off-limits to public snooping. And then there's the murky region known as "dark net." Uncharted by search engines, it's the Internet's seedy underbelly, home to anonymous users and secret networks that want to stay that way.

PERSON OF INTEREST

WHO?
Ralph Baer

WHAT is he famous for?
Inventing video games

WHEN?
1960s through today

WHERE?
United States

WHY is he important?
Love playing with your PlayStation? Its origins go back to 1966, when electrical engineer Ralph Baer invented what would become the Magnavox Odyssey, the first video game system. Despite its simple graphics and bleeping sound effects, the Odyssey established all the features of modern game systems: It hooked to your TV, used a handheld controller, and played a variety of games.

HOW does a 3-D PRINTER work?

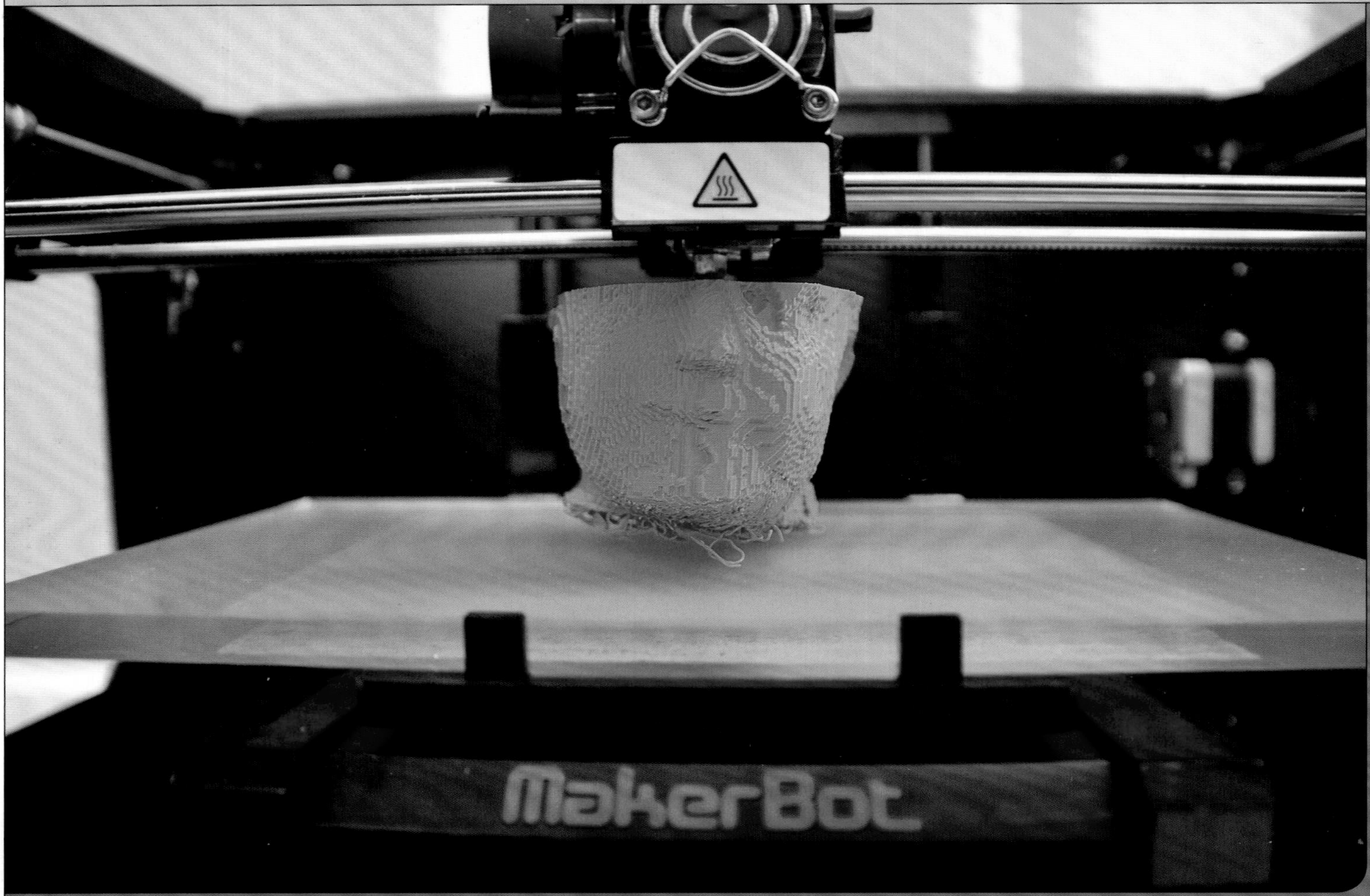

It sounds like something out of Tony Stark's (Iron Man's) lab: a machine that creates real-life objects just like a regular printer duplicates pictures and documents from your computer. But 3-D printers are real, and people use them to whip up everything from simple toys like chess pieces and rubber duckies to prototypes of complex inventions. Simply load the printer with a sort of plastic "ink" and select the object you wish to print from a "Thingiverse" of thousands of doodads (or design your own object). Then hit the Print button. Hot-ink guns on robotic arms move within the machine to "print" the object, layer by layer, until it's complete. Eventually, 3-D printers will evolve to create more complex goodies, including snacks!

How do air conditioners make my house cold?

The same way your refrigerator chills your soda. Both your fridge and your house's A/C absorb heat into coils filled with special refrigerant chemicals. The coils remove the heat from the house (or fridge), leaving the air inside comfortably chilly.

Why do microwaves make my food hot?

Introduced in the late 1960s as a faster way to fix supper, microwave ovens use a special frequency of radio waves—called microwaves—that causes the atoms in liquids and fats to vibrate. That vibration creates heat and cooks food much faster than a conventional oven.

How do touch screens work?

A touch-sensing interface is one of the reasons your tablet or smartphone is so smart. All touch screens generate an electrical field over the screen (although the technology used to generate the field varies by device). Your finger disrupts the field when you touch the screen, which reads this location and tells the device's operating system precisely where you touched or swiped.

MYTH MASHED

Why DID NASA INVENT TANG AND VELCRO?

Although the drink mix Tang and sticky Velcro tape will forever be associated with rockets to the moon and space stations (both Tang and Velcro were shot into space in the early days of the space program), NASA didn't invent either product. Still, plenty of other spin-offs—or technologies adapted for use here on Earth—came out of NASA-sponsored labs, including ...

MEMORY FOAM: The spongy material in your mattress was originally designed for aircraft seat cushions.

EAR THERMOMETERS: NASA developed heat sensors that doctors now use to take your temperature without sticking a thermometer under your tongue.

ARTIFICIAL LIMBS: NASA's research into robotic astronauts has resulted in more realistic and functional arms and legs for people who have lost theirs in accidents or combat.

INVISIBLE BRACES: Straightening your pearly whites no longer requires a mouthful of metal, thanks to a tough, transparent plastic originally created for missile systems.

Why does a boomerang return to its thrower?

These uncanny flying objects—which have been wielded as hunting weapons for thousands of years—always return to their tosser (as long as they're thrown correctly). The secret of the boomerang's round-trip flight lies in its shape. A curved design combines two wings joined in the middle. Once the boomerang wielder launches the weapon using a strong overhand toss (similar to chucking a baseball), the boomerang spins through space. Air passes over one wing faster than the other, creating a curved flight path that brings the boomerang back to its point of origin. The Guinness World Record for the longest boomerang throw is a staggering 1,402 feet (427 m)! It was a one-way trip; the boomerang got stuck in a tree.

What if you threw a boomerang in space?

It would return to your hand just like it would if you threw it on Earth—a fact verified by experiments on the International Space Station. It's the passage of air over a boomerang's wings, not the force of gravity, that's crucial to a boomerang's return flight.

WHY are COMPUTERS getting smaller (& smaller)?

Computers in the 1950s were the size of a house—literally. Today, your vastly more powerful smartphone fits in your jeans pocket. How could anything shrink in size while growing in power? The big breakthrough was the invention of the transistor, a tiny device that controls electronic signals. Like a nerve cell in the human brain, a transistor works with other transistors to store and process information in computing devices (and other gadgets). Transistors were installed on silicon microchips, which replaced much larger vacuum tubes in the 1950s. Many consider the transistor the greatest invention of the 20th century. In 1965, Gordon E. Moore, co-founder of the high-tech Intel Corporation, predicted that the number of transistors that could fit on a microchip would double every two years. Known as Moore's Law, his prediction held true. In 1971, computer makers could fit only about 4,000 transistors on a chip; by 2011, they could cram in over 2.5 billion. Today, engineers are searching for the transistor's successor.

Shrinking Thinking Machines

The Antikythera Mechanism Designed in 100 B.C.

INPUT METHOD: Knob and crank
SIZE: Approx. 1 foot x 6 inches x 4 inches (31 cm x 15 cm x 10 cm)
Recovered from a shipwreck off the Greek island of Antikythera in 1900, this toaster-size device may have been the world's first analog—or mechanical—computer. Archaeologists believe the Greeks used it 2,000 years ago to calculate the courses of constellations and predict eclipses. Smaller than a modern PC, the Antikythera Mechanism contained at least 30 bronze gears and was remarkably efficient for its size. It even had an instruction manual inscribed on copper plates.

Difference Engine Designed in 1837

INPUT METHOD: Punched cards
SIZE: About as big as your living room
Devised but never actually built by English mathematician Charles Babbage, this massive contraption relied on metal tumblers and cranks rather than electricity and transistors, yet it had all the components of a modern computer: a memory for storing numbers, a central processing unit for calculating math problems, an input device (punched cards) for entering information, and an output device in the form of a printer and a bell. (Which would've made the Difference Engine the first computer with sound effects!)

Apple II Designed in 1976

INPUT METHOD: Keyboard and cassette drive
SIZE: Smaller than a suitcase
The first successful mass-produced "microcomputer," the Apple II offered simplicity, the ability to upgrade, and style (for the time, at least) in a sleek beige box that hooked to your TV. Although primitive by today's standards, the Apple II sold in the millions and ushered in the era of personal computing. It was also one of the first personal computers that could play a decent home version of arcade games.

IBM Simon Designed in 1992

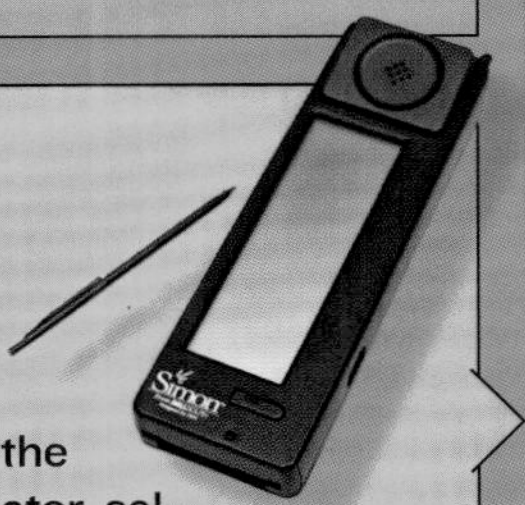

INPUT METHOD: Touch screen
SIZE: Brick-size
Considered the first "smartphone," this touch screen–controlled device combined the features of a computer (email client, calculator, calendar, appointment scheduler, etc.) with a cell phone (which transmits radio signals to the nearest "cell" antenna to communicate with other cell phone users). Paving the way for today's iPhones and tablets, it was the first phone that did other things and one of the first computers you could fit in your pocket.

ENIAC Designed in 1943

INPUT METHOD: Plugs and switches
SIZE: House-size
ENIAC (Electronic Numerical Integrator and Computer) was the world's first general-purpose electronic computer. Although it took days to program, ENIAC could perform thousands of calculations in a second. That power required some serious hardware. ENIAC was large enough to live in, weighed more than 30 tons (27 t), and took up the space of a typical single-family house. Built before smaller and more efficient transistors, ENIAC relied on more than 17,000 soda-can-size vacuum tubes that often malfunctioned when the massive machine was powered up. ENIAC's operators came up with a simple solution for that problem: They never turned it off. The computer ran continuously for more than seven years. It was even rumored (falsely) that ENIAC's massive power needs were responsible for occasional power outages in the nearby city of Philadelphia, Pennsylvania, U.S.A.

Continued on the next page

Google Glass Designed in 2011

INPUT METHOD: Voice commands and eye movement
SIZE: Fits on a pair of eyeglasses
The first in a new wave of "wearable computers," Google Glass combines a tiny computer with a pair of glasses and works like a smartphone for your eyeballs. The eyepiece displays all sorts of handy data—from text messages to directions (although Google Glass users run the risk of stumbling into traffic as they browse their email). Critics complain that the device's built-in camera represents an invasion of privacy.

Oculus Rift Designed in 2014

INPUT METHOD: Joypad, mouse, gesture commands
SIZE: As large as a pair of snow goggles
The long-awaited promise of exploring virtual reality comes true in this headset decked out with high-definition displays for each eyeball, creating a three-dimensional wraparound view that shifts with your head movements without any noticeable lag. It might be the closest you'll get to experiencing Harry Potter's reality-shifting Room of Requirement in real time (as long as you don't upchuck from motion sickness).

Quantum Computer To be designed in 2020

INPUT METHOD: Unknown. Possibly telepathy (seriously!)
SIZE: Smaller than your fist
With transistors and microchips shrinking to their dinkiest point, computer engineers are thinking small to create the next big thing. By using subatomic particles instead of transistors, the quantum computer of 2020 could pack a thousand times more processing power than today's computers in a case the size of a coffee cup.

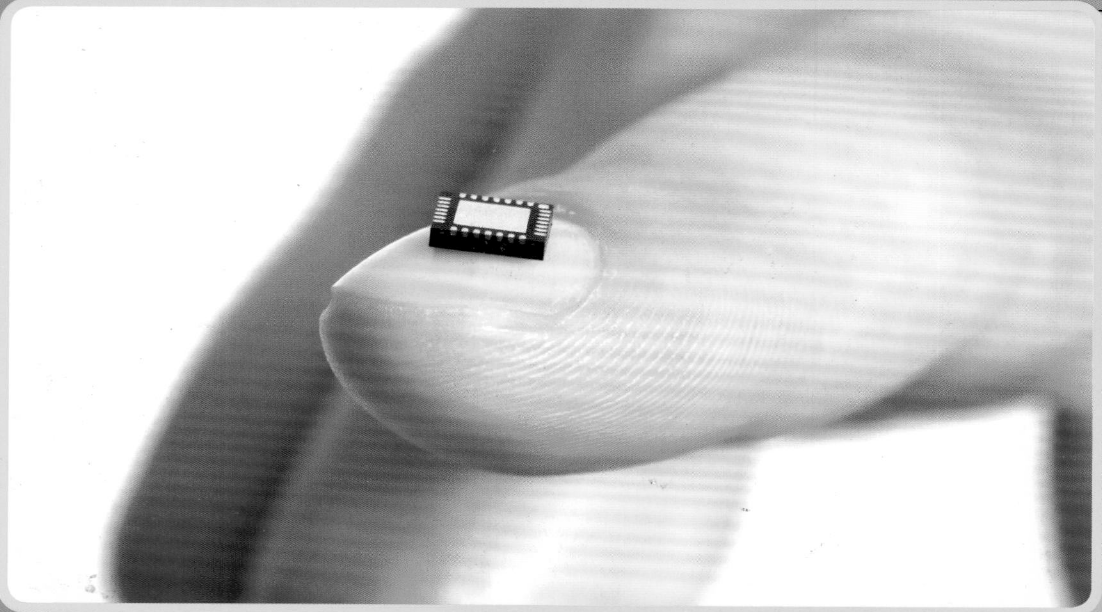

SAY WHAT?!

TO CELEBRATE the 50th birthday of the ENIAC computer, students at the University of Pennsylvania (where ENIAC was built) replicated the entire 1,800-square-foot (167-m²) machine on a microchip smaller than your thumbnail.

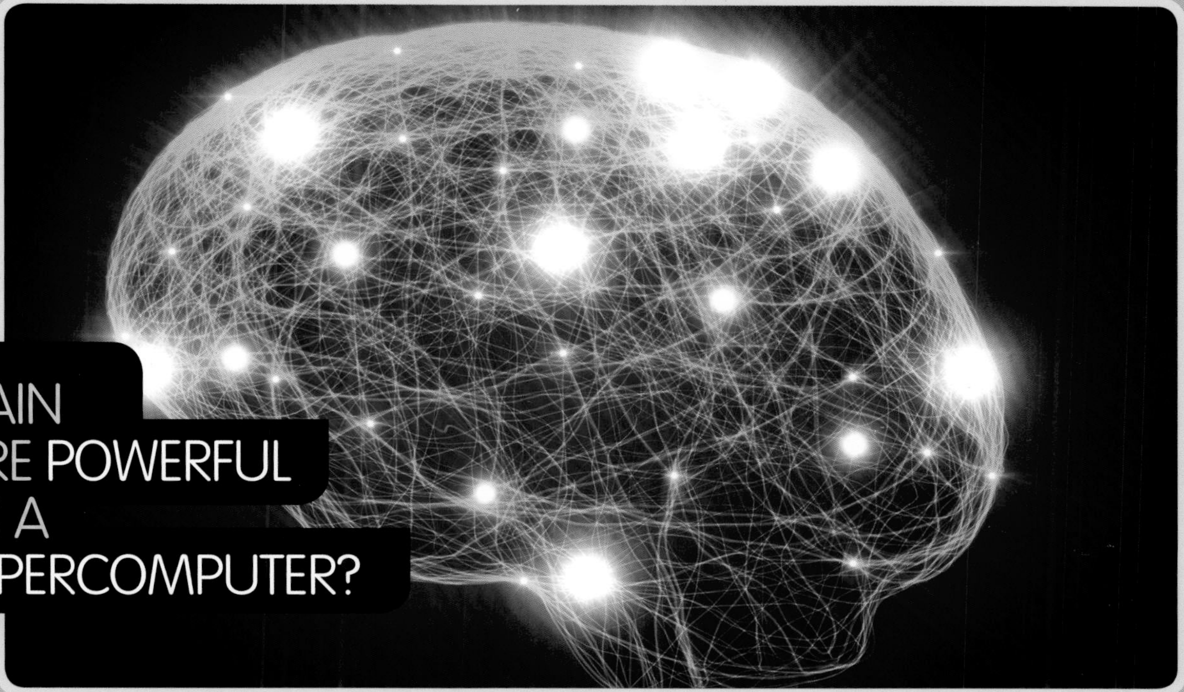

Is MY BRAIN MORE POWERFUL THAN A SUPERCOMPUTER?

It's not really fair to compare that three-pound (1.3-kg) melon of nerve cells in your noggin with a silicon-and-plastic computer the size of a master bedroom. Human brains process and store information in vastly different ways than a computer, for starters. But just for fun, let's compare the "hardware specs" of the "computer" on your shoulders with those of IBM's Watson, the artificially intelligent machine that used its vast resources of data and its ability to understand speech to beat two former champions on the TV quiz show *Jeopardy!*

	HUMAN BRAIN	WATSON SUPERCOMPUTER
Processing Power	2.2 billion megaflops	80 million megaflops
Memory Capacity	2,560 terabytes	16 terabytes
Power Consumption	20 watts	200,000 watts

THE WINNER
YOUR BRAIN!

Watson may have licked two humans in a game of trivia, but its thousands of processing cores and dozens of servers still can't come close to replicating the complexity and power of the neurons in your noggin. The human brain can achieve more than a trillion neural connections, and it has enough memory to hold 300 million hours of TV shows. Still, computer scientists suspect they'll be able to build a computer that replicates the brain's abilities by 2020.

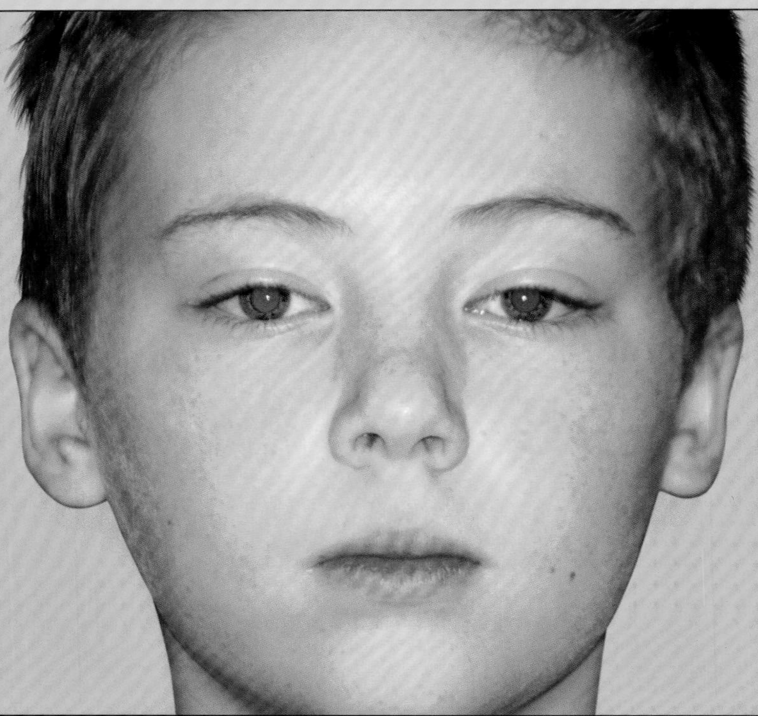

WHY do my EYES sometimes look red in photos?

My, what pretty blood vessels you have. When a camera's flash goes off in dim conditions, your pupils don't shrink fast enough to block the burst of light. The result (aside from a minute of bedazzled vision): Light reflects off the red blood vessels in your retina, giving you a devilish gleam in that family photo. Fortunately, most digital cameras have a red-eye-reduction mode that pulses the flash, giving your pupils time to adjust.

Why do traffic jams happen?

Sitting in bumper-to-bumper traffic is a real bummer—especially when you reach the end of the jam and don't see any reason for its cause. Researchers studying the problem have explained it with a mathematical model called a backward-traveling wave. When a driver on a busy highway suddenly slows to inspect an unexpected spectacle (such as an emergency vehicle or a fender bender) on the side of the road, every car behind follows suit, slowing more and more until cars far behind are forced to come to a halt. The only way to fix this frustrating phenomenon of human nature, researchers say, is to replace the humans with robots who don't care about roadside distractions.

Why do people hack computers?

Because they think it's fun, because they can, or because they want to commit cybercrime, the fastest-growing kind of crime. Hackers try to gain unauthorized access to the secret regions of the Internet: the computers of people, corporations, or governments. Their most valuable possession isn't money or gadgets or free video games. It's information! Hackers break into private networks to swipe secret info, which they can then sell or use for all sorts of dastardly purposes.

SAY WHAT?!

IMAGINE HAVING A ROBOT as a chauffeur. Google's self-driving car uses lasers to "see" the road and sensors to keep a safe distance from other cars. The car was involved in only one accident during extensive road testing—but a human was driving it in "manual mode" at the time.

Why do I need a mask or goggles to see underwater?

Human eyes have adapted to see clearly in the air, not underwater. When light hits the water, it bends, or refracts, in a way that counteracts the focusing effects of our corneas and lenses. Masks and goggles provide a barrier of air between our eyes and the water, resulting in clear vision. Unlike humans and other land-based animals, aquatic creatures evolved to see clearly underwater. The peepers of dolphins and alligators do double duty—they're able to focus above and below the surface.

Why do I need to wear glasses to see a three-dimensional movie?

Whether you're watching a cheesy 3-D classic through the old-fashioned red-and-blue glasses or a modern blockbuster through a sleek pair of high-tech shades, the 3-D effect relies on the supercomputer between your ears. Both types of glasses filter out individual images for each eye so that your brain can process the differences and perceive the illusion of depth.

Why is the sun bad for my gadgets?

Earth's atmosphere isn't the only place with stormy weather. Astronomers say space has its own weather system—controlled by the sun—and this weather can generate storms capable of damaging electronics on or around Earth. The storms start as dark sunspots that appear on the sun's surface (called the photosphere). These cool spots generate intense fields of magnetic forces thousands of times more powerful than those generated on Earth. Sometimes, during the most active part of the solar cycle, groups of sunspots can unleash explosive geysers of hot gases—called solar flares—sending radiation and charged particles toward Earth.

Our atmosphere and magnetic field shield us from all but the strongest of these storms of charged particles, but occasionally a flare is strong enough to disrupt the electronics in communication and navigation satellites and damage devices here on Earth. A massive solar storm in 1859 knocked out telegraph machines (the simple communication devices used before the invention of the telephone) across the U.S. and Europe. Some telegraph operators even reported getting zapped by their devices!

PERSON OF INTEREST

WHO?
Johannes Gutenberg

WHAT is he famous for?
Inventing the printing press

WHEN?
1450

WHERE?
Germany

WHY is he important?
You can trace the roots of the information age—the modern era marked by the spread of information and the explosive growth of the Internet—back to a workshop in Strasbourg, Germany, in the mid-1400s. Here, a blacksmith named Johannes Gutenberg took old printing technologies and added movable type (tiny metal pieces imprinted with letters) to create the first printing press. Before his invention, books were written by hand or using much slower printing technologies. They were luxuries only for the wealthy or officials of the church. Gutenberg's press could churn out thousands of pages per day, making books less expensive and information more widely available. Many consider his press one of the most important inventions in history.

SAY WHAT?!

HOW'D YOU LIKE to leave your mask on the beach when you snorkel? After centuries of free diving for fish and shellfish, the sea-dwelling Moken people of Southeast Asia have developed uncanny underwater vision. Studies show that Moken children can see more than twice as clearly underwater as European children.

HOW do solar panels convert sunlight into ENERGY?

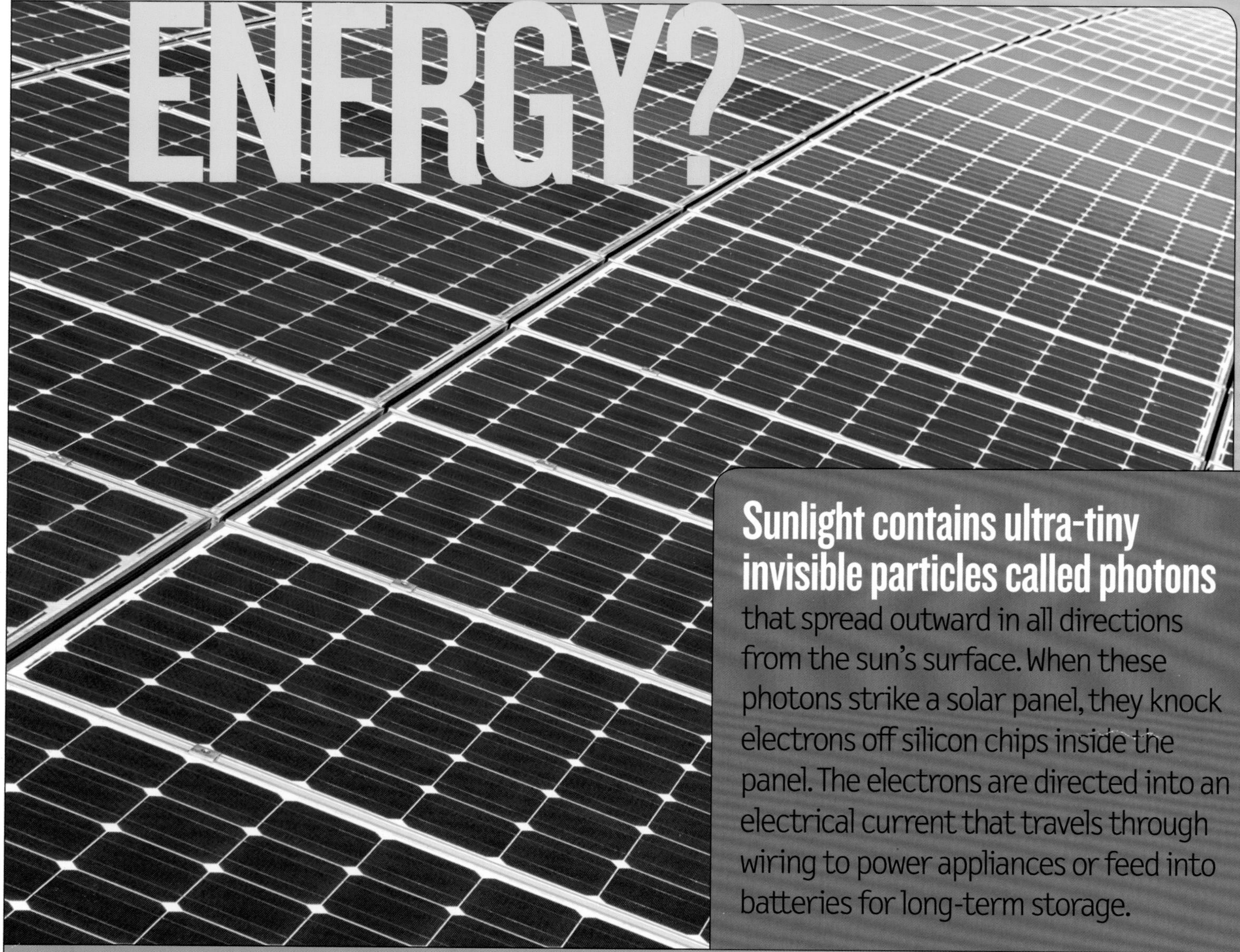

Sunlight contains ultra-tiny invisible particles called photons that spread outward in all directions from the sun's surface. When these photons strike a solar panel, they knock electrons off silicon chips inside the panel. The electrons are directed into an electrical current that travels through wiring to power appliances or feed into batteries for long-term storage.

How do turbines convert wind into energy?

When a breeze strikes a turbine—a windmill-like machine that converts wind into electricity—it spins propeller blades connected to gears inside the turbine's housing. The gears ramp up the spin of the blades, so that even a mild breeze results in a rapid spin of a shaft connected to the gears. The shaft turns magnets around a coil of special wires—a system known as a generator—to create electrical current.

Why aren't all batteries rechargeable?

You probably ask this question every time the double A's die in your Wii remote right when you reach the final level. To get to the bottom of why some batteries earn extra life in a recharging station while others are bound for the recycling bin, you first need to know what a battery is. It's simply a container filled with special chemicals that generate electricity through a chemical reaction. This reaction starts when you place the battery in your gadget and turn it on, completing a circuit that triggers electricity to flow from the battery's positive terminal, through the wiring of your gadget, and back to the battery's negative terminal (these terminals are marked with + and – symbols on your battery).

When all the chemicals in a standard, nonrechargeable battery have undergone the reaction process, the battery is dead. Time to drop it off at a recycling station (usually found in hardware stores). Rechargeable batteries, however, contain different chemicals that can react in the opposite direction, filling with electricity when you place them in a charger. Eventually, the special chemicals wear out and the reaction can no longer be reversed. But until that happens, you can recharge them again and again, giving your batteries more extra lives than you'll find in any video games.

Why do cars need gasoline?

Although more and more cars have electric engines (or hybrid gas-electric ones) to save on fuel costs and cut down on exhaust that contributes to climate change, the vast majority of automobiles on the road still rely on gasoline for their old-fashioned combustion engines. Applying pressure to the gas pedal mixes fuel and air in the car's engine, where a small spark ignites the mixture to create tiny explosions—the combustion process. Combustion makes the engine go *vroom, vroom,* spinning the tires and putting the car in motion.

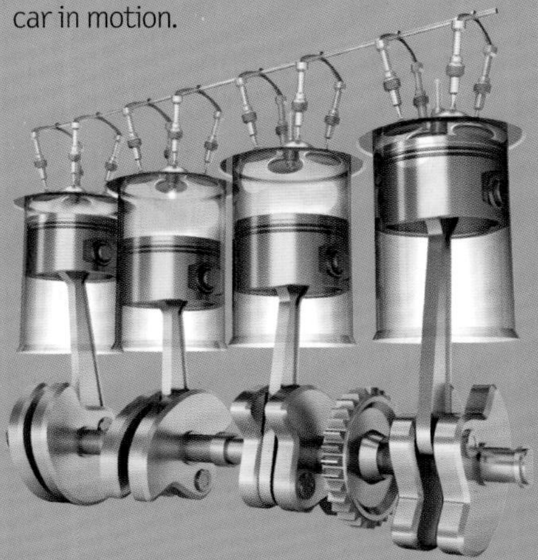

PERSON OF INTEREST

WHO?
Thomas Edison

WHAT is he famous for?
Inventing the lightbulb

WHEN?
1878

WHERE?
New York, USA

WHY is he important?
Thomas Edison didn't invent electricity—a natural form of energy that humans have known about since the time of the ancient Greeks—but he did figure out how to harness it to light a filament in a lightbulb as well as transmit it to homes through a grid system of wires. A genius tinkerer, Edison also invented the phonograph, a machine that records sounds and plays music (think of it as the great-granddaddy of your MP3 player).

Although Thomas Edison gets credit for inventing the lightbulb, a draftsman name Lewis Howard Latimer had a bright idea that revolutionized electric light. Latimer's carbon filament—the fiber inside the bulb that glows when charged with an electric current—stayed lit for much longer than Edison's quick-to-burn-out paper filament.

Solar SOARER

Imagine flying around the globe in a plane that doesn't burn a drop of fuel. It's no flight of fancy! A Swiss team of engineers and pilots has developed the *Solar Impulse,* a spindly airplane that soars on the power of sunshine. Solar panels line nearly every inch of the plane's passenger-jet-size wingspan, absorbing energy from the sun and storing it in lightweight batteries that power four electric propellers. The plane completed its first overnight flight in 2010, proving that it could harness enough solar power during the day to keep it aloft through the night. Don't plan to book a solar flight anytime soon, though—the *Solar Impulse* is strictly a one-seater aircraft, built to be as lightweight at possible. Even the pilot can't exceed 187 pounds (85 kg).

WHY do hot-air BALLOONS float?

Hot-air balloons are the oldest type of flight technology (predating the airplane by more than 120 years) for a reason: The principle behind "lighter-than-air" flight is simple. Heated air expands, becoming less dense—or lighter—than cool air, which is why hot air rises and cold air falls. Hot-air balloons carry a heat source (typically a flame) that warms the air inside the balloon. The less-dense air inside the balloon is lighter than the air outside of it, and the balloon takes flight.

Why DO HELIUM-FILLED BALLOONS FLOAT?

Helium balloons float for the same reason a beach ball floats in water. The balloon and the air inside it weigh less than the equivalent amount of water around it. As a result, the beach ball displaces the water surrounding it, pushing it away as it rises to the surface—a concept known as buoyancy. The same thing happens with a helium balloon. Helium is a special gas that weighs less than the surrounding air. Just like the beach ball in the water, the helium balloon pushes away the surrounding gas and rises above it.

Why do airplanes fly?

Planes soar with the greatest of ease because of two forces: thrust and lift. Thrust is generated by the engines, which use either propellers or jets to propel the plane forward. That forward motion moves air over the wings, which are shaped so that air passes faster over their tops than bottoms. The slower-moving air below the wings creates higher pressure than the faster-moving air above it. That difference in pressure creates lift, pushing the wings up. As long as a plane has thrust to propel air over the wings, it has lift. If a plane loses thrust, the wings "stall" and the plane plummets.

Why do gliders stay in the sky?

Now you know that flying machines need thrust and lift to get off the ground. Lacking engines, gliders must make up for their lack of thrust by maximizing lift. They have skinny bodies and sprawling wings constructed of ultralight materials. These massive wings provide more lift with less air moving over them than conventional plane wings. Glider pilots seek out "thermals," columns of heated air that rise up from the ground. Thermals are invisible, but they typically form over dark patches of terrain—parking lots or dirt fields. The pilots circle inside the column, letting the heated air push them higher and higher, until they reach the desired altitude. Then they leave the column and glide slowly back to the ground. Glider pilots can also simulate thrust by flying into strong winds.

How do helicopters fly?

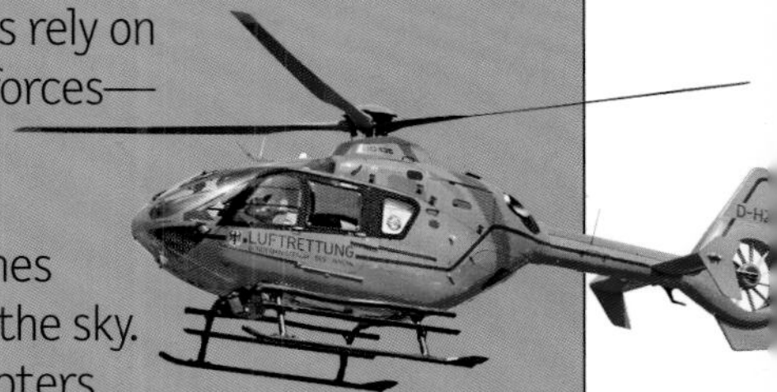

Helicopters rely on the same forces—thrust and lift—that propel planes miles into the sky. And helicopters have wings just like planes, except, in their case, the wings aren't fixed to the fuselage (which is why planes are also called fixed-wing aircraft). A helicopter's wings are on the propellers—or "rotors"—that whirl above the whirlybird. The helicopter's engine spins the rotors, which thrusts them through the air and creates lift, pulling the helicopter vertically into the air. The pilot can control the shape (or "angle of attack") of the rotors to control the amount of lift, as well as angle them forward or backward to determine the direction of flight. The smaller tail rotor, meanwhile, counteracts the rapid spin of the main rotor so that the helicopter doesn't whirl out of control (the tail rotor also controls turns). Balancing these rotor systems takes some serious multitasking skills and hand-eye coordination (helicopters are trickier to fly than airplanes), but then "rotary-wing aircraft" are much more nimble in the air, able to take off vertically, hover, and dart in any direction.

SAY WHAT?!

THE SPACE SHUTTLES became giant gliders when they left orbit. They'd reenter the atmosphere at 16,465 mph (26,498 kph) and glide to stop on a runway without using an engine.

HOW do AIRPLANES land?

To land the plane, the pilot lines it up with the runway many miles from the airport. Then he or she slowly reduces engine power, which in turn reduces thrust and slows the plane down. With less air moving over the wings, the plane gradually loses lift and descends closer to the ground. Pilots carefully time the reduction in thrust and lift so that the plane touches down gently at the start of the runway (although in passenger planes, a computer-controlled autopilot typically handles the landing).

Why are some plane rides bumpy?

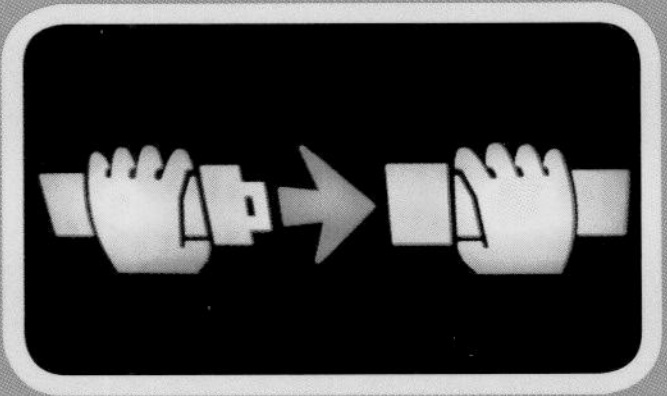

It hits you like a speed bump out of thin air—literally. The plane lurches, your orange juice sloshes on the tray table, and the "Fasten Seat Belt" light illuminates overhead. Turbulence—aka chop or bad air—is as much a part of air travel as bagged pretzels and bad in-flight movies. It's the reason pilots wear their seat belts at all times, although it's not dangerous (planes are built to withstand even the most severe turbulence). Thunderstorms and pockets of warm air called updrafts create turbulence, but pilots can usually spot these areas of bad air and steer clear. What pilots can't see are jet streams, fast-moving rivers of air that course through the atmosphere at altitudes that planes fly. Flying "upstream" in these rivers or skimming along the banks can make even the largest passenger planes rock. If it happens on your flight, don't panic! (Although you might want to hold on to your orange juice.)

Why do airplanes have pressurized cabins?

You can neither see it nor feel it, but the air around you is both crucial to your survival and actually weighs something (which is why scuba and oxygen tanks are lighter when they're empty). Air is thickest and heaviest at sea level, where humans have evolved to live. Planes, on the other hand, fly faster and more smoothly at high altitudes, around 35,000 feet (11 km). Way up there, the air is thin and frigid. Fly this high without your own air supply and you'd pass out from lack of oxygen. So, using a complex mechanical system that takes air from the engines, airplane cabins are "pressurized" to maintain the air pressure of an altitude that the passengers and pilots find comfortable.

Why CAN SAILBOATS SAIL INTO THE WIND?

Seeing a sailboat travel downwind makes sense even to landlubbers. The wind pushes the sails and the boat moves forward. But seeing a sailboat travel upwind is baffling—especially once you learn that the wind is "pulling" the boat. How is that possible? Simple physics!

It might not look like it, but a sailboat's sails—especially modern triangular sails—are really just giant wings. Like an airplane wing, each sail is shaped so that air moves faster over one side than it does over the other. This creates lift on the surface of the sail facing the wind, which "pulls" the sail (and the boat to which it's attached) forward at an angle against the wind even as the wind pushes the boat away in the downwind direction. This downwind slippage—known as leeway—is counteracted by a wing that you can't see: a heavy fin called a keel that runs down the center of the boat underwater. The keel's weight and shape counteract the force of the wind striking the sail above the water, keeping the boat from sliding downwind or being pushed over by the force of the wind (which is why you often see sailboats leaning over; the weight of the keel is keeping the boat from capsizing).

By controlling the angle of the sails, a captain can chart a course against the wind. Sailing directly into the wind is impossible, however, because the captain always needs to keep the wind at the correct angle to pull the sails forward. By sailing a series of zigzags—or "tacking"—across the wind, the captain can chart course to destinations that lie completely upwind.

WHY don't we have FLYING CARS yet?

Science fiction from the last century predicted we'd all be zipping through the sky in the family car by now, so why are we still stuck on the ground in highway traffic? Inventors have developed many flying car prototypes—such as the Moller Skycar and the Terrafugia Transition—over the decades, but these flying machines are still too tricky for the average driver to operate without a pilot's license. They also often involve time-consuming transformations—wings that fold, propellers that tuck away, and the like—to get airborne, making them more like planes that can drive on the road than true flying cars. And then there's the safety factor. Drivers in malfunctioning cars can simply pull over to the side of the road. Pilots in malfunctioning flying cars better have a parachute.

Why don't we have teleporters yet?

Crowded airports, delays, jet lag—travel by plane can be a real pain. Imagine zipping to Hawaii for a surf session, then zapping to Italy for a slice of pizza, all in the time that it takes some planes to taxi for takeoff. Believe it or not, teleporting technology already exists, but it isn't quite the crew-beaming transporter from *Star Trek*.

Using a process called quantum teleportation, scientists have figured out how to transfer the characteristics of one atom (the basic unit of matter) to a distant atom. The technology might eventually be used to transmit objects across the solar system. Teleporting people, however, is a trickier matter. The object being "teleported" is essentially destroyed at its point of origin and duplicated at its destination. Hmmm ... maybe jet lag doesn't sound so bad after all.

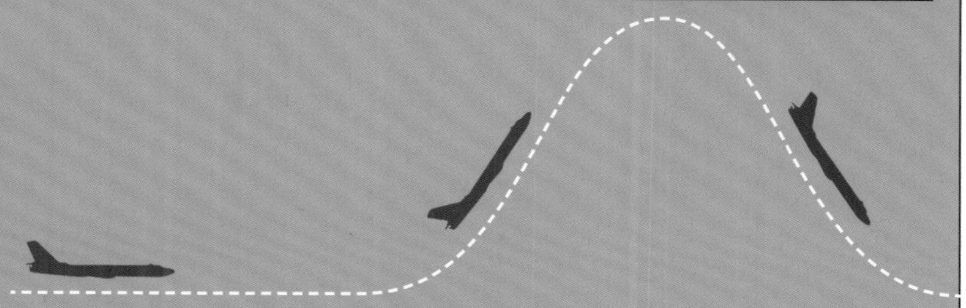

Why haven't we developed antigravity yet?

Actually, we have—but it's not cheap. Wannabe (and well-to-do) astronauts can climb aboard the *G-Force One* to fly and bounce around the airplane's cabin in simulated free fall. The modified 727 flies special acrobatic maneuvers that re-create weightlessness for up to 30 seconds at a stretch. Such "reduced gravity aircraft" aren't new—NASA has been using them for decades to help astronauts adjust to the sensation of free fall—but a company called the Zero Gravity Corporation is offering civilians a similar experience for $5,000 a ticket!

Why hasn't someone created a device to translate other languages in real time yet?

Software company Microsoft is working on a "universal translator" right now. This high-tech program not only translates your speech into the language of your choice, but it also plays your words aloud in your own voice when you make calls over the Internet using a smartphone or computer.

ANIMALS

WHY HUNT FOR intelligent life in outer space when scientists are finding signs of smarts throughout the animal kingdom here on Earth? In this chapter, you'll go on safari for answers to some of nature's biggest questions. Are dogs smarter than cats? How do dolphins communicate? And why do bugs bug us? Get ready: Things are about to get hairy.

6
WILD WHYS

WHY do animals PLAY?

It might seem obvious why kitties pounce on mouse-shaped toys and puppies nip at each other's ears in play battles. Many species of animals—particularly in the mammal and bird kingdoms—engage in such "purposeless activities." Surely they're practicing skills that will help them later in life, right? But that convenient theory doesn't survive scientific scrutiny.

OH YEAH!?

What kind of scientific scrutiny?

Kittens forbidden from frolicking in lab experiments (by some seriously coldhearted scientists, no doubt) were no worse at catching mice as adults than cats that enjoyed a play-filled kittenhood. Same goes for coyotes, rodents, and other animals that engage in playful activities. Playtime doesn't appear to reinforce social bonds in studies of closely knit animals such as meerkats or lions, either. Researchers are at a loss for why animals waste precious energy engaging in purposeless activities—especially since those activities might result in injury.

C'mon, there has to be some reason behind all the horseplay!

Wait, do you mean actual horseplaying? Researchers discovered something interesting from watching young horses—called foals—at play: Foals that frolicked in the fields were more likely to survive to their first birthday. That must mean such "purposeless activity" plays some role in an animal's survival. One theory, tested on lab rats, showed that rodents allowed to play were less stressed. (Rats that wrestle make chirping sounds that might be the rodent equivalent of gut-busting laughter.) Rats raised with playmates and fun objects developed bigger brains than rats that grew up in empty, boring cages. Just goes to show: Goofing off is good for you!

WILD RECESS

HOW DO THESE ANIMALS PLAY?

ELEPHANTS? SLEDDING!

Young elephants love to slide down hillsides on their behinds and pile into each other.

DOLPHINS? SURFING!

These original wave warriors use their bodies like surfboards to ride the faces of shore-breaks and the wakes of powerboats.

AFRICAN WILD DOGS? TUG-OF-WAR!

Before they grow into fearsome pack hunters, African wild dog puppies play fight over strips of impala skin.

RAVENS? SNOWBOARDING!

These black birds ride down snow-covered roofs and hillsides on sticks, on small objects, or even on their backs. Once they hit the bottom, the radical ravens don't need to wait in line for a chairlift. They fly back to the top and ride again!

MEERKATS? WRESTLING!

These feisty members of the mongoose family launch into playful battle royales on the dusty plains of southern Africa. Sometimes the entire family—up to 30 members—will join in, tumbling and pinning one another to the ground. No wonder a meerkat group is called a mob!

SHOREBIRDS? SKYDIVING!

Young gulls and other shorebirds that open clams by dropping them onto hard surfaces have been spotted releasing clam-size rocks from the air, then diving to catch the rocks before they hit the ground.

WHAT'S the SMARTEST animal on Earth?

That's easy: *You are.* Or, rather, the human species, aka *Homo sapiens,* aka people.

OKAY, what's the smartest animal on Earth AFTER humans?

Gosh, where to start? IQ in animals is hard to measure, considering that they live in such different worlds from us. (A cuttlefish is an Einstein when it comes to blending in with its environment.) Scientists agree that the following creatures are especially brainy ...

OCTOPUSES are extremely clever when faced with puzzles (such as figuring out how to open a jar to get at a tasty fish or escaping from aquariums). They'll even gather shells, rocks, and other objects to fortify their lairs. Equipped with more complex brains than other invertebrates (animals without a backbone, such as insects, worms, and snails), octopuses are the smartest spineless creatures.

ORANGUTANS, CHIMPS, and other **PRIMATES** lead busy social lives.

NIGHTINGALES and **CROWS** are hardly birdbrained. Nightingales can learn to sing 60 different songs. Crows use tools to open nuts.

PIGS are fast learners. Researchers have taught them how to play video games and even take a shower when they're hot. (Turns out pigs don't really "sweat like pigs.")

ELEPHANTS live in complex family groups (and have been known to paint pachyderm masterpieces when provided a few art supplies).

But one animal in particular, the **DOLPHIN,** shares all these smarty-pants characteristics: tool-use, social networking, creativity, and communication. More than 30 species of dolphins—including orcas (aka killer whales) and the Atlantic bottlenose dolphin made famous on TV and in aquarium shows—roam the world's oceans and rivers. They team up in groups called pods to accomplish tasks. Their brains are nearly as large as ours. They complement their eyesight through echolocation: a method of bouncing sounds off obstacles and the fish around them. They even have their own extreme sport: acrobatic leaps and spins that would make freestyle snowboarders jealous. And they talk to each other using what seems like a learned language instead of the instinctive barks, yips, grunts, shrieks, and other sounds that most animals are born using.

How do dolphins communicate?

Starting from birth, dolphins squawk, whistle, click, and squeak. Sometimes one dolphin will vocalize, and then another will seem to answer. Members of a pod will communicate in different patterns at the same time, like people chattering at a party. And just as you gesture and change facial expressions as you talk, dolphins communicate nonverbally with varied body postures, jaw snaps, bubble blowing, and fin caresses.

What do dolphins talk about?

Scientists suspect dolphins "talk" about everything from basic facts, like their age and gender, to their emotional state. When the going gets tough, they'll call other pod members for backup. They even have names—so-called social whistles—to summon one another. Intensely social animals, dolphins probably communicate a lot about their relationships.

Why haven't we figured out how to talk to dolphins yet?

Although researchers have taught captive dolphins how to read sign language, deciphering dolphin-speak is tricky because their language is so dependent on what they're doing (whether they're playing, fighting, or going after tasty fish). It's no different for humans. Think about when you raise a hand to say hello. That same gesture could also mean goodbye. Crossing guards raise their hand to say stop. A salesclerk might do it to tell you something costs five bucks. Imagine you're an alien from another planet trying to make sense of it all. Now you know what it's like to study dolphin communication.

DECODING DOLPHIN

What DOES IT MEAN WHEN DOLPHINS ...

... rub fins?

They're saying hi. Dolphins meeting up will caress each other's pectoral (or side) fins. Researchers think it's a greeting, like when we shake hands.

... clap their jaws?

They're yelling "back off!" Dolphins sometimes snap their jaws when staking out territory, warning other dolphins to keep away.

... swim in sync?

They're trying to get a date. Pairs of male dolphins will develop elaborate underwater routines to impress females.

... bend their bodies into an S-shape?

The dolphin might be signaling that it's getting ready to charge. Watch out!

... approach from behind?

The dolphin is playing. Dolphins approach head-on when they're feeling less playful and more aggressive.

SAY WHAT?!

SCIENTISTS STUDYING a species of fish called herring noticed the fish produced a fartlike "raspberry" sound at night by releasing a stream of bubbles from an opening alongside their butts. Only other herring can hear this high-frequency noise, which helps them cluster in protective schools. In other words, herring communicate through farting!

WHY do skunks STINK?

Mess with a skunk and you'll be sorry! Glands in their butts are loaded with an oily, sticky, stinky musk they can squirt up to ten feet (3 m) away. The spray reeks of sulfurous chemicals called thiols that can potentially knock out, burn, and even kill animals that take a direct hit. Skunks, which are nocturnal (active at night), developed this chemical weapon to deter predators that hunt using smell in the darkness. Most of the time, skunks don't even need to use their butt blasters. An angry display is often all it takes to frighten away predators, which have learned to associate the skunk's white stripe with an awful stink.

What OTHER ANIMALS HURL FOUL FLUIDS?

BOMBARDIER BEETLES

Talk about packing heat! This breed of beetle can squirt a boiling mix of volatile chemicals from the business end of its abdomen. The spray melts attacking insects and sears human skin.

ZORILLAS

You think a skunk is stinky? It's got nothing on the striped polecat, aka the zorilla, aka the smelliest animal on Earth! Like a skunk, this member of the weasel family can squirt a stream of sticky fluid from its butt at any animal that crosses its path. The polecat's spray is almost supernaturally stinky.

HAGFISH

Nearly blind and not very bright, hagfish bumble around the deep ocean looking for their next meal. If a bigger fish starts trouble, it's slime time! The hagfish encases itself in a cocoon of protective mucus and emits enough extra goo to clog the predator's gills. If the slimed fish survives this suffocating coup de gross, it learns a valuable lesson: Never hassle a hagfish!

TURKEY VULTURES

With a featherless face made for digging into maggot-ridden roadkill, turkey vultures are already the uncontested leaders of the dirty-bird club. But you haven't really seen their rotten side until you've made one mad. These bad birds defend themselves by barfing up whatever decomposing flesh they've recently devoured, along with powerful stomach acids.

HIPPOS

When an African hippopotamus emerges from a local mudhole to mark its territory with poop and pee, it doesn't waste any time spreading its waste. The big beast whips its tail to fan feces and urine in every direction. Scientists aren't certain why hippos spray their excrement to and fro, but they suspect it might serve to mark territory and attract mates. Um, how romantic?

WHAT'S the DIFFERENCE between...

... insects?

CHARACTERISTICS: Six legs and three body segments

SAMPLE SPECIES: Ants, bees, butterflies, cockroaches, and mosquitoes

SPECIAL ABILITIES: Insects are the only arthropods (the animal division that includes insects and arachnids) that can fly. Some dragonflies can zoom up to 30 miles an hour (48 kph)!

... bugs?

CHARACTERISTICS: Specialized mouth parts and hardened front wings

SAMPLE SPECIES: Cicadas, aphids, shield bugs, and bedbugs

SPECIAL ABILITIES: All bugs are insects, but not all insects are bugs, which are defined by strawlike mouths made for sucking the sap from plants or (in the case of bedbugs) blood from living hosts.

... arachnids?

CHARACTERISTICS: Eight legs and two body segments

SAMPLE SPECIES: Spiders, ticks, mites, and scorpions

SPECIAL ABILITIES: Spiders can spin webs of unbreakable silk to snare prey. They instill greater fear in humans than any other animal, despite the fact that spiders are relatively harmless compared with insects.

Why do creepy-crawlies creep us out?

Pest control is a billion-dollar business for a reason: Insects and arachnids are the all-stars of nastiness. They reproduce like crazy (a single female aphid, for example, can produce 600 billion offspring in one season)! They have horrible eating habits (houseflies vomit digestive juices on everything they eat and then slurp it up like a sickening soup). They sting or bite (Australia's funnel-web spider can kill you if you don't get the antivenom). Their furry legs and murderous jaws (called mandibles) inspire sweat-inducing phobias (intensely strong feelings of distress triggered by specific things).

What kind of phobias?

People afraid of insects suffer from entomophobia. Arachnophobia is the fear of spiders.

Why don't we just kill all those pests?

Because they have us outnumbered! More than 80 percent of all the species on Earth belong to this wildly diverse group of creatures, and biologists are discovering new bugs all the time. Each square foot of your backyard is crawling with them: grubs, ants, spiders, beetles, centipedes, and grasshoppers. Your bedroom floor is a habitat for dust mites. You have microscopic bugs clinging to your body right now. Feeling itchy yet? Oh, and think about this the next time you squash a bug: They're crucial to our survival.

Why are insects crucial to our survival?

Because the world would be a lifeless brown ball of dust without them. Many of these creepy creepers feast on feces (poop) and dead plant and animal matter while adding nutrients to the soil for plant life, which is also pollinated by bees and other buzzing insects. Plants in turn are food for other animals and produce oxygen from carbon dioxide. Insects keep the whole process running smoothly, keeping Earth clean and green.

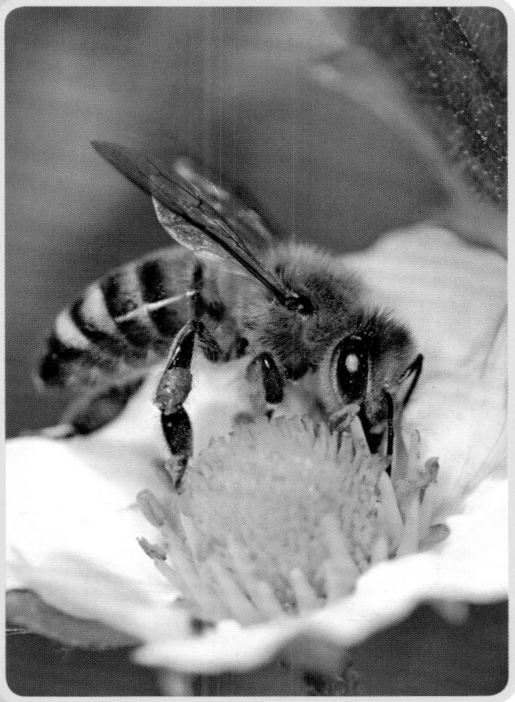

Why DO INSECTS HAVE SHELLS INSTEAD OF SKIN?

They wear their skeletons on the outside of their bodies, and they can change these shells just like we change our clothes. When a bug outgrows its bony skin, it sheds it—a process called molting—and grows a new one. The old armor is left behind, although giant centipedes will actually eat their discarded skeletons. Hey, at least you can't call them litterbugs!

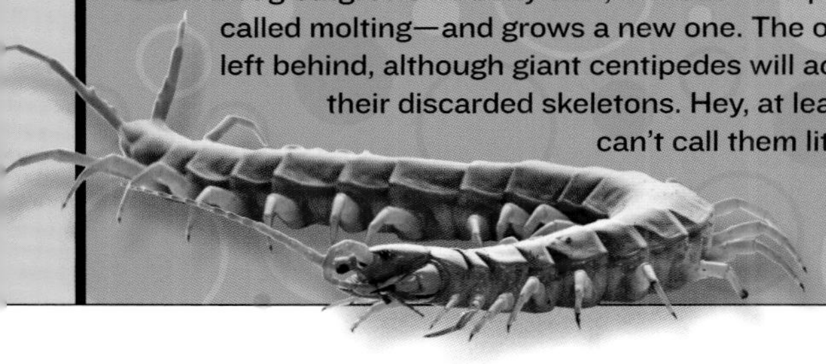

. . . SO why DO CRABS AND LOBSTERS HAVE SHELLS?

Because they're arthropods—the same animal group that includes insects and arachnids. If it has at least six legs, a segmented body, and wears its skeleton like a suit of armor, it's an arthropod! The next time you're eating a tasty lobster tail, you're snacking on a bug!

WHY do some people EAT insects?

In many parts of the world, insects are just another food group. And why not? Bugs are rich in protein and vitamins. They require fewer resources to raise than cows, pigs, and chickens. Unlike bottom-feeding shrimp, which we pop in our mouths without a second thought, many bugs live on a wholesome diet of grass, leaves, and flowers. Bugs also devour farmers' crops, so eating pest insects helps protect our veggies. Win-win!

Why shouldn't the thought of eating insects bug me?

Because you're probably already eating them. Farms, food-delivery trucks, and food-packaging plants are hardly bug-free environments. Insects cling to the food and crawl through the machinery. In the United States, the Food and Drug Administration puts a limit on how many insect parts (and rat hairs and other nasty stuff) can end up in your apple sauce, frozen broccoli, canned mushrooms, ketchup, and other packaged foods, but those itty-bitty bug bits add up. You eat about two pounds (.9 kg) of shredded insect every year. It's ground into everything during the food-production and packaging processes.

What DO BUGS TASTE LIKE?

Depends on the insect. According to people who engage in entomophagy, or eating insects for food ...

... giant water bugs taste like a salty Jolly Rancher candy.
... scorpions taste funky and bitter, like spoiled crab meat.
... grasshoppers taste like spicy popcorn.
... mopane caterpillars taste like beef jerky.
... palm weevil larvae taste like bacon soup.

Okay, I'm ready to bite a bug. Where can I place my order?

Almost anywhere. Eighty percent of people on Earth include insects as a regular part of their diet. That means you'll find bugs on the menus in every continent—even North America. The Insectarium, a museum infested with insects (kept safely in displays) in New Orleans, Louisiana, U.S.A., serves an assortment of buggy treats, including "Chocolate Chirp Cookies" baked with dry-roasted crickets. Or you can search online for Larvets, an extra-crunchy snack festively packaged in three tasty-sounding varieties: barbecue, cheddar cheese, and Mexican spice. The secret ingredient: farm-raised insect larvae from Hotlix, makers of "the original candy that bugs." Other crunchy Hotlix treats include Scorpion Suckers and Cricket Lick-Its.

WHY are killer bees KILLERS?

They're the product of a lab experiment gone wrong! This highly aggressive breed of honeybee escaped from a Brazilian lab in 1957, and they have been heading north ever since. They'll pursue any threat until it drops—and then continue stinging and stinging and stinging! A swarm chasing a Texas man nailed him more than a thousand times! Known to scientists as Africanized bees, they were dubbed "killer bees" by the media.

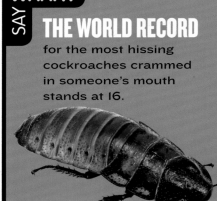

Why are honeybees disappearing?

Beginning in 2006, beekeepers across the United States reported alarming losses of their hives. Honeybees were fleeing their queens and colonies, never to return. The phenomenon—called colony collapse disorder—continued to spread, and by 2013 beekeepers were reporting average losses of 45 percent of their hives. Honeybees are vital pollinators for everything from apples to almonds, avocados to onions (not to mention the source of all honey), and bee researchers are scrambling to figure out what's causing the disappearing act. Current suspects include parasites, viruses, and pesticides, and many believe it's a combination of all three.

WHAT?! SAY

THE WORLD RECORD for the most hissing cockroaches crammed in someone's mouth stands at 16.

Why are cockroaches so hard to kill?

They've crept through Earth's crannies for 300 million years and survived the worldwide calamity that wiped out the dinosaurs. Cockroaches keep on crawling and crawling and crawling for all sorts of reasons. They're more active at night, when it's easier to hide from predators—and the bottom of your shoe. The roughly 4,500 species of roaches around the world have evolved to fill nearly every ecological niche (including humid sewers, where they reproduce by the millions). Hardier than most insects, roaches are resistant to radiation and can go a month between meals. They'll eat almost anything—including human eyelashes! But it's just as well that these brown bugs are such extreme survivors. Their anything-goes diet rids the world of organic garbage. And while roaches might make your skin crawl, they're a gourmet snack for rodents, birds, lizards, and other small animals.

Why is it so hard to swat a fly?

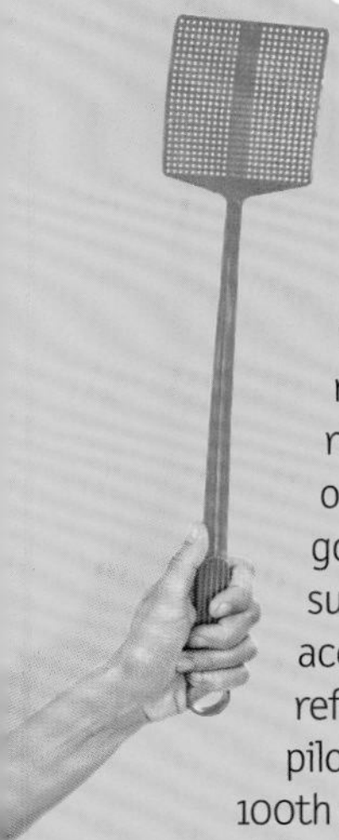

Anyone who has wasted time trying to bat this buzzing bug would swear it had powers of teleportation, as it magically disappears at the moment of impact before reappearing an instant later over the potato salad. The good news is flies don't have superpowers. They're just aces at flying and have reflexes faster than any fighter pilot's. How fast? In less than a 100th of a second—or a 50th of the time it takes to blink—a fly can detect an incoming threat from any direction (thanks to large eyes designed to detect movement), perform a roll to change direction, and zip away at full throttle. Scientists credit the flies' amazing reaction time to a special neuron—or brain cell—running from the bugs' itty-bitty brains to their muscles. It's like they have an instant connection between their eyes and their wings.

Why do moths fly into flames and bounce off lights?

No one knows for sure why moths (along with other winged insects) will make a beeline for lightbulbs or burn up in candle flames. The most popular theory is that moths navigate at night by flying parallel to the brightest light source, which in the time before man-made campfires and electricity was the moon or stars. The moon makes a good navigational aid because it never gets any closer, helping the moth keep a straight flight path. Trying to fly parallel to a streetlight or flame short-circuits the moth's flight computer, causing the moth to fly in tighter and tighter circles until it eventually bounces off the light or burns up.

Why are mosquitoes the world's most dangerous animal?

Mosquito bites in Africa and elsewhere claim the lives of millions of people each year—far more victims than those killed by sharks and crocodiles. These buzzing, bothersome flies spread malaria, dengue fever, and other diseases that are fatal if left untreated.

Why do crickets chirp?

If these busy little bugs have ever kept you up at night with their incessant singing, blame the boys. Male crickets make a racket to attract female crickets and to keep other males from intruding on their turf.

MYTH MASHED

How do crickets make that chirping sound?

A male cricket's musical instrument is his wings rather than his legs. A strange, tooth-covered vein runs along the bottom of each wing. When he's ready to make some noise, a cricket holds both wings open to amplify the sound—like a natural speaker—then rubs one wing's teeth over the other until the lady crickets start to swoon.

Why do fireflies glow?

It's not a teeny-weeny lightbulb or a spark that lights up a firefly's insides. In fact, this insect's fiery glow doesn't produce any heat at all. It's the product of a chemical reaction inside the bug's body. By mixing chemicals and oxygen, the firefly switches its night-light on and off and controls its intensity, providing mood lighting for summer evenings in the backyard.

Fireflies are born with their built-in night-lights. They glow as larvae to warn predators not to eat them (firefly bodies contain yucky-tasting chemicals; one taste teaches most predators to snack elsewhere). In their adult forms, fireflies flash to identify each other and attract mates. Female fireflies go for guy flies with the brightest, flashiest light show.

WHY are coral reefs so COLORFUL?

Coral reefs are often called the "rain forests of the sea," but they're more like undersea cities for fish, eels, lobsters, and the many other organisms that live here. The workers that build these cities are the corals themselves—minuscule creatures that create a tough limestone skeleton to live in. The structures you see are the skeletons of thousands of coral polyps piled up over the centuries. Corals invite algae roommates into their limestone homes to help them survive and produce the reef's trademark vivid colors. The algae convert sunlight to food and oxygen for the corals, which in turn nourish the algae with their waste.

Why ARE CORAL REEFS IMPORTANT?

Not only do coral reefs account for 25 percent of all life in the ocean, but they also serve as the sea's early-warning system. The delicate relationship between corals and their algae roommates is vulnerable to the slightest changes in global climate and ocean health. A jump of even two degrees in water temperature sends the algae packing their bags, leaving the coral with a sickly bleached look. Pollution can poison the sensitive corals in their shallow habitats. When the corals go bad, the rest of the ocean could follow.

Why is the ocean glowing like this?

Because it's home to billions of microscopic creatures called *Pyrodinium bahamense* that shine when disturbed—a phenomenon called bioluminescence. The best spot to see it in action is Laguna Grande, a bay on the northeastern corner of Puerto Rico. Every splash makes the water flash, and darting fish create lightning bolts in the deep.

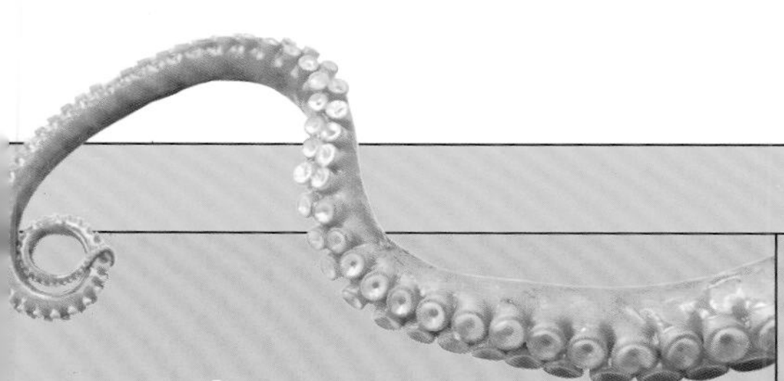

Why don't octopus arms ever get tangled?

With our two arms, two legs, and a dozen joints, humans have it easy when it comes to telling limb from limb. The octopus, on the other hand, has a much more complicated body plan. Its eight boneless arms can form joints at any point, bending in all directions like cooked spaghetti noodles. And each arm bristles with hundreds of tooth-tipped suckers that stick to any fleshy surface. Imagine trying to untangle a string of holiday lights covered in glue. You'd think an octopus would spend every day just trying to keep its arms from tangling into one impossible knot, but these undersea wonders have two foolproof systems for keeping their limbs straight ...

SMART LEGS: Each of the octopus's eight arms has a mind of its own: a network of roughly 400,000 neurons that controls the arm without input from the animal's main brain. These micro-brains help the arms work together rather than clump together.

SUCKER-PROOF SKIN: Octopus skin excretes a special chemical. When the suckers brush against the creature's other arms, they sense the chemical and automatically avoid latching on. The octopus can override this reflex if it wants to (say, if it's battling another octopus). Scientists think octopuses also rely on these chemicals to detect and identify each other.

Why do whales beach themselves?

Marine biologists can't always tell why pods of whales and dolphins—sometimes by the hundreds—will swim onto a beach and strand themselves in the surf, often dying en masse unless people manage to shove the behemoths back out to sea. Sometimes the whales are sick with pneumonia or some other illness. Sometimes they've suffered attacks from sharks or other whale species. Quirks in the Earth's magnetic field—which whales follow as part of their biological navigation system—might also play a role. Mass strandings have been recorded as far back as 2,300 years ago, but some scientists speculate that strandings are on the rise today because of pollution and an increase in ocean noise caused by ship traffic and submarine sonar systems.

Why do sharks attack people?

Before you run screaming from the water, let's get one thing clear: Shark attacks are incredibly rare. Far more people are injured by their toilets each year than by a hungry shark. You have a 1 in 3,700,000 chance of being killed by a shark. And for every person who dies in the jaws of one of these fearsome fish, about two millions sharks perish at the hands of humans.

But shark attacks do happen—an average of 19 attacks per year in the United States (and one fatal attack every two years). Researchers believe such attacks are typically a case of mistaken identity. A shark sees a swimmer's hands and feet flashing in the murk and confuses them for the scales of a tasty fish. A surfer is a dead ringer for a sea lion or turtle when seen from below. Most shark attacks on humans are bump-and-runs—a quick taste of wet suit or surfboard or skin that tells the shark it has bitten the wrong animal. A bump from a little species might result in a few stitches. Bump-and-runs from great white sharks, which reach more than 20 feet (6 m) in length, can be much more serious.

Q: tips

How can I dodge jaws?

- Sharks tend to target lone swimmers, so swim in a group.
- Leave the water immediately if you're bleeding.
- Stay out of the water during the dawn and twilight hours, when sharks are on the prowl.
- Don't wear shiny watch-bands or jewelry that sharks might mistake for fish scales.
- Avoid swimming in river mouths, areas between sand-bars, or near drop-offs.
- Don't swim near fishermen or diving seabirds. No reason to become shark bait!

- Wear a disguise. A company in Perth, Australia, designed a line of wet suits to make surfers, divers, and snorkel-ers appear less appetizing to sharks. The suit's bold stripes mimic the coloration of dan-gerous marine creatures, such as sea snakes and lion-fish, which sharks avoid.

SAY WHAT?!

KILLER WHALES (which are actually members of the dol-phin family and not whales) in Argentina will beach them-selves on purpose to gobble up sea lion pups on shore, and then wriggle their way back into the deeper water.

WHY do zebras have STRIPES?

Scientists have a few theories about the fashionable fur of these African equids (the family of mammals that includes horses). Some suspect it's a type of camouflage to keep these herd animals from standing out in a crowd. The stripes break up the animal's shape (a tactic known as disruptive coloration) as well as help it blend in with its neighbors, making it hard for a lion to see where one zebra ends and the next one begins. A more recent theory suggests that the zebra's coloration repels bloodsucking insects, which don't like to land on stripes. The stripes might be a natural pest control.

Why do leopards, jaguars, and cheetahs have spots?

For the same reason tigers have stripes: to help them hide while hunting. The cats' coloration blends with tall grass and the shifting shadows beneath trees and brush. Leopards, for instance, become virtually invisible when they sneak up on prey before pouncing at the last instant.

Can animals change their spots?

Yes, dozens of animals can alter their appearance to match the season or the scenery. The fur of the arctic fox, for instance, shifts from brown to white in the wintertime. But the fox has nothing on the disguise mastery of octopuses, squid, and cuttlefish. Color- and texture-shifting cells in their skin let them mimic rocks and morph into corals. Toxic-to-the tummy mollusks called nudibranchs rely on their diet to change colors—the brighter the better (poisonous animals often bear bright, colorful markings as a warning to predators). And while chameleons can also shift the color of their skin at will, they do it to communicate rather than to blend in with their surroundings.

MYTH MASHED

Why DO POLAR BEARS HAVE WHITE FUR?

The largest land carnivore might look white and fluffy, but its fur isn't white at all. Each hair is actually see-through, with a hollow core that traps heat. The fur only looks white because of the way it reflects light (just like snowflakes look white even though they're transparent). If you were brave—and foolish—enough to brush aside the polar bear's dense coat, you'd see that its skin is actually as black as its nose!

Why do penguins look like they're wearing tuxedos?

Because these flightless birds have a type of camouflage known as countershading, meaning their tops and bottoms don't match. A penguin's belly is a lighter tone to match the day-lit surface of the water above, while its back is dark to blend in with the murk below. Their counter-coloring helps them hide from predators such as leopard seals.

Why are flamingos pink?

These big, bent-beaked birds are born with drab feathers. As they age, the flamingo's plumage turns pink from the bacteria and a vitamin-rich pigment called beta-carotene in the bird's shrimp-filled diet.

SILLY QUESTION, SERIOUS ANSWER

Would my skin color change if I ate like a flamingo?

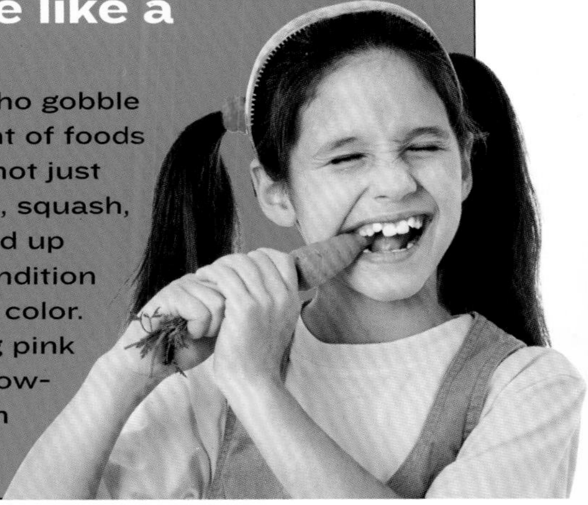

Actually, yes! People who gobble up an excessive amount of foods rich in beta-carotene (not just shrimp but also carrots, squash, sweet potatoes) will end up with carotenemia, a condition that changes their skin color. Instead of the shocking pink of flamingo plumage, however, their skin takes on a subtle yellowish tint.

WHY do birds have FEATHERS?

Light and strong, feathers serve 101 functions: They help birds fly, keep them warm and dry, protect them from the sun, act as camouflage, attract mates with their colorful designs, and much more.

Why do birds have hair when they hatch?

A baby chicken might look like a ball of fuzz with legs and a beak, but that's not hair covering its itty-bitty body. Rather, it's a layer of fine feathers called "down," which traps heat to keep the chicks toasty. (Down is such a good insulator that it's used as stuffing in pillows, jackets, and sleeping bags.) As the baby birds grow, they sprout tougher, more feathery-looking feathers on top of the down.

Why do mammals have fur?

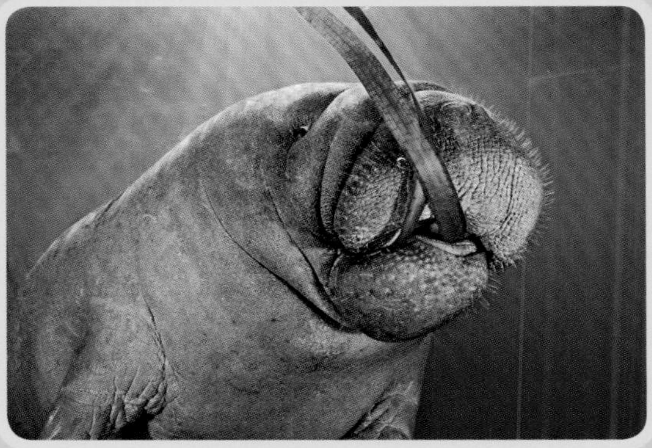

Warm-blooded mammals evolved with fur to retain body heat and act as a trap for smelly chemicals, called pheromones, that convey all sorts of information about each animal. All mammals have some type of hair—even marine mammals such as manatees and dolphins (dolphins are born with whiskers that eventually fall out).

Why do humans have fur only atop their heads?

That's not quite true. We all have fine hairs on our bodies (and thicker clumps of hair in our armpits and other places to catch those stinky pheromones). But our patchy pelts look bald compared with the lustrous fur of felines, polar bears, or sea otters (which have the thickest hair on Earth). Scientists aren't certain why humans evolved to become less hairy in the past six million years or so, but they have a few theories. Primates may have shed their fur as they adapted to life on sweltering savannas (as opposed to the cool forests of our earlier ape ancestors). Modern humans don't need body hair to stay warm. That's what clothes are for.

Why does this animal look like a cross between a lion and a tiger?

Because it's a "liger," a hybrid offspring of a male lion and female tiger. It has the faint stripes of a tiger and the shaggy mane of a lion.

Why does this animal look like a cross between a horse and a zebra?

Because it's a "zorse," the hybrid offspring of a female zebra and a male horse. The two equines are sometimes combined for use as pack animals in Africa.

Why DO SNAKES HAVE SCALES?

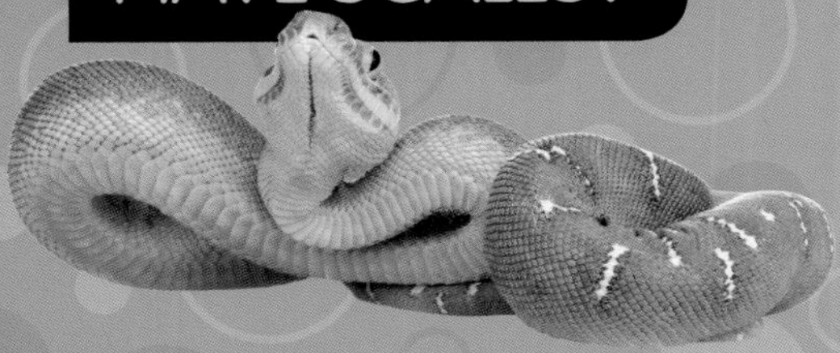

Don't let a snake's slimy appearance fool you. Snake scales are dry and smooth. Scales on the body and head are like a natural suit of armor (which a snake sheds in one piece periodically throughout its life). Snakes evolved without legs, so they glide on the scales of their bellies to get around.

... Okay, why do fish have scales then?

Just like reptiles, fish have scales on their bodies for protection against predators and hazards in the environment. Shark scales are particularly tough. Sharks are armored with teeth-like scales called dermal denticles. These overlapping, diamond-shaped ridges point toward the shark's tail, reducing drag and boosting swimming speed. They work so well that Olympic swimsuit makers incorporated denticle designs in their fabrics.

WHY can camels survive so long without DRINKING water?

If you think the secret to a camel's success in the desert lies in its humps, you're right. If you think those humps are flush with fresh water like gurgling water coolers, you're wrong. A camel's humps are filled with fat—enough fat to supply the animal with energy and hydration for long hauls through the desert. Camels can also adjust their body temperature to deal with the baking sun, and their brains have a sort of natural air-conditioning. But it's really the humps that keep them going (plus the scant bit of moisture they get from nibbling on desert plants).

Do CAMELS EVER GET THIRSTY?

Sure, but not very often. Their humps provide them with enough energy for up to seven months in the winter (but less than a week in the peak heat of the summer). You can tell when a camel needs to wet its whistle by the size of its hump, which actually shrinks as the camel uses up its stored fat.

Why do giraffes have long necks?

Zoologists have a few ideas. Some say giraffes developed long necks to swing like baseball bats when competing for mates—but the most common theory is actually the simplest: Giraffes evolved with sky-high skulls to help them munch on leaves out of reach of other animals. Despite their towering necks, though, giraffes have the same number of neck vertebrae (special bones on the spinal cord) as humans—and even mice!

Why do lizards lose their tails?

To survive! Weak points in the tail help it break free when a predator pounces or a bird swoops in for the kill. The squiggling tail distracts the predator while the lizard flees to safety. Eventually, the tail regrows and the lizard is ready to lose it all over again.

Why are geckos so good at sticking to stuff?

It's not gluey goop or suction cups that make these little lizards stick. Instead, their toes are coated with millions of microscopic hairs that attach to surfaces at a molecular level, creating a bond so strong that one gecko could support 280 pounds (127 kg).

What other animals have regenerative powers?

Conchs can regrow their eyes, starfish can sprout new limbs, and zebrafish can mend their muscles, but no animal matches the amazing regenerative abilities of the axolotl, a friendly faced salamander that lurks in lakes near Mexico City. They can sprout lopped-off legs in a matter of months. Broken hearts and damaged brains grow back good as new.

Do all animals age?

Not quite! A bell-shaped ball of jelly called *Turritopsis nutricula*—aka the immortal jellyfish—lives up to its nickname. When the going gets tough, this creature reverts to its earliest stage of development and begins the aging process from scratch, hitting the reset button on its life. That would be like you transforming into a baby whenever you wanted!

Why do vampire bats drink blood?

This special species of bat, found in the night skies above the jungles of Central and South America, dines exclusively on the blood of pigs, chickens, and other farm animals. Zoologists suspect that vampire bats evolved from ancient bats that ate bloodsucking insects. The bloodthirsty bats developed adaptations that made it easier to slurp blood directly from their victims. These adaptations include heat sensors in the nose, a grooved tongue made for lapping, razorlike teeth, and an anti-clotting substance in vampire bat spit, which keeps a victim's blood flowing smoothly for the feast. The substance's name: Draculin.

LIGHTNING ROUND

What IS THE FASTEST . . .

... land animal? CHEETAH

Cheetahs can sprint for up to 60 seconds at speeds reaching 75 miles an hour (120 kph).

... two-legged land animal? OSTRICH

Although they're flightless birds, ostriches can zoom 43 miles an hour (70 kph) and use their wings for steering when being pursued by a predator.

... fish? MARLIN

This shimmering sport fish can zoom to 80 miles an hour (129 kph) when trying to escape the hook of a fishing line.

... animal overall? PEREGRINE FALCON

This master raptor achieves speeds over 240 miles an hour (386 kph) when it dives, making it the fastest creature on Earth.

... fastest animal based on body size? HUMMINGBIRD

A dive-bombing hummingbird is speedier (relatively speaking) than the space shuttle on reentry. Scientists have declared these birds the world's fastest animals relative to their size.

... human? JAMAICAN OLYMPIC ATHLETE USAIN BOLT

This aptly named sprinter has reached speeds above 23 miles an hour (37 kph).

WHY are sloths so SLOW?

These tree-climbing natives of the South and Central American rain forests live their lives like they're on permanent vacation, creeping so slowly that some sloths actually grow moss on their backs. (Although they always look sleepy, sloths doze for only a reasonable 9.6 hours a day, according to a 2008 study.) Their diet—which consists of leaves, flowers, and bits of fruit—is to blame for their slow-motion lifestyle. After all, imagine how sluggish you'd be if all you ate were salad greens, and you had to climb to every room in your house.

SILLY QUESTION, SERIOUS ANSWER

Why did the chicken cross the road?

Because it couldn't fly over it. No matter how hard they flap their wings, chickens can hope for little more than a short glide and a soft landing. They aren't really "flightless birds," a group that includes ostriches, emus, and cassowaries. The breastbones of these birds can't support the powerful muscles required to pump wings and achieve liftoff. (Penguins, meanwhile, are a different type of flightless birds built for underwater "flight.") Flightless birds lost their ability to fly through evolution, but chickens became flightless over time through selective breeding, which made them too heavy for liftoff. After all, farmers hardly want their prized poultry soaring north for the winter. The chicken's ancestor—the red jungle fowl, which is still around today—has retained the ability to fly.

Why do bats sleep upside down?

Bats aren't strong enough to take off from the ground like birds. By hanging upside down, they can drop right into the air and start flying. High-up tree branches and other roosting spots also give bats a place to hide from predators during the day. Unlike your hands (which require muscle power to hold a tight grip), bats' feet close automatically on branches the instant they start hanging upside down.

Why do lions and tigers roar?

Because they have something important to say, and they want every animal within five miles (8 km)—the range of a lion's roar—to get the message. The sole social members of the feline family, lions roar to communicate with the rest of their pack (called a pride). A male lion on patrol will roar to let the females (called lionesses) know that the pride's territory is free from rogue lions (or lions without a pride), or he might roar to tell other lions to keep their distance. Although not as loud as lions, lionesses roar to call their cubs home or shout for help in the hunt. Tigers, which are solitary animals like all other cats, unleash their roars to convey a simpler message: Keep out of my territory.

How do they roar?

Of all the cats, lions and tigers produce the loudest roars—loud enough to rattle the suspension of any nearby vehicles. Fatty folds in the throats of these big cats vibrate to create and amplify that sandpapery roaring sound with just a little bit of air pressure from the lungs. Leopards and jaguars—the only other cats that can roar—also have these folds.

Why do wolves howl?

A wolf pack relies on teamwork to hunt prey and defend its territory. By working together, a pack can take down much larger animals. And nothing builds team spirit like a good group howl, one of nature's most haunting sounds. Wolves howl in a chorus often: when they wake up, before a hunt, perhaps even for fun. Audible up to ten miles (16 km) away in the right terrain, a howl also functions as the pack's long-distance phone service. Wolves will howl to call members to a meeting site, warn of danger to the pups, or tell neighboring packs to keep off their land.

Why are some wolves "lone" wolves?

Although wolves are social animals that like to live in happy pack families, some wander the wilderness without ever finding a mate, while others lose their pack members to tragic fates. These lone wolves face many hardships not experienced by those living in packs. Unable to use teamwork to bring down large animals, they must settle for easier-to-kill prey such as birds, beavers, and rodents—mere morsels compared with typical pack feasts. Wherever they wander, lone wolves have to be extra wary: They risk a vicious attack if they enter another pack's territory.

Why does a kangaroo carry its offspring in a pouch?

Kangaroos (along with koalas, opossums, and Tasmanian devils) are marsupials, a type of mammal that nurtures its defenseless newborns in a pouch outside its body. While other types of mammals (known as placental mammals) grow their offspring inside the womb, marsupials give birth relatively early and continue their pregnancies in their pouches. The pouch fulfills all the life-support functions of the womb until the baby kangaroo (called a joey) is ready to hop on its own two feet. Sometimes, older and younger joeys will squeeze into the same pouch. Bet you'll never complain about your room being cramped again.

Why DO WE THINK BABY ANIMALS ARE CUTE?

There's a reason you say "awww" whenever you see a puppy or a smiling baby. We have evolved to think that any creature with a big head, large eyes, and a button nose—features that most human babies share—is cute. Anyone who has had to babysit knows that toddlers require a lot of time and attention—more than the offspring of other animals. Evolution has wired our brains to think babies are cute, which makes us more willing to drop everything we're doing and care for them. In fact, studies show that babies who are considered extra cute get extra attention. Animals with similar facial features—from kitties to koalas—also set off our cuteness response.

WHY do dogs chase their TAILS?

Dog experts disagree over why canines chase their tails in a race they can't win. Some breeds—German shepherds, Finnish bull terriers, and miniature terriers—hit the spin cycle more than others, leading scientists to think tail-chasing is tied to genetics. But studies show puppies that aren't properly socialized (for instance, they're removed from their littermates too early) grow up to be habitual tail-chasers. Another cause could be a lack of vitamins in a dog's diet. Some trainers suspect this hyperactive habit is a sign of a bored dog that wants to play; other trainers think tail-chasers are overstimulated by other dogs in the house or rowdy kids nearby. In any case, most dogs can be broken of the habit through patient training.

Why does my dog spin in circles before lying down?

They say old habits die hard—and this particular one goes back to Fido's ancestors. Wolves and wild dogs turn in circles to tamp down the grass and drive out bugs before dropping for a nap. Your pup inherited that same behavior as instinct, whether he or she is settling down in the backyard or on the bed's comforter.

Why do dogs sniff each other's behinds?

Spot's sense of smell is a hundred times more sensitive than yours, and he lives in a world where odor is information. Glands on a dog's backside transmit all sorts of info about his or her identity, including age, sex, social status, and much more. So when dogs sniff each other's stinky parts, they're really just saying hello.

Why does my dog like to roll in stinky stuff?

Fallen leaves, cow plops, roadkill—all sorts of repulsive piles seem like paradise to your pooch, who has a nasty habit of rolling in filth the instant he or she gets outside (usually right after a bath). But remember, a dog's nose is a hundred times more sensitive than a human's. What smells sweet to us—such as dog shampoo—might seem just plain awful to your dog, so he or she will roll in something smelly to overpower the shampoo odor. Some experts believe dogs instinctively roll in poop or dead critters to cover their scent or share these foul finds with pack members. In this case, unfortunately, you're part of your dog's pack!

Why does my dog pant when she gets hot?

When a dog pants, she's turning on the air-conditioning. Panting sucks in and circulates air to cool her body. Unlike their human best friends, dogs don't sweat through their skin. They do it through the pads of their paws, but not enough to cool off on a hot afternoon (you'd feel the same way if you played fetch in a fur coat).

Why is my dog's nose cold and wet?

Veterinarians think dogs secrete a thin layer of snot—or just lick their noses—to keep them wet, which may help them detect the direction of interesting odors.

MYTH MASHED

Why is a cold, wet nose a sign of a healthy dog?

It's not! Dogs with warm, dry noses are just as healthy as those with cold, wet ones.

Why does my dog dig holes?

When you try to stop Spot from shoveling away the soil in the backyard, you're waging a battle against instincts inherited from his wolf ancestors. Dogs dig holes for several reasons, including ...

TO COOL OFF: Freshly dug dirt makes a great escape from the heat on summer days.

TO BURY TREASURES: Just like wolves that bury food for survival, dogs feel an instinctive urge to hide precious items—such as bones and chew toys—for later retrieval.

TO HAVE FUN: Some dog breeds (especially terriers and others bred to hunt burrowing rodents) just enjoy digging.

TO KEEP THEMSELVES OCCUPIED: Certain dogs suffer separation anxiety when they're left alone all day. Digging gives them something to do.

Why does my dog hate the mail carrier?

The easiest way to answer this question is to trade places with your pooch. As a social pack animal, you consider it your job to guard your territory and look after the rest of your pack (in your case, the humans you live with). Feeling at home in Fido's fur? Good. Now consider this: Nearly every day, a strange human approaches your territory, often while the rest of your pack isn't home. It's an intruder! The stranger rattles the front door, trying to get in. You must protect the house! You bark and growl and leap against the door, doing everything in your power to scare away the intruder. And it works! The stranger wanders away to the next house. Mission accomplished ... until tomorrow.

WHY does my cat hack up HAIR BALLS?

Cats groom themselves throughout the day using their sandpapery tongues to comb food and dirt from their fur. Unfortunately, they gobble down gobs of loose hair with all that gunk. Feline bellies aren't equipped to digest strands of fur, so, *kersplat!* The hair comes out the same way it went in, and you discover soggy fuzz balls all over the house. Hey, a few hair balls are better than a filthy feline!

SILLY QUESTION, SERIOUS ANSWER

Can humans get hair balls like cats?

Sure, if you have a habit of chewing on your hair. Human hair balls are called bezoars. Medieval Europeans even carried them as good-luck charms!

Why does my cat sometimes put icky "treasures" on my doorstep?

Because your kitty thinks your stalking skills could use some work. Biologists think cats share their kills out of motherly instinct. Mama cats bring minced mice and battered birds to their kittens to teach them hunting skills. Trying to stop your cat from hunting and sharing is like asking your brother to stop stinking up the bathroom—it's a battle against nature!

Why do cats purr?

Although only lions, tigers, leopards, and jaguars can roar, all cats can purr. Researchers aren't quite sure why cats produce this pleasant rumbling sound, but they think it starts as a way for mommas to reassure kittens that they're safe. Once cats grow up, purring evolves to convey general contentment. Some scientists think that a cat's purring sound might even help it develop stronger bones!

Why aren't cats as friendly as dogs?

Researchers can point to a few reasons why Fido and not Miss Whiskers is famously known as man's and woman's "best friend." For starters, dogs are pack animals, descended from wolves, while cats are solitary and less social. Dogs are hard-wired to get along with others. Plus, pooches and people go way back—as far back as 30,000 years ago, when humans began tossing morsels to wolves in return for protection and help with hunting. Cats, by contrast, have lived with us for only the past 8,000 years or so. Although dogs and cats have developed a deep relationship with humans, canines are more attuned to our feelings and needs.

What do you mean, dogs are friendlier? My cat loves me!

Of course your cat loves you, but it's possible your cat might love someone else, too. That's what researchers discovered when they strapped tiny National Geographic cameras to the collars of 60 house cats and let them roam the suburbs of Athens, Georgia, U.S.A. The cat's-eye footage revealed that at least one cat in the study lived a double life, splitting his time between two families who each thought they were the cat's true owners. The two-timing tabby would scratch at one house's door, nuzzle the owners, tuck into dinner, then scamper to the other house for a second dose of food and affection.

So which is smarter: cat or dog?

Ah, now here's a question that has dog and cat owners fighting like, well, cats and dogs. Without a doubt, both of these treasured pets are clever, but research has shown that mutts edge out kitties when it comes to overall smarts. Pooches have bigger brains, learn to understand hundreds of human words, and can be trained for all sorts of important jobs. Cats have a far less impressive work résumé (they're much more difficult to train), although they can learn tricks and are experts at manipulating their masters with one perfectly pitched meow (studies have shown that cats learn which noises get our attention). Researchers believe that dogs became brainier as they evolved alongside humans and had to cope with our demands and problems. Social animals tend to be smarter.

Which OF THESE ARE REAL JOBS FOR TRAINED ANIMALS?

Seeing Eye dog
HELPS THE BLIND

Carrier pigeon
CARRIES MESSAGES

Therapy dog
CHEERS UP SICK, INJURED, OR ELDERLY PEOPLE

Delicacy-digging pig
DIGS UP TRUFFLES, A GOURMET FOOD

Monkey waiter
SERVES SUPPER AT A JAPANESE TAVERN

Elephant artist
PAINTS WITH ITS TRUNK

Combat dog
BACKS UP SOLDIERS IN COMBAT

Herding dog
PROTECTS AND DIRECTS SHEEP AND CATTLE

Draft dog
PULLS CARTS AND SLEDS

Waterskiing squirrel
SELF-EXPLANATORY

Do cats really have nine lives?

Of course not, but they sure seem like they do! Cats possess grace and a sense of balance that borders on the supernatural. Their most stupendous superpower is the "righting reflex": the ability to spin in midair and land on their paws no matter which way they fall. Cats that take a tumble from great heights also spread their legs and bodies to slow the descent. This natural parachute combined with their righting reflex has helped kitties survive accidental falls from skyscrapers.

Answer: Actually, all these creature careers are real and held by trained animals across the globe.

WHAT'S the world's LARGEST animal?

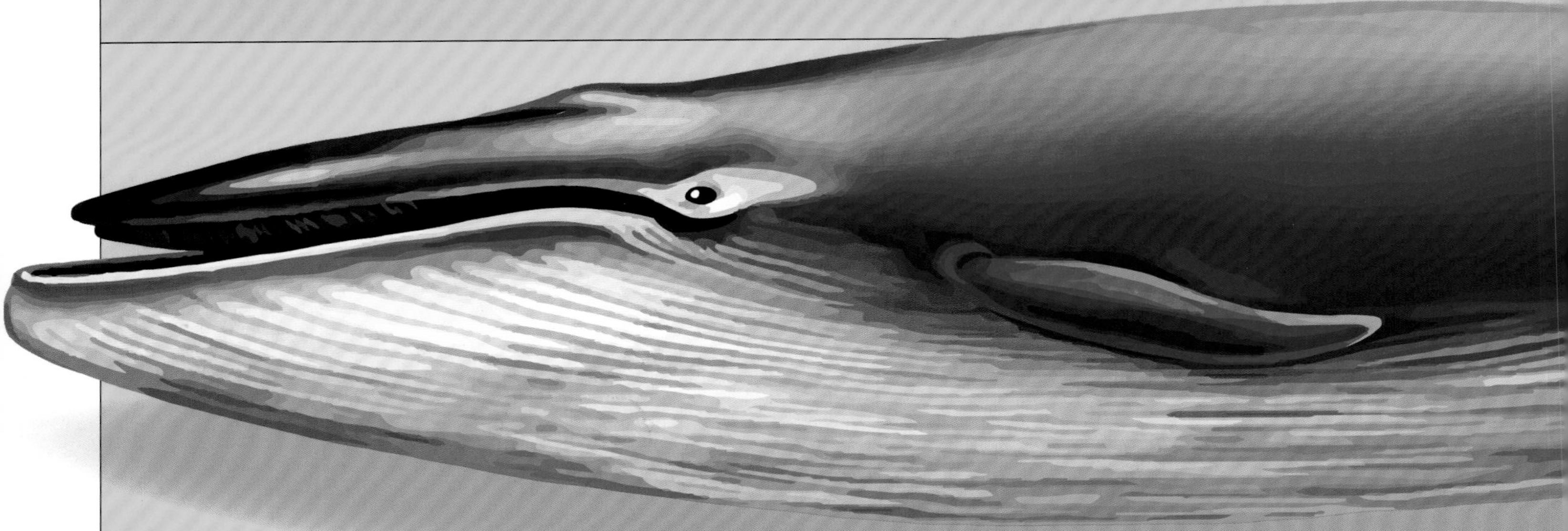

This one's easy. Nothing tops the titanic size of the blue whale, the largest animal that ever lived. The largest specimens grow to the length of a basketball court. A blue whale's heart is as big as a compact car. Its tail flukes are as wide as a soccer goal. Folds in the skin of the whale's throat allow it to stretch like a pelican's, ballooning to monstrous proportions as it consumes tiny shrimplike crustaceans called krill—up to four tons (3.6 t) per day! Once found in every ocean except the high Arctic, blue whales were hunted nearly to extinction. The species began to bounce back after hunting was outlawed in the 1960s, but only a tiny fraction of their original numbers remains.

SAY WHAT?!

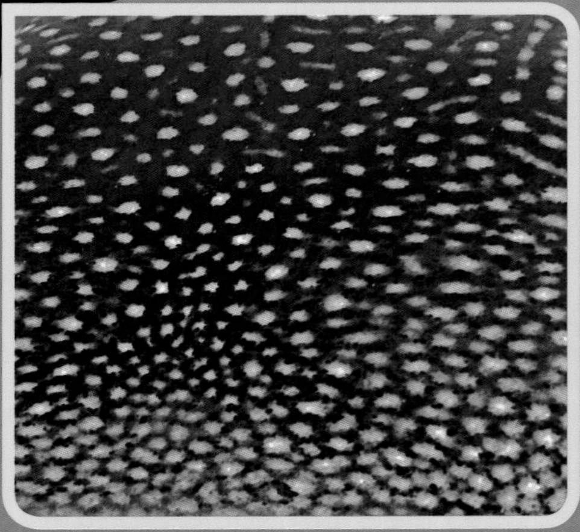

AS THICK AS THE WALLS of a bank vault, whale shark skin is six inches (15 cm) deep—the thickest of any animal's—and covered in constellations of yellow spots. Marine biologists photograph these spots to identify whale sharks. Like fingerprints, the spots are unique to each animal.

What's THE LARGEST ...

... LAND ANIMAL?

AFRICAN ELEPHANT

Topping 13 feet (4 m) at the shoulder, African elephants are just a bit bigger than their Asian cousins. You can tell the two species apart by their ears: Africa elephant ears are shaped like their home continent.

... BIRD?

OSTRICH

These flightless birds grow up to nine feet tall (2.7 m). They also lay the largest egg of any bird. One ostrich egg can weigh as much as two dozen chicken eggs.

... SPIDER?

GOLIATH BIRDEATER

The size of a catcher's mitt and sprouting inch-long fangs, this relative of the tarantula feeds on rodents and even birds that wander into its burrow. The giant huntsman spider of Southeast Asia has longer legs, but the Goliath birdeater beats it in body size.

... FISH?

WHALE SHARK

It grows up to 46 feet long (14 m), rivaling a humpback whale in size. Its mouth can open large enough to swallow a human whole. (Relax, these gentle giants eat only pinhead-size plankton).

... LIVING THING?

HONEY MUSHROOM

Just feet below the floor of Malheur National Forest in Oregon, U.S.A., sprawls the world's largest living organism: the honey mushroom. For more than 2,500 years, it has spread its fungal filaments through the soil and grown to the size of 1,600 football fields. Now that's one humongous fungus!

POP **CULTURE**

THIS BOOK ANSWERS some big, deep, and important questions. But you'll find none of them in this chapter. Instead, get ready to raid the realms of sports, film, celebrities, and even soft drinks for answers to questions you never knew you wanted to ask.

7 THE WHYS OF OUR LIVES

WHY do paparazzi take photos of CELEBRITIES?

It's the price of fame. When movie stars, pro athletes, politicians, and other famous folks are out and about, crews of camera-wielding paparazzi tag along hoping to capture the celebs not looking their best. Paparazzi stalk stars because the perfect unflattering photo can be worth a fortune—sometimes in the millions of dollars—to gossip magazines, TV shows, and websites. Celebrities, meanwhile, are striking back by releasing their own pics on photo-sharing sites before the paparazzi can get their cameras ready.

Why do people spread gossip?

Researchers have found that between 65 and 80 percent of all conversations could be considered gossip—idle chatter and rumors about people's private lives. Surprised? Don't pretend you've never dished some dirt yourself! But gossip isn't all bad, and it does serve a purpose. According to one study, only about 5 percent of it is mean-spirited. The rest is considered crucial to making people feel connected and establishing the rules for a functional society.

Why was the first space shuttle a big deal for *Star Trek* fans?

NASA intended to name its first shuttle, built in the 1970s as a test craft for atmospheric flights, the *Constitution*. But after a letter-writing campaign by fans of the sci-fi show *Star Trek*, President Gerald Ford asked NASA to name the shuttle *Enterprise* (the starship from the show). Ford never admitted that he was influenced by the *Star Trek* show or campaign, however. Regardless, *Star Trek* fans were thrilled—even though this real-life *Enterprise* never launched into space.

NAME-DROPPING

Why ARE LEGOS CALLED LEGOS?

The company that makes the famous snap-together bricks took its name from the Danish phrase *leg godt*, which translates to "play well."

Why WAS *RETURN OF THE JEDI* RENAMED FROM *REVENGE OF THE JEDI*?

Director George Lucas changed the title of the third Star Wars movie from *Revenge of the Jedi* after realizing that true Jedis wouldn't seek revenge.

Why IS NINTENDO'S MARIO CHARACTER NAMED MARIO?

Originally appearing as a carpenter named Jumpman in the *Donkey Kong* arcade game, Mario was renamed after the landlord of Nintendo's American warehouse. Mario's profession changed to plumber when he appeared again in *Mario Bros.*

PERSON OF INTEREST

WHO?
J. K. Rowling

WHAT is she famous for?
Introducing the world to a boy wizard

WHEN?
1997 through today

WHERE?
England

WHY is she important?
The "boy who lived" first sparked to life in the imagination of J. K. Rowling when she was riding a train from Manchester to London in 1990. Rowling's own mother was dying of an illness at the time, which influenced her tale of an orphaned boy and the villainous Voldemort's quest to conquer death. Low on money and raising her daughter alone, Rowling released her first novel, *Harry Potter and the Philosopher's Stone* (known as the *Sorcerer's Stone* in the U.S.) seven years later, followed by six sequels. Her creation spawned blockbuster movies and even a theme park. She's now one of England's wealthiest people and possibly the most famous English author since William Shakespeare.

WHY do roller coasters (and dips in the road) make my stomach TINGLE?

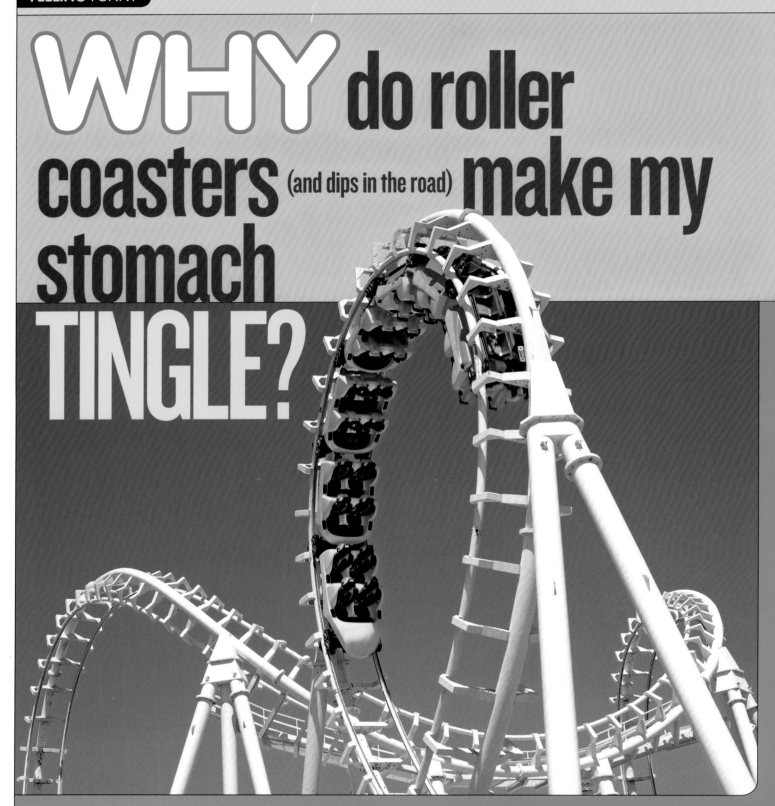

Your body's guts have a lot of give. When you encounter a sudden change in direction and speed, your organs jostle against each other until forces of gravity and momentum reassert themselves and pull everything back into place. Drops on roller coasters (and, to a lesser extent, dips in the road) counteract the forces of gravity and throw your body into a sudden free fall. For an instant, with nothing pushing against it, your stomach rises and you feel that funky sinking feeling that makes roller coasters so much fun and/or terrifying.

Why does drinking a soda with caffeine make me hyper?

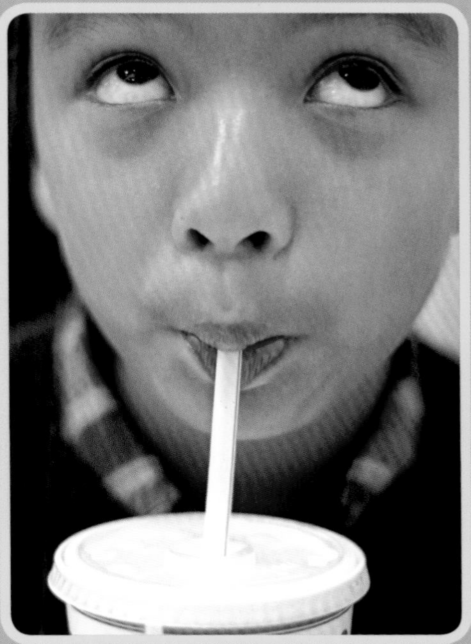

Caffeine—a chemical extracted from coffee beans, cacao (the source of chocolate), cola nuts (used in, you guessed it, cola), and tea leaves—offers no nutritional value, yet some adults can't start their day without a jolt from their cup of joe. The caffeine in coffee, tea, energy drinks, pop, and chocolate stimulates the central nervous system, delivering a boost of energy while clearing away the cobwebs of drowsiness (which is why people feel charged up after chugging down a caffeinated drink). But caffeine's effects are temporary. Once the caffeine wears off, you're left feeling drained and foggy. You might even have a headache. Drinking too much caffeine will cause your heart to race and your hands to shake. And good luck getting to sleep if you slurp a soda before bedtime.

Why does biting tinfoil make my teeth tingle?

It's just an unfriendly reminder that you have fillings (or some other metal dental work). When two different metals come into contact, an electrical charge passes between them. That's the zap you feel when tinfoil touches the metal in your mouth. The jolt travels from the tin to your tooth's nerve through the filling. People without dental work won't experience this sensation—yet another reason to brush and floss regularly!

SAY WHAT?!

THINK YOU COULD HANDLE that sinking feeling in your stomach for ten dizzying seconds? The aptly named Drop of Doom at Six Flags Great Adventure in Jackson, New Jersey, U.S.A., offers the world's tallest drop: a 41-story plunge that reaches speeds up to 90 mph (145 kph).

MYTH MASHED

Why are "right-brained" people more creative and "left-brained" people better at math?

Your brain is split into two symmetrical (or mirror-image) halves known as hemispheres, connected by a ribbon of white matter known as the corpus callosum, through which both halves communicate. It's common knowledge that the right side of the brain is the source of music concertos, masterpiece paintings, and deep emotions, while the left side specializes in solving logic problems and dealing with numbers. But in this case, common knowledge is incorrect. While the various lobes have their specialties (language, memory, sensory perception, etc.), experiments show that both hemispheres pull their weight during every task. While the left hemisphere excels at detecting words in sounds, for example, the right hemisphere detects the emotions in those words.

WHY do meals look TASTIER in commercials (than in real life)?

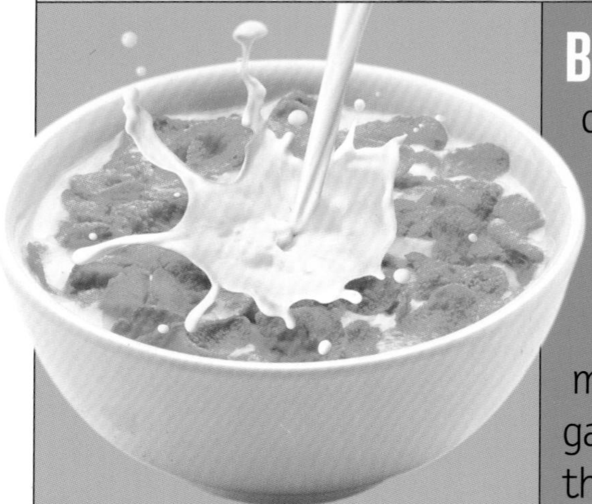

Because they're not real meals. Each dish, dessert, and drink has been carefully prepared and arranged by a "food stylist," a special food photographer who uses all sorts of sneaky tricks to make dishes look scrumptious for commercials, cookbooks, and menus. The stylist stuffs baked chicken with napkins to plump it up and paints burgers with burnt matches to simulate grill marks. Milk is substituted with kindergarten glue so cereals don't look soggy. Dish soap is dabbled on the surface of drinks to give that fresh-poured look. Um, yum?

Why do spicy foods melt my mouth?

That bowl of four-alarm chili is waging chemical warfare on your tongue. Chili peppers contain capsaicin (pronounced cap-SAY-ah-sin), a substance that triggers the sensations of pain and heat when it touches your tongue (or, in the case of the hottest peppers, even your hands). Pepper plants likely evolved this compound to keep away nibbling animals. Spicy-food connoisseurs build up a resistance to capsaicin by gradually eating progressively hotter peppers until they can nibble thermonuclear meals while working up only a mild sweat.

What are the hottest peppers?

A chemist named Wilbur Scoville developed a scale to answer this very question in 1912. His system measures the heat factor of chili peppers in multiples of 100 "Scoville units," as rated by human tasters with iron tongues! The higher the rating, the hotter the pepper. Here's a peppering of peppers from all parts of the Scoville scale spectrum ...

Green Bell Pepper
0 Scoville units

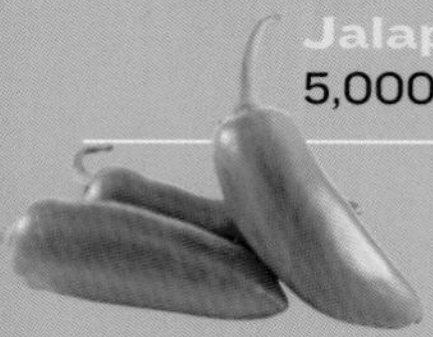

Jalapeño Pepper
5,000 Scoville units

Tabasco Pepper
50,000 Scoville units

Habanaga Pepper
500,000 Scoville units

Ghost Pepper
1,000,000 Scoville units

SAY WHAT?!

THE GHOST PEPPER IS SO HOT that it will burn your skin unless you wear gloves. The capsaicin concentration in ghost pepper is even higher than the amount used in pepper spray, a nonlethal weapon wielded by police.

Q: tips

How DO I COOL MY MOUTH IF I EAT SOMETHING SPICY?

- Don't guzzle water! Although a splash of icy H_2O might provide momentary relief, it will only scatter the scorching capsaicin chemical throughout your mouth, spreading the pain.
- Do drink milk, which actually works like a vacuum to slurp the capsaicin from your pain receptors. The colder the milk, the better.
- If you don't have milk, you can eat another dairy product such as cottage cheese, yogurt, or—best of all—ice cream!
- Mix a tablespoon of sugar into a glass of water, then swish the water around in your mouth and spit it out. The sugar in the water bonds with the capsaicin, clearing it from your mouth.

WHY do doughnuts have HOLES?

For the same reason bagels have holes—so they're not a gooey mess inside. Although doughnuts and bagels are cooked in different ways (fried and baked, respectively), both are dense with dough when they're solid disks. To help them cook evenly all the way through, bakers punch out the middles. The holes also helped bakers display doughnuts on sticks when they were introduced in the late 1800s.

Why does cotton candy melt in my mouth?

When a candy maker and a dentist teamed up to invent a new kind of treat in 1899, they dubbed it "fairy floss" for a reason: As soon as their fluffy confection hit the mouth, it seemed to magically disappear like a fairy in the forest. Thirty years later, fairy floss became known by its more popular name, cotton candy, but its magical properties remained. The secret lies in the recipe. Cotton candy is made of sugar heated—or caramelized—in a special machine, colored by food coloring, and spun at high speeds into thin strands. Despite its fluffy appearance, cotton candy is still basically sugar. And like sugar, it dissolves in water—in this case, the saliva in your mouth.

Okay, so why does sugar melt in water?

Sugar is made of molecules of sucrose, a compound held together by relatively weak bonds. When the sucrose molecules mix with water, the water molecules surround and break the bonds holding together the sugar molecule. The sugar is still in the water, of course (which is why the water tastes sweet), but now it's dissolved into the new sugar-and-water mix, called a "solution." Hot water dissolves sugar more quickly—and can hold more of it—because the heat spreads its molecules farther apart, making room for more sucrose.

Why does bubble gum lose its flavor?

Chewing gum is a funny kind of food—the only kind you're allowed to play with. Go ahead and chew it, snap it, and blow it into bubbles, but whatever you do, don't swallow it. Gum's rubbery properties are a product of its ingredients, including synthetic rubber and softeners that keep it from turning into a chalky block in your mouth. Synthetic rubber? Softeners? Yummy! Or not, which is why gum makers add "flavorings"—the closest thing to food in the ingredients list. And like food, these sweeteners mix with the saliva in your mouth and sink to your stomach each time you swallow. Eventually, all the sweeteners head south, leaving you with a flavorless lump of softened rubber to spit into the nearest trash can.

FOOD FOULS

Why IS IT CONSIDERED CRUDE TO ...

... CHEW WITH YOUR MOUTH OPEN?

It is not only nasty to show fellow diners your "see-food diet"—it's also dangerous. Eating while saying "ahhh" usually means you've bitten off more than you can chew.

... EAT WITH YOUR ELBOWS ON THE TABLE?

This rule goes back to medieval times, when diners sat shoulder-to-shoulder at narrow feasting tables with no elbow room to spare.

... READ AT THE TABLE?

Dinnertime is also meeting time for most families, when everyone can discuss the day without smartphones and laptop screens getting in the way.

... REACH ACROSS THE TABLE?

Stretching your arm in front of neighbors at the table disrupts their meals—and is a good way to accidentally upend the gravy boat.

... SLURP YOUR NOODLES?

Depends on where you eat 'em! While eating sounds are considered uncouth in many countries, noodle slurping is actually a respectful sign of enjoyment in Japan.

MYTH MASHED

Why DOES GUM STICK TO YOUR STOMACH FOR SEVEN YEARS IF YOU SWALLOW IT?

Mom warned you that gum doesn't digest; it just sits in your stomach soaking in a stew of digestive juices and taking up space. Acids and enzymes in your stomach make short work of gum's sugars and flavor additives, but its synthetic-rubber base is one tough glob to digest. That doesn't mean gum just swirls around and around in your belly like a penny in a washing machine. Like clockwork, your stomach empties its contents into the intestine for further digestion. Any gum gobs, corn kernels, or other tough-to-digest treats go along for the ride. It all gets pushed to the colon and passed in your poop, looking much as it did when you ate it. Not that we suggest you go looking.

WHY do Twitter messages have a limit of 140 characters?

From the get-go, messaging-app Twitter was designed to let people share text messages over mobile phones rather than computers. Most phones can display only a limited amount of characters, so Twitter's designers restricted its message length to meet those limits.

Why do people try to make "viral" videos?

Sometimes they just want to share funny footage (everyone loves a cute-kitty video!), but more often than not, they want your attention. Viral videos grow in viewership like a snowball rolling down a hill. The more people who pass around the videos and share them with friends, the more popular the videos become! Video creators stand to make a few bucks from websites that pay a little moolah for every view. Advertising companies concoct viral videos in an attempt to build buzz around a product or piece of entertainment by tricking people into talking about it online. Next time you see something stupendous, think twice before hyping it. You might be giving someone free advertising!

Why is this guy running on water?

He's trying to trick you into buying a pair of shoes. This is an example of viral marketing. Millions of Web surfers fell for an online video demonstrating the art of "liquid mountaineering," aka running on water, in summer 2010. The footage featured a group of athletes sprinting farther and farther across the surface of a chilly lake (the secret, apparently, is to pump your feet while wearing the right shoes). It was also totally fake—an advertisement for the brand of shoes worn in the video.

Why do people take part in Internet memes?

A meme is an idea or a behavior that spreads from person to person while subtly changing over time. Internet memes spread through emails, social media, and on message boards. Unlike viral videos, memes invite people to participate in the behavior or customize the message. Web surfers hope their cheesy tweaks will gain them Internet fame.

What are some famous memes?

Spend enough time exploring the Internet and you're bound to see ...

GRUMPY CAT: People write suitably unhappy captions on photos of this perpetually depressed-looking house cat.

PLANKING: Planking pranksters pose facedown in public spots for photos they upload to the Internet.

DIET COKE AND CANDY: Backyard chemists harness the chemical reaction between Diet Coke and a certain candy to create frothy soda geysers.

LOLCATS: Photos of cute cats are captioned with silly, grammatically incorrect messages from the kitty's point of view, the most famous phrase being "I can has cheezburger?"

PERSON OF INTEREST

WHO?
Shigeru Miyamoto

WHAT is he famous for?
Designing your favorite games

WHEN?
1980s through today

WHERE?
Japan

WHY is he important?
You may not know his name, but you certainly know his games. *Donkey Kong, Super Mario Bros., The Legend of Zelda, Mario Kart*—all of these landmark titles (along with their characters and many sequels) are the creations of Shigeru Miyamoto, a game designer at Nintendo since the late 1970s. Miyamoto has been called the Steven Spielberg of video games for a reason: His creations combine crowd-pleasing thrills and charming characters with deep, secret-filled game play.

Why ARE SOME PEOPLE MEAN ON THE INTERNET?

Armies of jerks lurk on the Internet. And even the most mundane topics set off these cyberbullying "trolls," who pick fights over everything from politics to sci-fi plots to sports stats to the merits of a particular pop star. Psychologists think they know why the Internet brings out the worst in people. Humans are social animals and evolved with brains wired for face-to-face interaction. The Internet, for all it has done to spread knowledge and shrink the world, has in some ways pushed people farther apart. Web browsers remove people's faces from conversations while adding anonymity, letting complete strangers behave badly without consequences. Research has shown that people are more likely to criticize others if they're not in the same room. So while you can't do anything to curb cattiness online, you can choose to treat others with respect. And escaping the lair of the Internet troll is as easy as hitting the Back button.

WHY do people believe in BIGFOOT?

Bigfoot believers point to the eyewitness accounts—more than 3,000 in all— of towering apelike creatures said to wander the wilderness of the Pacific Northwest and elsewhere. Roughly 10,000 supposed Bigfoot tracks have been reported since the early 1800s—although these prints vary wildly. (Older tracks show four toes; newer ones have five.) Today the beast is a central figure in cryptozoology, the study of legendary creatures, and cryptozoologists (people who study said legendary creatures) think Bigfoot represents a "missing link" between humans and our hairy ancestors. Yet despite decades of Bigfoot hunting, no one has recovered a body of the beast—a fact often cited by nonbelievers as proof that Bigfoot is bogus.

Why do people believe in the Loch Ness Monster?

The first reports of something fishy in Loch Ness, Scotland's second largest lake, go back 2,000 years, when a fearsome tattooed tribe known as the Picts chiseled the image of a finned creature onto large stones nearby. Five centuries later, according to one written account, an Irish monk shouted a prayer to repel a monster poised to gobble a Loch Ness bather. A series of high-profile sightings in the 1930s transformed "Nessie" from a creature of folklore into a cryptozoology superstar. More than 4,000 eyewitness accounts of a massive lake monster—some verified by lie-detector testing—have been reported since. As with those of Bigfoot, many of these sightings and photographs were proven as hoaxes, but that hasn't dampened the enthusiasm of true Nessie believers. Their number one Nessie suspect: the plesiosaur, a long-necked marine dinosaur that was supposed to have died out with *T. rex* and his kin 65 million years ago.

Nessie skeptics believe the sightings are simply cases of mistaken identity. Otters, dog-paddling deer, and large sturgeon can look mysterious when their backs break the surface of the lake. High-tech sonar searches have turned up nothing conclusive from the lake's murky depths. And yet the search for Nessie continues. At least one website maintains a live camera view of the lake, encouraging viewers to keep a round-the-clock watch for suspicious activity. The ancient Picts may have recorded Nessie in stone; modern creature hunters can now tag the beast online.

Why are sailors and pilots afraid of the Bermuda Triangle?

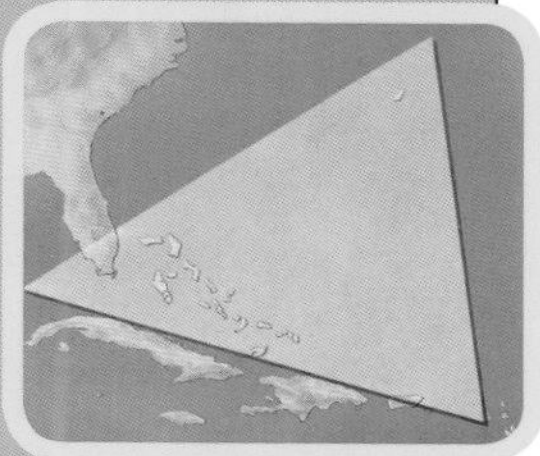

A vast region of the Atlantic bounded by Bermuda, Miami, and Puerto Rico, the Bermuda Triangle is notorious for swallowing planes, boats, and ships. According to one report, 75 planes and hundreds of yachts have gone missing in the Bermuda Triangle in the past century. The most famous disappearing act was Flight 19, a group of five U.S. Navy torpedo bombers that took off on a training mission in 1945 and vanished over the Atlantic Ocean. Search crews found no trace of the planes or the 14 men aboard them.

Navigators going back to the days of Christopher Columbus reported confusing compass readings in the Bermuda Triangle. Pilots have complained of an eerie electrical fog that interferes with their instruments. Believers in the paranormal suspect the Triangle is a gateway to another dimension or home to mysterious ship-wrecking technology from the lost city of Atlantis. Even without any supernatural shenanigans, this eerie area is certainly an easy place to get lost. Swift currents and sudden storms send ships swirling in circles. Shipwrecking reefs lie just under the surface in some places; the seafloor dips into trenches five miles (8 km) deep in others. The Triangle has been a superhighway for sea traffic since the early days of exploration, so it makes sense that the region would see more accidents than less-traveled areas. Wreckage not set adrift by the strong currents could sink into the region's trenches, never to be seen again.

Why DO PEOPLE BELIEVE IN GHOSTS?

Researchers who study the paranormal (or phenomena beyond the boundaries of science) believe that people leave behind energy when they die—especially when they die a traumatic death—and that energy shows itself as "spectral" activity.

... so, what sort of spectral activity?

Creepy moans, creaky stairs, flickering lights, sudden chills, shadowy figures, and even human-shaped forms dressed in old-fashioned getups. Using high-tech gadgets, pursuers of the paranormal skulk through old houses, graveyards, and other allegedly haunted spots hoping to document ghostly goings-on. They've yet to uncover any conclusive evidence, but that hardly seems to matter: A third of all Americans claim they believe in ghosts.

WHY do we SAY ...

"... tip of the iceberg"? When we know only a little bit about a big problem, we say it's just the tip of the iceberg. Icebergs are typically huge. Some are larger than the U.S. state of Rhode Island. One Antarctic iceberg rivals the size of Sicily, the largest island in the Mediterranean. Most of that icy mass lies below the surface of the water. Only about one-eighth of an iceberg—the famous "tip" from the expression—is visible from above.

"... blind as a bat"?

Because many bats hunt at night and rely on a sonar system to "see" using reflected sound waves—a system known as echolocation—people once assumed these flying mammals were blind. Hence, anyone with poor eyesight might be called "blind as a bat." But although many species of bats have small eyes, they can all see quite clearly. In fact, researchers have learned that bats will trust their eyes more than their sonar when flying in low light. Bats evolved echolocation to hunt for bugs at night, which gave them a survival edge over mammals and birds that competed for food during the daylight hours. So think twice before you call someone blind as a bat—unless you actually want to compliment their eyesight!

"... butterflies in my stomach"?

It is a familiar sensation to anyone who has faced a pop quiz, given a speech in front of classmates, or asked a special someone on a date. Your mouth goes dry, your palms get wet with sweat, your heart goes pitter-patter, and your stomach starts to flutter (hence the expression). Of course, you don't really have a butterfly bouncing around in your belly. These uneasy feelings are your body's natural reaction to dangerous or stressful situations—a reaction known as the fight-or-flight response. Your brain triggers the release of chemicals that increase the circulation in your muscles, which restricts blood flow to your stomach and causes the fluttery effect. It's your body's way of getting ready to fight or flee a threat—a holdover from when your ancestors had to contend with saber-toothed predators. Hey, that pop quiz doesn't seem so bad now.

"... stick your head in the sand"?

It's a strategy stolen from ostriches, which supposedly nudge their noggins into the ground to avoid danger. When people would rather not face a threatening situation or awful reality, they're said to have their heads in the sand. The expression has just one problem (well, two problems if you consider it unhealthy to hide from reality): It's based on a myth. Ostriches don't really stick their heads in the sand. They do drop down and press their necks against the ground to hide from threats, but they keep their heads out so they can see what's going on.

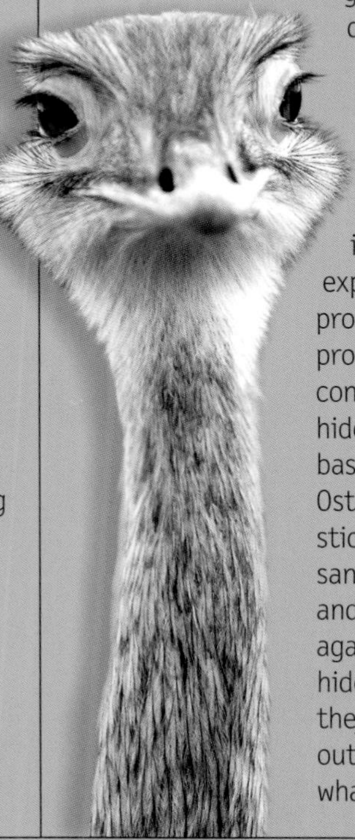

"... you can't teach an old dog new tricks"?

When someone (for instance, an older relative) seems stubborn about learning something new (say, how to turn on a computer), he or she might shrug and use this tired expression. And when that person does, clue him or her in to this fact: With the proper training, even stubborn breeds of mutts can learn to heel, sit, and roll over well into their golden years.

"... crying crocodile tears"?

Friends (or foes) who express phony sadness to gain sympathy are said to shed "crocodile tears." The expression is an old one, based on the myth that alligators and crocodiles cry when they devour their victims. Crocodilians do indeed cry when they eat, but scientists are stumped by the cause. Some researchers suspect that the hissing noises crocodiles make while eating unclogs their sinuses and turns on the waterworks. Saltwater crocodiles, meanwhile, cry to purge excess salt.

Does ANYONE APPRECIATE CROCODILE TEARS?

Humans don't, but some insects sure do. While some bugs drink blood, certain species of moths, bees, and butterflies drink tears. To them, tears are tasty and nutritious, filled with minerals and salts that they need to survive. Most of these "lacryphagous" insects sip the tears of mammals—even humans! Researchers around the world have also seen bees and butterflies slurping liquid from the eyes of alligators and crocodiles, who don't seem to mind sharing their tears.

What's the difference between ...

	CROCODILES	ALLIGATORS
Typical habitat	Swamps, rivers, lakes, and seas across the world	Swamps, rivers, and lakes in the southern portions of the United States and in China
Physical features	Long, pointy heads and generally lighter in appearance	Shorter, rounder snouts and darker in appearance
Ferociousness	Highly aggressive and prone to attacking humans	Timid around humans; rarely attack
Largest ever captured	20 feet, 3 inches (6.2 m) long and 2,370 pounds (1,075 kg)	14 feet, 8 inches (4.5 m) long and 880 pounds (400 kg)

WHY is American football called "FOOTBALL" (when players use their hands)?

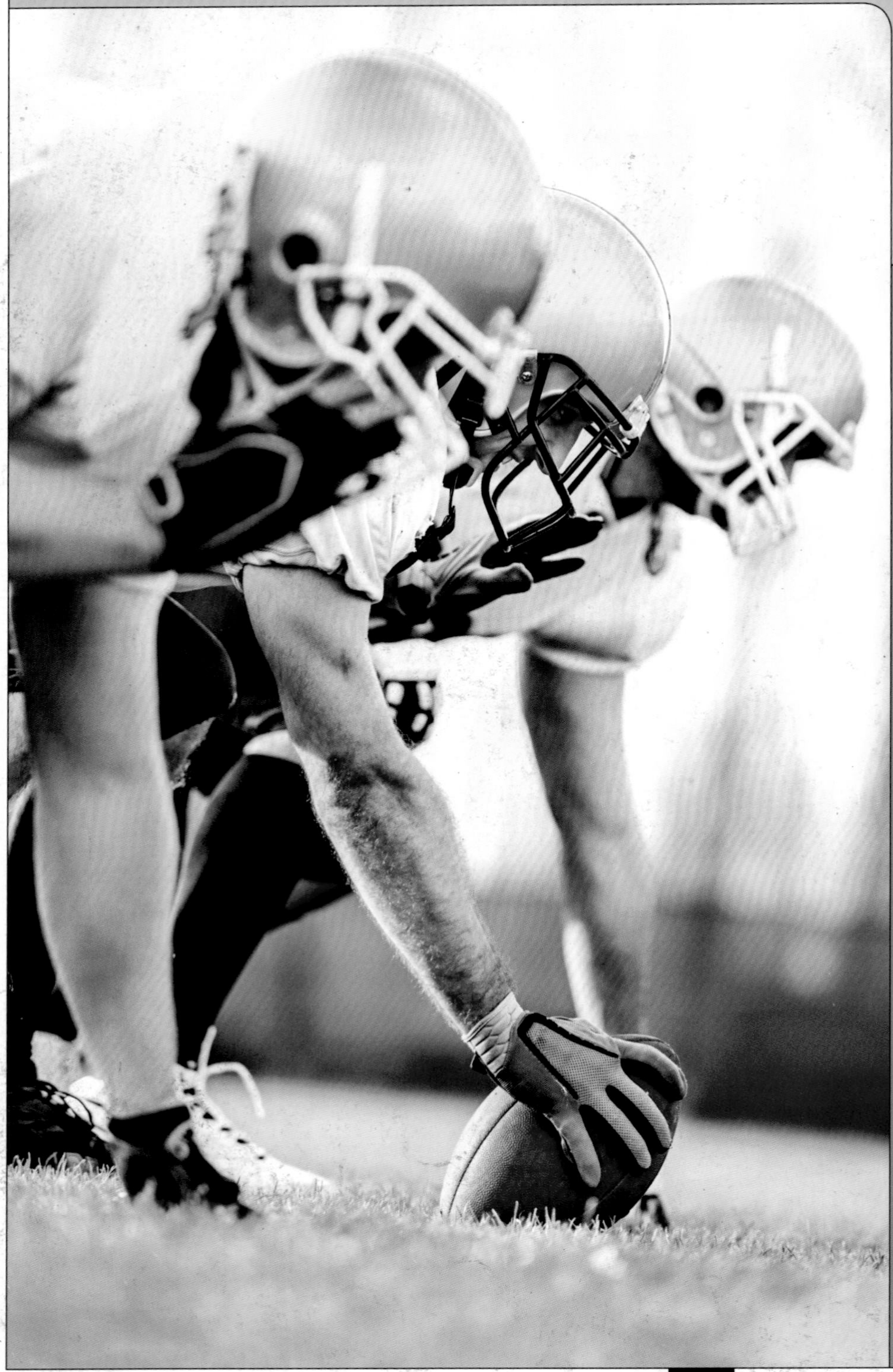

Sports historians debate over the origin of football's name. One explanation is that, in the mid-1800s, American football evolved from the game of rugby, a rough-and-tumble sport that, in turn, evolved from a much bloodier medieval game called campball. In both rugby and campball, players use their feet as well as their hands to move the ball around, although tossing the ball forward is a no-no. Rules changed all the time in the early days of American football. Even forward tosses were illegal until 1906, when they were introduced to make the sport safer. Players' use of feet in the game's early days likely played a role in its name.

Why are American footballs oblong instead of round?

The technical name for a football's shape is a "prorate spheroid." And while you'd think this shape—so perfect for long-distance passing and bouncing willy-nilly during mad scrambles—was the result of careful design by football's inventors, it really just happened by accident. In the earliest days of football, as the sport was still evolving, the "pigskin" was just an ordinary round ball. During the first college match between Princeton and Rutgers in 1869, the ball leaked and sagged into a lopsided shape. As the sport evolved into more of a passing game, its lopsided ball evolved with it, becoming the prorate spheroid we know today.

Why are American footballs called "pigskins"?

Modern footballs are covered with cowhide (aka leather) stretched over a plastic or rubber balloon, so it makes more sense to call them "cowskins" than pigskins. In fact, pig's skin was probably never used to cover even the earliest balls. But in the days before rubber and plastic, sports balls were made from another piece of pig anatomy: the bladder. Turns out the airtight innards of a pig made a great plaything—as long as you didn't mind inflating it with your mouth.

Why is baseball called "America's pastime"?

Good question, considering that the slow-paced sport has been surpassed in popularity by American football (according to fan polls and ratings for televised games, anyway). Yet professional baseball has been mixed up with American culture—and history—longer than any other sport. Soldiers played it to pass the time during the American Civil War. American football, basketball, and soccer might deliver faster action and greater spectacle, but baseball leagues have more team rivalries, a greater wealth of stats for true fans to memorize, and a richer roster of heroes (such as Jackie Robinson, the first African American to play Major League Baseball). Teams play just about every day during baseball season, making the game more accessible to fans who want to spend the afternoon at the ballpark—a classic American setting.

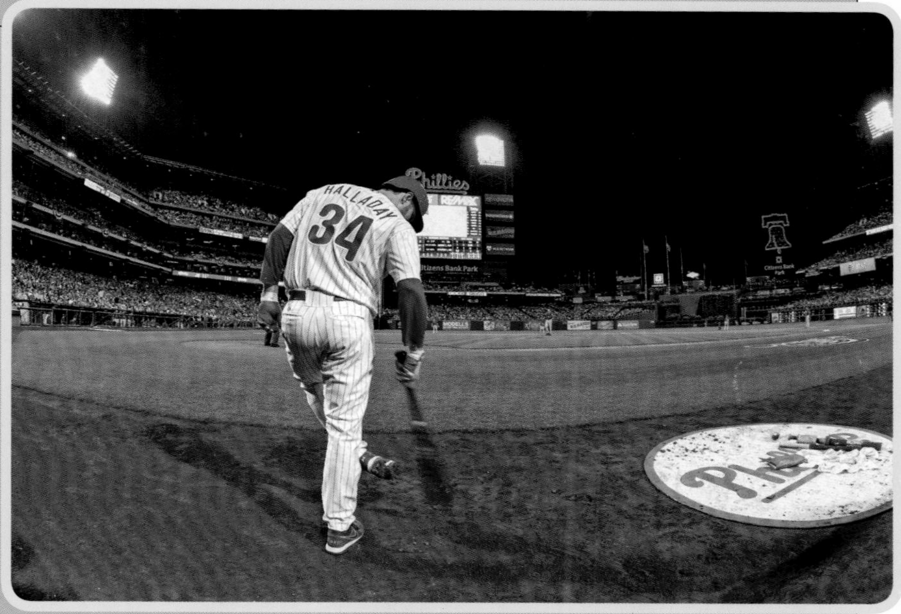

Why do baseball players tap their shoes with the bat before hitting?

Like most athletes who compete in outdoor sports, baseball players wear shoes bristling with cleats (or spikes) to give them traction on the soft ground. Before they step up to home plate, batters usually trek through the soft dirt surrounding the on-deck circle (where they warm up). By knocking each shoe with the bat at home plate, players shake the soil off their cleats, improving their traction for the mad dash around the diamond.

Why IS THE SPORT OF FOOTBALL CALLED "SOCCER" IN THE UNITED STATES AND CANADA?

The name "soccer" isn't an American invention. It originated in England, where in 1863 the Football Association formed to promote and standardize the game we play with our feet today. That form of the sport became known as "association football," or "soccer" for short. Even English people called football "soccer" as recently as 40 years ago.

WHY does the Zamboni machine take to the ice during HOCKEY GAMES?

You think hockey players take a beating during a typical game? Take a look at the ice after the first period! The skate blades carve chasms into the ice as the players race around the rink, bodychecking each other and performing zigzagging fake-outs known as dekes. Repairing the mini-crevasses would take more than an hour by hand, so in the 1940s inventor Frank Zamboni developed a machine that smoothed the ice in minutes.

Why do surfers wax the tops of their boards and snowboarders wax the bottoms?

For two very different reasons: stickiness versus speed. Surfboards are (usually) made of fiberglass, which gets slippery when wet. A layer of sticky wax—often mixed with a little sand—creates some traction on top of the board, making it easier for surfers to paddle, pop up, and scoot around without slipping overboard. Snowboarders (and skiers), on the other hand, apply wax to the bottoms of their boards to create a waterproof barrier. This barrier reduces friction between the board and the snow, boosting speed and improving control for sick tricks in the terrain park.

Why do basketball hoops have nets?

To make every shot count. Basketball nets have a slight funnel shape so that they flutter when the ball passes through them. The fluttering lets players, fans, and referees know when the ball actually went into the basket.

Why do racehorses need jockeys?

The diminutive athletes who ride thoroughbreds at the Kentucky Derby and other horse races admit that they play just a small role in each event. But while horses in other parts of the world have been trained to race without riders (and robots have replaced jockeys in camel races), racing experts claim thoroughbreds are so fast (up to 35 mph/56 kph) that they require some human guidance to get around the turns. Indeed, horses that buck their riders at the start of a race will usually stop once they reach the first turn. Jockeys also develop deep relationships with their horses, keeping them calm during the hectic events of race day.

Why do figure skaters spin faster when they pull in their arms and legs?

It's a simple but crowd-pleasing trick from Figure Skating 101. Skaters pull into a spin, cross their free leg over their other knee, then tuck in their arms. The tighter the tuck, the faster the spin, until the skater looks like a tornado on ice. But while the "scratch spin"—aka the "blur spin"—is relatively easy to pull off, the physics behind it goes by the complicated name of the "conservation of angular momentum." We'll keep it simple: Because of a force known as inertia, wider objects require more energy to spin than narrower ones. Apply the same amount of spin force to two objects—a wide one and a narrow one—and the narrow one will spin much more rapidly. So when figure skaters perform scratch spins, their goal is to start wide—with arms and leg outstretched—and end narrow. As they pull in their arms and free leg, they gradually require less energy to spin, which increases the speed of their rotations until they're a blur of sequined tights and pearly whites.

Why do baseball and American football players smear black stuff under their eyes?

Before the game, players apply a stripe of "eye black" grease under each eye to reduce glare from the sun and stadium lights.

SAY WHAT?!

THE DARK FUR AROUND THE EYES of a meerkat, a sort of African mongoose, works just like a football player's eye black: reducing glare as it scans the skies for threats.

WHY does music make me MOVE?

We tap our toes. We sway in our seats. We shimmy across the dance floor. Grooving to the beat engages the parts of our brains that process speech and movement, which leads some scientists to believe our sense of rhythm is simply a fringe benefit of having communication skills. Other researchers believe humans developed the ability to boogie to strengthen our social bonds, which helped us work together and flourish as a species. After all, every culture in history has developed some sort of music. But whether you think you can dance or not, we all have rhythm. One study suggests we're born with it.

Do animals have a sense of rhythm, too?

Anyone who's stumbled across a video online of Snowball the dancing cockatoo knows the answer to this question. Parrots and sea lions have demonstrated the ability to bob their heads to a beat (Snowball likes to boogie to "Everybody" by the Backstreet Boys). Our close primate relatives chimps and bonobos also seem to have a simple sense of rhythm. Scientists are still trying to figure out why these and possibly other animals know how to boogie, but in the meantime we can all enjoy the silly videos online.

Why were female roles played by men in classical theater?

If you saw a performance of William Shakespeare's *Romeo and Juliet* in the 1500s, you might wonder why the production wasn't called *Romeo and Romeo.* Women weren't allowed on stage during the period known as the English Renaissance (or in ancient Greece or during many other periods in history). The reasons were often rooted in religion (England at the time was under the influence of a devout group known as the Puritans) or a strange sense of propriety. It was thought that women on stage demeaned themselves or somehow tempted the male members of the audience. The result: Female roles went to men or boys who pretended to be women. Women didn't first take the stage until the end of the Renaissance, in the late 1600s.

Why is Peter Pan usually portrayed by a female on stage?

The Harry Potter of his day, Peter Pan—aka "the boy who wouldn't grow up"—was introduced to the world by Scottish author and playwright J. M. Barrie in 1904. The Broadway producer who funded the play thought that a male actor didn't fit the part of an eternal boy, so he suggested that Peter Pan should be played by a woman. An actress was chosen for the role in both the American and English versions, and the tradition of casting a woman to play Peter has continued almost ever since (although Peter has been played by a man in nearly every movie version of the tale).

Why does time fly when you're having fun?

For the same reason car trips and lame chores seem to take forever. Studies show that your brain perceives the passage of time at different speeds depending on whether you're bored or busy. When you're taking a timed test or focused on accomplishing a complex goal, the minutes seems to race by. Likewise, time flies when you're playing a fun game, watching an exciting movie, or engrossed in a good book. Speaking of which, you've just reached the finale of *Why?* Here's hoping the last 1,111 questions zipped right on by!

PERSON OF INTEREST

WHO?
Michael Jackson

WHAT is he famous for?
Becoming the "King of Pop"

WHEN?
1958 to 2009

WHERE?
United States

WHY is he important?
Like the "King of Rock" Elvis Presley before him, Michael Jackson dominated his own genre of music—pop music—and spread its influence and popularity around the globe. He was the artist behind the best-selling album of all time (1982's *Thriller*). He popularized the "moonwalk" and "robot" dance moves. He helped turn music videos into a new kind of mainstream entertainment. Michael Jackson was a pop phenomenon for most of his life, going back to his childhood with his siblings in the Jackson 5. He passed away in 2009, but the King of Pop's legacy still reigns.

Boldface indicates illustrations.

N

O

P

Q

R

S

Abbreviations:
CO: Corbis; GI: Getty Images; IS: iStockphoto; NGC: National Geographic Creative; SS: Shutterstock

Cover (UP LE), Lew Robertson/Digital Vision/GI; (UP CTR), x-ray: NASA/CXC/Univ.Potsdam/L.Oskinova et al; Optical: NASA/STScI; Infrared: NASA/JPL-Caltech/NASA; (UP RT), Malyugin/SS; (LO LE), Anda Stavri Photography/Flickr RF/GI; (LO CTR), Image Source/GI; (LO RT), WitR/SS; back cover (UP), jimmyjamesbond/IS; (CTR RT), Greg Amptman/SS; (CTR), beboy/SS; (LO CTR), SERG_AURORA/IS; (LO LE), GlobalP/IS; 1, Production Perig/SS; 2-3, Galyna Andrushko/SS; 4, Beboy_ltd/IS; 5 (UP RT), James Looker/PC Gamer Magazine via GI; 5 (CTR RT), Flip Nicklin/Minden Pictures; 5 (LO RT), Skyhobo/IS; 5 (LO LE), Kenneth Garrett/NGC; 6 (CTR LE), NASA/JSC/ISS; 6 (LO LE), ventdusud/IS; 7, spe/SS; 8-9, Pete Saloutos/SS; 10 (LO), Eugenio Marongiu/SS; 11 (UP LE), Svisio/IS; 11 (UP RT), PomInOz/IS; 11 (LO LE), RyFlip/SS; 11 (CTR RT), Utekhina Anna/SS; 11 (LO RT), urfin/SS; 12 (UP LE), SumHint/SS; 12 (CTR LE), Dieter Meyrl/IS; 12 (UP CTR), alex-mit/IS; 12 (CTR CTR UP), spyross007/IS; 12 (CTR CTR LO), Benjamin Ordaz/SS; 12 (LO CTR), 7activestudio/IS; 12 (UP RT), Lightspring/SS; 12 (CTR RT UP), 7activestudio/IS; 12 (LO RT), Lightspring/SS; 12 (CTR RT LO), BlueRingMedia/SS; 13 (UP RT), Alila Medical Media/SS; 13 (CTR RT), 02creationz/SS; 13 (LO RT), Dim Dimich/SS; 13 (LE), Cynthia Turner; 14 (CTR LE), Sebastian Kaulitzki/SS; 14 (LO RT), vgstudio/SS; 14 (CTR RT), Kozorez Vladislav/SS; 15 (CTR LE), cokacoka/IS; 15 (UP RT), Mike Kemp/Rubberball; 15 (LO RT), Tatiana Ivkovich/SS; 15 (LO LE), IvonneW/IS; 16 (LE), mevans/IS; 16 (CTR RT), ranplett/IS; 16 (LO RT), shumpc/IS; 17 (UP RT), THEGIFT777/IS; 17 (LO RT), rosliothman/IS; 17 (CTR), Nocturnal654/IS; 17 (CTR LE), kyoshino/IS; 18 (LO LE), Lucky Business/SS; 19, Springer Medizin/Science Photo Library RM/GI; 20 (LE), GlobalP/IS; 20 (LO), Wavebreak/IS; 21 (LE), roundhill/IS; 21 (RT), imageBROKER/Alamy; 21 (LO), artJazz/IS; 22, stokkete/IS; 23 (UP LE), shorrocks/IS; 23 (UP RT (REM)), Southern Illinois University/Photo Researchers RM/GI; 23 (UP RT (eyes)), Allan Hobson/Photo Researchers RM/GI; 23 (CTR), gielmichal/SS; 23 (LO LE), Vibrant Image Studio/SS; 23 (LO CTR), Ron and Joe/SS; 23 (LO RT), 3dsguru/IS; 24 (LE), grafikwork/SS; 24 (RT), Netta07/SS; 25 (UP CTR), PeterHermesFurian/IS; 25 (UP RT), WhitneyLewisPhotography/IS; 25 (CTR), AlexMotrenko/IS; 25 (LO CTR), topneba/IS; 25 (LO RT (1)), aastock/SS; 25 (LO RT (2)), stevanovicigor/IS; 25 (LO RT (3)), David Pereiras/SS; 25 (LO RT (4)), Nastco/IS; 25 (LO RT (5)), Mosich/IS; 25 (LO RT (6)), PhotoAlto/Alamy; 25 (LO RT (7)), Westend61 GmbH/Alamy; 26 (RT), BlueOrange Studio/SS; 26 (LE), OK-Photography/IS; 27 (UP), aastock/SS; 27 (CTR LE UP), StevenWolf/IS; 27 (CTR LE LO), WestLight/IS; 27 (CTR RT), Alan Bailey/SS; 27 (LO), morrowlight/SS; 28 (LO), cate_89/IS; 28 (UP), andrewsafonov/IS; 29 (CTR LE), Andrea Izzotti/SS; 29 (UP RT), HeavenUSA/IS; 29 (CTR RT), InspiredFootage/IS; 29 (LO RT), Dan Kosmayer/SS; 29 (fingerprint1), jurisam/IS; 29 (fingerprint2), leezsnow/IS; 29 (fingerprint3), jgroup/IS; 29 (UP LE), Zemler/SS; 30 (LO LE), mari_art/IS; 30 (CTR), ersin ergin/SS; 30 (UP RT), g-stockstudio/SS; 31 (UP RT), princessdlaf/IS; 31 (CTR LE), Juniors Bildarchiv GmbH/Alamy; 31 (CTR RT), AvailableLight/IS; 31 (LO), piovesempre/IS; 32 (CTR LE (1)), Kasiam/IS; 32 (CTR LE (2)), vikif/IS; 32 (CTR LE (3)), amphaiwan/SS; 32 (CTR LE (4)), OxfordSquare/IS; 32 (CTR LE (5)), donatas1205/IS; 32 (CTR LE (6)), Stargazer/SS; 32 (LO LE), BeholdingEye/IS; 32 (RT), wavebreakmedia/SS; 33 (UP RT), Africa Studio/SS; 33 (CTR LE), bluecinema/IS; 33 (LO LE), Halfpoint/IS; 33 (CTR RT), FuzzMartin/IS; 33 (LO RT), Luna2631/SS; 33 (UP RT inset), trucic/SS; 34 (LE), YinYang/IS; 35 (UP CTR), Alexilus/SS; 35 (UP RT), richcarey/IS; 35 (CTR LE), eurobanks/IS; 35 (LO RT), pkline/IS; 36 (UP LE), Stiggdriver/IS; 36 (LO LE), Ljupco Smokovski/SS; 36 (CTR RT), Cimmerian/IS; 36 (LO RT), iLexx/IS; 37 (UP LE), Olha Rohulya/SS; 37 (UP CTR LE), D. Kucharski K. Kucharska/SS; 37 (CTR LE), luismmolina/IS; 37 (UP RT), valzan/SS; 37 (LO), xrender/SS; 38 (LE), Nataliia Romashova/SS; 38 (CTR RT), decade3d/SS; 38 (LO), Nikolai Pozdeev/SS; 39 (UP LE), pzRomashka/IS; 39 (LO LE), bikeriderlondon/SS; 39 (LO RT), Elena Stepanova/SS; 40 (RT), gerenme/IS; 40 (LO LE), Andrey_Popov/SS; 41 (UP LE), FuatKose/IS; 41 (UP RT), Serhiy Kobyakov/SS; 41 (CTR), SuperStock/Alamy; 41 (LO RT), jarenwicklund/IS; 42 (UP), Chiyacat/SS; 42 (LO LE), decade3d/IS; 42 (LO RT), Ermolaev Alexander/SS; 43 (LE), UpperCut Images/Alamy; 43 (UP RT), TimArbaev/IS; 43 (CTR RT), Netta07/IS; 43 (LO CTR), isatori/IS; 43 (LO RT), pjohnson1/IS; 43 (LO CTR LE), julichka/IS; 44 (LO LE), drbimages/IS; 44 (UP RT), ra3rn/IS; 44 (UP CTR), Ivaylo Ivanov/SS; 44 (CTR RT), hddigital/SS; 45 (UP LE), Pasko Maksim/SS; 45 (LO LE), CREATISTA/IS; 45 (LO CTR), DNY59/IS; 45 (UP RT), Plume Photography/SS; 46 (LO RT), sergign/SS; 46 (LO LE), Shawn Pecor/SS; 46 (UP), Lighthousebay/IS; 47 (UP LE), Vladimir Gjorgiev/SS; 47 (LO LE), Suzanne Tucker/SS; 47 (CTR), cristi_m/IS; 47 (UP RT), tbmphoto/IS; 47 (LO RT), Vladimir Gjorgiev/SS; 48 (UP LE), ozgurdonmaz/IS; 48 (LO), ATIC12/IS; 49 (UP LE), Pascal Parrot/Sygma/CO; 49 (CTR LE), bibikoff/IS; 49 (CTR RT), Sebastian Kaulitzki/SS; 49 (LO), ATIC12/IS; 50-51, Reto Stöckli, NASA Earth Observatory; 52 (LO), ISS/NASA/JSC Gateway to Astronaut Photography of the Earth; 52-53, Ro-Ma Stock Photography/Photolibrary RM/GI; 53 (RT), ldambies/SS; 54, Dimitri Vervitsiotis/Photographer's Choice RF/GI; 55 (UP LE), U.S. Air Force photo/Senior Airman Matthew Lotz; 55 (CTR LE), tricia/IS; 55 (UP RT), NASA/Scott Andrews; 55 (LO RT), plumley1/IS; 56 (LE), Sportstock/IS; 56 (LO RT), rook76/SS; 57 (UP RT), Spotmatik/IS; 57 (CTR LE), Devonyu/IS; 57 (CTR RT), Anna Grigorjeva/SS; 57 (LO RT), klenger/IS; 58 (UP LE), Kues/SS; 58 (UP CTR), Mopic/SS; 58 (LO CTR), Publiphoto/Science Source; 58 (LO RT), Stocktrek Images, Inc./Alamy; 58 (UP RT), B Christopher/Alamy; 59 (UP LE), Richard Bizley/Science Source; 59 (UP CTR), leonello calvetti/Alamy; 59 (UP RT), Publiphoto/Science Source; 59 (CTR LE), Walter Myers/Science Source; 59 (CTR), Sergey Krasovskiy/Stocktrek Images/CO; 59 (LO LE), CoreyFord/IS; 59 (LO RT), B Christopher/Alamy; 60 (UP RT), James L. Stanfield/NGC; 60-61 (LO), DEA Picture Library/De Agostini/GI; 61 (UP CTR), Sam DCruz/SS; 61 (UP RT), Panhandlin/IS; 61 (LO), J Zapell/USDA; 62 (UP), adventtr/IS; 62 (LO), kovtynfoto/SS; 63 (CTR), OlgaLis/SS; 63 (UP RT), Greg Epperson/SS; 63 (LO RT), Tom Van Sant/Geosphere Project, Santa Monica/Science Source; 64-65, Gary Hincks/Science Source; 65 (LO RT), Dave Kaup/Reuters/CO; 66 (UP LE), Triff/SS; 66 (LO RT), Monika Bright, University of Vienna, Austria/NOAA; 67 (UP LE), Tony Lomas/IS; 67 (UP CTR), Svisho/IS; 67 (CTR LE), yurybosin/IS; 67 (LO CTR), Teerasak/SS; 67 (LO LE), Martina Roth/SS; 67 (LO RT), Cathy Keifer/SS; 68 (CTR RT), Ivan_Sabo/SS; 68 (LO LE), Joel Carillet/IS; 68 (LO RT), Courtney Keating/IS; 69 (UP LE), Dobermaraner/SS; 69 (CTR LE), Greg Amptman/SS; 69 (UP RT), Rich Carey/SS; 70 (CTR RT), Robynrg/SS; 70 (LO LE), Peter Burnett/IS; 71 (CTR RT), E. R. Degginger/Alamy; 71 (CTR LE), studiocasper/IS; 71 (UP), Sumikophoto/SS; 71 (LO CTR), Fabrice Coffrini/AFP/GI; 71 (LO LE), Hilary Morgan/Alamy; 71 (LO RT), Fred Ward/CO; 72 (RT), -A1A-/IS; 72 (LO LE), Dirk Freder/IS; 73 (LO CTR), song_mi/SS; 73 (LO LE), rainaraina/IS; 74 (LO CTR), Atsuhiro Muto/National Snow and Ice Data Center/AP Photo; 74 (CTR CTR LO), James Mattil/SS; 74 (CTR), neridesign/IS; 75 (LE), luchschen/IS; 75 (UP), Eduard Moldoveanu/SS; 75 (LO), SPbPhoto/SS; 76, BluesandViews/IS; 77 (LO), ssuaphoto/IS; 77 (RT), Jeff Schmaltz, MODIS Rapid Response Team, NASA/GSFC; 77 (UP), Beboy_ltd/IS; 78, Mihai Simonia/SS; 79 (LE), muratart/SS; 79 (UP), Eric Van Den Brulle/The Image Bank/GI; 79 (LO), JDCarballo/SS; 79 (LO back), Michael Rosskothen/SS; 79 (RT), ImageTeam/SS; 80-81, NASA,ESA, M. Robberto (Space Telescope Science Institute/ESA) and the Hubble Space Telescope Orion Treasury Project Team; 82-83, Mark Garlick/Science Source; 84 (UP), rwhitacre/IS; 84 (LO), NASA/JPL-Caltech ; 85 (CTR LE), NASA and STScI; 85 (CTR RT), Viktar Malyshchyts/SS; 85 (LO), NASA/JPL-Caltech; 85 (UP), NASA/JPL-Caltech; 86, NASA, ESA, S. Beckwith (STScI), and The Hubble Heritage Team (STScI/AURA); 87 (RT 1), NASA, ESA, and the Hubble Heritage Team (STScI/AURA); 87 (RT 3), Triff/SS; 87 (RT 5), Valerio Pardi/SS; 87 (RT 7), Zurijeta/SS; 87 (UP LE), Stocktrek Images, Inc./Alamy; 87 (RT 6), Galina Savina/SS; 87 (RT 2), NASA/JPL-Caltech; 87 (RT 4), NASA/NOAA; 87 (LO LE), Dess/IS; 88-89, Milky Way: Ken Eward, National Geographic Society; 88 (LO), Nelson Marques/SS; 90 (LO LE), SOHO/NASA; 90 (UP RT), letty17/IS; 91 (CTR RT), hidesy/IS; 91 (CTR LE), John R Foster/Science Source/GI; 91 (LO), Ivan Bastien/IS; 91 (UP CTR), Sedlacek/SS; 91 (UP RT), biletskiy/SS; 92 (UP), AstroStar/SS; 92 (LO), Procy_ab/IS; 93 (LO LE), chrisboy2004/IS; 93 (LO RT), Ranger 9/NASA; 93 (UP RT), Charles M. Duke Jr./NASA; 93 (UP), Anson_iStock/IS; 94-95, Bobboz/SS; 96 (CTR), NASA/JPL-Caltech/Cornell Univ./Arizona State Univ.; 96 (LO LE), parameter/IS; 96 (LO CTR), NASA/JPL/Space Science Institute; 96 (LO RT), NASA and Erich

Karkoschka, University of Arizona; 97 (LO RT), NASA, ESA, J. Clarke (Boston University), and Z. Levay (STScI); 97 (UP), NASA/JPL; 97 (LO CTR), NASA, ESA, and E. Karkoschka (University of Arizona); 97 (CTR RT), NASA/JPL-Caltech/Space Science Institute; 98 (CTR), CVADRAT/SS; 99 (CTR), NASA; 99 (UP), Ralf Juergen Kraft/SS; 99 (LO), NASA ESA/ATG medialab; 99 (CTR LE), NASA/JPL-Caltech; 100 (CTR), ISS/NASA; 100 (LO), ITAR-TASS Photo Agency/Alamy; 101 (UP CTR), NASA; 101 (CTR LE), Henrik Lehnerer/SS; 101 (CTR RT), NASA/JPL; 101 (LO LE), Stocktrek/GI; 101 (LO CTR), Neil Armstrong/NASA; 101 (UP LE), Michael Collins/NASA; 101 (LO RT), NASA/JSC; 101 (UP RT), NASA; 102, NASA/Rick Wetherington and Tony Gray; 103 (UP), TodorovNikifor/IS; 103 (CTR RT), Library of Congress; 103 (LO), Mark Rademaker/Pixel Pusher; 104, ISS/NASA; 105 (UP), John_Kasawa/IS; 105 (LO), NASA; 105 (CTR), Petty Officer 3rd Class Richard Brahm/U.S. Coast Guard; 106 (CTR), Albert Ziganshin/SS; 106 (LO), NASA/JPL; 107 (LO CTR), NASA/JPL-Caltech/USGS; 107 (CTR), NASA/JPL-Caltech/MSSS; 107 (LO RT), ZargonDesign/IS; 107 (UP RT), NASA; 107 (LO LE), NASA/JPL/Space Science Institute; 107 (UP LE), Harvard-Smithsonian Center for Astrophysics/David Aguilar; 108 (CTR), NASA/JPL-Caltech; 108 (LO LE), NASA; 109 (CTR LE), NASA/ESA/JPL-Caltech/Yale/CNRS; 109 (CTR), Bill Ingalls/NASA; 109 (CTR RT), Danita Delimont/Alamy; 109 (UP RT), Martin Capek/SS; 110 (CTR), NASA/JPL-Caltech; 110 (LO), NASA/JPL-Caltech/UCLA/MPS/DLR/IDA; 111 (CTR RT), rgmeier/IS; 111 (CTR LE), StephanHoerold/IS; 111 (LO RT), 20thCentFox/Courtesy Everett Collection; 111 (UP LE), solarseven/IS; 112 (CTR), Maciej Frolow/Photographer's Choice/GI; 112 (CTR RT), PaulFleet/IS; 112 (LO LE), NASA; 113 (LO RT inset), ESA/Rosetta/MPS for OSIRIS Team MPS/UPD/LAM/IAA/SSO/INTA/UPM/DASP/IDA; 113 (CTR), Marc Ward/SS; 113 (LO RT), jimmyjamesbond/IS; 113 (UP), Monsignor Ronald Royer//Science Photo Library/CO; 114-115, fotoVoyager/IS; 116, nathanphoto/IS; 117 (UP), elnavegante/IS; 117 (CTR), Philippe Wojazer/AFP/GI; 117 (LO), Kenneth Garrett/NGC; 118, estt/IS; 119 (UP), Syda Productions/SS; 119 (LO), CO; 119 (CTR LE), U.S. Marines; 119 (RT), Horizons WWP/Alamy; 120, pius99/IS; 121 (CTR RT), H.M. Herget/NGC; 121 (LO), Magzmichel/IS; 121 (UP LE), Viacheslav Lopatin/SS; 121 (UP), f9photos/SS; 121 (UP CTR), Michael S. Yamashita/CO; 121 (UP RT), Barna Tanko/SS; 122 (LO RT), The Natural History Museum/Alamy; 122 (CTR), O. Louis Mazzatenta/NGC; 122 (LO LE), Richard Barnes/NGC; 123 (LE), Popperfoto/GI; 123 (LO CTR), Kenneth Garrett/NGC; 123 (LO LE), Kenneth Garrett/NGC; 123 (RT 1), Jennie Hills/Science Museum/Science & Society Picture Library/GI; 123 (RT 3), Westend61 GmbH/Alamy; 123 (RT 2), The Print Collector/Alamy; 123 (UP), Kenneth Garrett/NGC; 123 (RT 4), Charles & Josette Lenars/CO; 124 (LO LE), Catherine Lane/IS; 124 (goat), Eric Isselee/SS; 124 (UP LE), MarkHatfield/IS; 124 (carrots), andersphoto/SS; 124 (grain), Veronika111/IS; 125 (UP LE), f9photos/IS; 125 (UP CTR LE), elnavegante/IS; 125 (LO), gmutlu/IS; 125 (CTR LE), De Agostini/GI; 125 (CTR), De Agostini/GI; 125 (UP CTR), View Stock RF/GI; 126 (LO LE), Bragin Alexey/SS; 126-127 (UP), Pakhnyushchy/SS; 126-127 (Background), Jonathan Weiss/SS; 126 (CTR RT), Brian Green/Alamy; 127 (LO CTR), Eric Fowke/Alamy; 127 (salt), vikif/IS; 127 (stone), Keren Su/CO; 127 (beads), Mike Linley/Dorling Kindersley/GI; 127 (spices), Svetl/IS; 127 (knife), mala_ja/SS; 127 (squirrel), IrinaK/SS; 127 (cocoa beans), AndrisTkachenko/IS; 127 (seeds), Chad Zuber/SS; 128 (UP), Maciej Noskowski/IS; 128 (LO), hipproductions/IS; 129 (LE), Jacques de Guise, French School, Bibliotheque Municipale, Boulogne-sur-Mer, France/Bridgeman Images; 129 (UP RT), Fulcanelli/SS; 129 (CTR RT), North Wind Picture Archives/Alamy; 130, Gannet77/IS; 131 (LO), Christie's Images/CO; 131 (CTR), adoc-photos/CO; 131 (UP), The Print Collector/Alamy; 132 (UP), RG-vc/SS; 132 (LO LE), viki2win/SS; 132 (CTR), INTERFOTO/Alamy; 132 (CTR), INTERFOTO/Alamy; 132 (LO CTR RT), Pgiam/IS; 132 (LO RT), flowgraph/IS; 133 (LE), KPG Payless2/SS; 133 (LO RT), ostill/SS; 133 (UP RT), KPG Payless2/SS; 133 (Background), KPG_Payless/SS; 134 (LO RT), Chico Sanchez/Alamy; 134 (LE), oscar_killo/IS; 134 (LE back), ROMAOSLO/IS; 135 (LO RT), Pasticcio/IS; 135 (UP), Gannet77/IS; 135 (CTR), Library of Congress; 136, American School/Private Collection/Peter Newark American Pictures/Bridgeman Images; 137 (CTR LE), solkanar/SS; 137 (UP RT), World History Archive/Alamy; 137 (UP LE), RussellSirmans/IS; 137 (CTR), AntonSokolov/SS; 137 (LO CTR), North Wind Picture Archives/Alamy; 137 (LO RT), North Wind Picture Archives/Alamy; 138-139 (Background), Johner Images/Alamy; 138 (LO), Jim Gibson/Alamy; 139 (UP inset), rimglow/IS; 139 (UP), Science Source/GI; 139 (LO), AP Photo; 140 (LE), Pgiam/IS; 140 (RT), DanielaAgius/IS; 141 (UP RT), Kemal Taner/SS; 141 (UP LE), rypson/IS; 141 (CTR LE), gorillaimages/SS; 141 (LO CTR), best-photo/IS; 142-143, NASA/JSC; 144, Anton Balazh/SS; 145 (LO RT), elwynn/SS; 145 (CTR LE), Tomislav Pinter/SS; 145 (UP), scanrail/IS; 146 (LO RT), RuthBlack/IS; 146 (CTR), lelepado/IS; 146 (LO LE), egal/IS; 146 (LO CTR), RuthBlack/IS; 147 (UP RT), simoningate/IS; 147 (UP LE), Marina Sun/SS; 147 (UP CTR LE), Viktor1/SS; 147 (UP CTR RT), Jos Beltman/SS; 147 (CTR), marvinh/IS; 147 (LO), Chad Tomlinson; 147 (CTR RT), Jens Wolf/dpa/CO; 148, Alen Gurovic/Alamy; 149 (UP), galinast/IS; 149 (RT), svetik15/IS; 149 (CTR), exopixel/SS; 149 (LO), gavran333/IS; 150, Krystian Nawrocki/IS; 151 (UP), Louisa Gouliamaki/AFP/GI; 151 (CTR RT), CO; 151 (UP LE), CO; 151 (CTR LE), SSPL/GI; 151 (LO RT), Hadrian/SS; 151 (LO LE), Rob Stothard/GI; 152 (UP RT), James Looker/PC Gamer Magazine via GI; 152 (UP LE), ferrantraite/IS; 152 (LO), LeonidSad/IS; 152 (CTR RT), Science Photo Library/CO; 153 (UP), Chris George/Alamy; 153 (LO), Seth Wenig/AP Images; 153 (UP), Henrik5000/IS; 154 (LO), Phillip Bond/Alamy; 154 (CTR), chuyu/IS; 155 (LO LE), Ayse Pemra Yuce/SS; 155 (UP LE), Dougberry/IS; 155 (LO RT), pavlos christoforou/Alamy; 155 (UP RT), Culture Club/GI; 156 (LO LE), ssuaphoto/IS; 156 (CTR LE), Gyuszko-Photo/SS; 157 (CTR), alex-mit/IS; 157 (UP LE), Tom Wang/SS; 157 (UP RT), Library of Congress; 157 (LO RT), Laurent Gillieron/epa/CO; 158, MariuszBlach/IS; 159 (CTR RT), Fentino/IS; 159 (UP), travellight/SS; 159 (LO LE), mevans/IS; 159 (LO), NASA; 160, Strathdee Holdi Ltd./IS; 161 (UP LE), Christophe Testi/SS; 161 (CTR LE), Jodi Jacobson/IS; 161 (UP RT), kickstand/IS; 162, Rex USA; 163 (UP LE), Paramount/Courtesy Everett Collection; 163 (RT), Mark Williamson/Oxford Scientific RM/GI; 163 (LO), Anatolii Babii/IS; 164-165, Frank Stober/F1online RM/GI; 166 (UP LE), 101cats/IS; 166 (LO LE), frenc/IS; 166 (UP RT), vladimir zakharov/Flickr RF/GI; 166 (LO RT), mari_art/IS; 167 (UP LE), phil gould/Alamy; 167 (LO LE), madcorona/IS; 167 (CTR), Dave King/Dorling Kindersley/GI; 167 (UP RT), alarifoto/IS; 167 (CTR RT), A M Seward/Alamy; 167 (LO RT), Johann Schumacher/Photolibrary RM/GI; 167 (CTR LE), Tory Kallman/SS; 168 (UP RT), tanoochai/SS; 168 (UP LE), Marjan Visser Photography/SS; 168 (LO LE), SensorSpot/IS; 168 (CTR LO LE), Vincent J. Musi/NGC; 168 (CTR), Enjoylife2/IS; 168 (LO CTR), Tsekhmister/SS; 168 (LO RT), Augusto Stanzani/Ardea; 169, Flip Nicklin/Minden Pictures; 170 (LO), steele2123/GI; 170 (RT), Daniel Cox/Photolibrary RM/GI; 171 (UP LE), Satoshi Kuribayashi/Minden Pictures; 171 (UP CTR), Cultura RM/Alamy; 171 (LO LE), Mark Conlin/Alamy; 171 (UP RT), ADIBILIO/IS; 171 (LO RT), Stuart G Porter/SS; 172 (UP), Antrey/IS; 172 (CTR), rpbirdman/IS; 172 (LO), elthar2007/IS; 173 (UP LE), mrkob/SS; 173 (CTR LE), Moncherie/IS; 173 (CTR RT), proxyminder/IS; 173 (UP CTR), weter 777/SS; 173 (LO RT), dial-a-view/IS; 173 (LO LE), fivespots/SS; 174, Lion1st/SS; 175 (LO), Yuri/IS; 175 (plate), Bipsun/SS; 175 (crab meat), DebbiSmirnoff/IS; 175 (candy), Gaertner/Alamy; 175 (jerky), Cathy Britcliffe/IS; 175 (water bug), Yaping/SS; 175 (scorpion), johnaudrey/IS; 175 (caterpillar), Maxfocus/IS; 175 (bacon), Floortje/IS; 175 (weevil), Dr. Morley Read/SS; 175 (grasshopper), proxyminder/IS; 175 (popcorn), Glenn Price/SS; 176 (UP), age fotostock/Alamy; 176 (LO LE), Soyka/SS; 176 (LO CTR), South_agency/IS; 177 (UP LE), Antagain/IS; 177 (LO LE), Jeka/SS; 177 (UP CTR) Steve Hellerstein/Alamy; 177 (LO CTR) Irin-k/SS; 177 (LO RT), ivkuzmin/IS; 178 (LO LE), Richard Whitcombe/SS; 178 (LO RT), Martin Dohrn/Nature Picture Library; 178 (UP), strmko/IS; 179 (UP LE), QiuJu Song/SS; 179 (LO), D. Parer & E. Parer-Cook/Ardea; 179 (UP CTR), webguzs/IS; 179 (CTR RT), Gilmanshin/SS; 180, MattiaATH/SS; 181 (UP RT), AndreAnita/IS; 181 (leopard), Eric Isselee/SS; 181 (cheetah), Eric Isselee/SS; 181 (jaguar), Anan Kaewkhammul/SS; 181 (CTR LE), Karen Grigoryan/SS; 181 (CTR LO RT), Le Do/SS; 181 (CTR UP RT), javarman/SS; 181 (LO RT), 3sbworld/IS; 182 (CTR), Victor Tyakht/SS; 182 (LO), asharkyu/SS; 183 (UP RT), Christian Charisius/Reuters/CO; 183 (CTR), Darren Baker/SS; 183 (LO LE), GlobalP/IS; 183 (UP LE), Stephen Frink Collection/Alamy; 183 (LO CTR), Ted Kinsman/Science Source; 183 (LO RT), HO/Reuters/CO; 184 (CTR RT), muratart/SS; 184 (CTR), Zhukov Oleg/SS; 185 (UP CTR), dossyl/IS; 185 (CTR UP RT), Universal Images Group Limited/Alamy; 185 (UP LE), Christian Musat/SS; 185 (CTR LE), GlobalP/IS;

185 (UP RT), Maros Bauer/SS; 185 (CTR LO), Jane Burton/Nature Picture Library; 185 (LO LE), Joel Sartore/NGC; 185 (CTR LO RT), Frank Leung/IS; 185 (LO RT), Kaliva/SS; 186 (LO RT), anshu18/IS; 186 (UP), Roy Toft/NGC; 187 (UP LE), 13/Natphotos/Ocean/CO; 187 (UP RT), Stayer/SS; 187 (LO), Eric Isselee/SS; 187 (CTR), Iakov Filimonov/SS; 188 (LO RT), IvanMikhaylov/IS; 188 (UP), Christina Gandolfo/Alamy; 188 (LO LE), Charles Mann/IS; 189 (LO LE), Judith Dzierzawa/IS; 189 (UP), stevecoleimages/IS; 189 (CTR), LifeJourneys/IS; 189 (LO RT), damedeeso/IS; 190 (LO RT), Redzaal/IS; 190 (CTR), Arman Zhenikeyev/SS; 191 (UP), Achim Prill/IS; 191 (CTR LE), SJ Allen/SS; 191 (LO), Splash News/CO; 192 (LO RT), Kim Briers/SS; 192 (LO LE), Hiroya Minakuchi/Minden Pictures; 192-193 (CTR), Nature Art/SS; 193 (CTR LO RT), picturepartners/SS; 193 (UP RT), TobiasBischof/IS; 193 (CTR LE), Coffeemill/SS; 193 (LO LE), marcinhajdasz/IS; 193 (LO RT), USDA Photo; 193 (CTR RT), Audrey Snider-Bell/SS; 194-195, EpicStockMedia/SS; 196 (CTR LE), FelixRenaud/IS; 196 (LO), PathDoc/SS; 197 (UP), NASA; 197 (CTR), LeventKonuk/IS; 197 (CTR LE), 20thCentFox/Everett Collection, Inc.; 197 (LO LE), ilbusca/IS; 197 (LO RT), CBW/Alamy; 197 (CTR RT), Suzanne Plunkett/Reuters/CO; 198, Skyhobo/IS; 199 (UP), rarpia/IS; 199 (LE), stocksnapper/IS; 199 (LO), Pete Pahham/SS; 199 (RT), jianying yin/IS; 200 (CTR), Lauri Patterson/IS; 200 (LO), Okea/IS; 201 (UP RT), lisafx/IS; 201 (UP LE), HandmadePictures/SS; 201 (LO LE), Javier Correa/SS; 201 (CTR), lawcain/IS; 201 (CTR LE), Jesús Arias/IS; 201 (CTR LO), Swapan Photography/SS; 201 (LO RT), Maria Bobrova/IS; 202 (CTR RT), a-wrangler/IS; 202 (UP), Pablo631/IS; 202 (LO LE), vinicef/IS; 202 (CTR LE), Celiafoto/SS; 203 (LO), pkline/IS; 203 (UP), Isa-R/IS; 204 (CTR LE), EricVega/IS; 204 (UP), Anatolii Babii/IS; 204 (LO), Annette Kiesow; 205 (UP CTR), Champ Harms; 205 (LO CTR LE), Nils Jorgensen/Rex USA; 205 (UP RT), estrella225/IS; 205 (UP CTR LE), MediaPunch Inc/Rex USA; 205 (CTR RT), Kevork Djansezian/GI; 205 (CTR), ZUMA Press, Inc./Alamy; 205 (LO), Big_Ryan/IS; 206, Roberto A Sanchez/IS; 207 (UP RT), dieKleinert/Alamy; 207 (UP LE), Keystone/GI; 207 (CTR RT), Stephen Frink Collection/Alamy; 207 (LO LE), Nadya Lukic/IS; 208 (UP), Robert Harding World Imagery RF/Alamy; 208 (LO), Umkehrer/IS; 209 (CTR LE), machaon/IS; 209 (UP CTR), cruphoto/IS; 209 (UP RT), rozowynos/IS; 209 (LO), BIOphotos/IS; 209 (CTR RT), Nagy-Bagoly Arpad/SS; 210, skynesher/IS; 211 (UP LE), TRITOOTH/IS; 211 (CTR LE), Danny Lawson/PA/AP Photo; 211 (CTR RT), Brian Garfinkel/GI; 211 (LO LE), strickke/IS; 212 (CTR), Mark Spowart/Alamy; 212 (LO LE), piskunov/IS; 212 (LO RT), Mike Cherim/IS; 213 (UP LE), PhilAugustavo/IS; 213 (CTR LE), Mikhail Pogosov/SS; 213 (CTR RT), Photodisc/GI; 213 (LO LE), IPGGutenbergUKLtd/IS; 213 (LO RT), tratong/SS; 214 (LO LE), Kursad/IS; 214 (LO RT), Christopher Smith/The Times/AP Photo; 215 (UP), 4x6/IS; 215 (CTR LE), Walt Disney/Everett Collection; 215 (UP RT), David Hanlon/IS; 215 (CTR RT), Steve Granitz/WireImage/GI; 215 (LO), ArtMarie/Vetta/GI

STAFF FOR THIS BOOK
Becky Baines, *Project Editor*
James Hiscott, Jr., *Art Director/Designer*
Chad Tomlinson, *Designer*
Lori Epstein, *Senior Photo Editor*
Annette Kiesow, *Photo Editor*
Jennifer Agresta, *Fact-Checker*
Michael Libonati, *Special Projects Assistant*
Paige Towler, *Editorial Assistant*
Rachel Kenny and Sanjida Rashid, *Design Production Assistants*
Michael Cassady, *Rights Clearance Specialist*
Grace Hill, *Managing Editor*
Joan Gossett, *Senior Production Editor*
Lewis R. Bassford, *Production Manager*
Rachel Faulise, *Manager, Production Services*
Susan Borke, *Legal and Business Affairs*

PUBLISHED BY THE NATIONAL GEOGRAPHIC SOCIETY
Gary E. Knell, *President and CEO*
John M. Fahey, *Chairman of the Board*
Melina Gerosa Bellows, *Chief Education Officer*
Declan Moore, *Chief Media Officer*
Hector Sierra, *Senior Vice President and General Manager, Book Division*

SENIOR MANAGEMENT/KIDS PUBLISHING AND MEDIA
Nancy Laties Feresten, *Senior Vice President;* Jennifer Emmett, *Vice President, Editorial Director, Kids Books;* Julie Vosburgh Agnone, *Vice President, Editorial Operations;* Rachel Buchholz, *Editor and Vice President,* NG Kids *magazine;* Michelle Sullivan, *Vice President, Kids Digital;* Eva Absher-Schantz, *Design Director;* Jay Sumner, *Photo Director;* Hannah August, *Marketing Director;* R. Gary Colbert, *Production Director*

DIGITAL
Anne McCormack, *Director;* Laura Goertzel, Sara Zeglin, *Producers;* Emma Rigney, *Creative Producer;* Bianca Bowman, *Assistant Producer;* Natalie Jones, *Senior Product Manager*

The National Geographic Society is one of the world's largest nonprofit scientific and educational organizations. Founded in 1888 to "increase and diffuse geographic knowledge," the Society's mission is to inspire people to care about the planet. It reaches more than 400 million people worldwide each month through its official journal, *National Geographic,* and other magazines; National Geographic Channel; television documentaries; music; radio; films; books; DVDs; maps; exhibitions; live events; school publishing programs; interactive media; and merchandise. National Geographic has funded more than 10,000 scientific research, conservation, and exploration projects and supports an education program promoting geographic literacy.

For more information, please visit nationalgeographic.com, call 1-800-NGS LINE (647-5463), or write to the following address:

National Geographic Society
1145 17th Street N.W.
Washington, D.C. 20036-4688 U.S.A.

Visit us online at nationalgeographic.com/books

For librarians and teachers: ngchildrensbooks.org

More for kids from National Geographic: kids.nationalgeographic.com

For information about special discounts for bulk purchases, please contact National Geographic Books Special Sales: ngspecsales@ngs.org

For rights or permissions inquiries, please contact National Geographic Books Subsidiary Rights: ngbookrights@ngs.org

Trade edition ISBN: 978-1-4263-2096-5
Library edition ISBN: 978-1-4263-2097-2

Printed in China
15/RRDS/1

TO MY FRIEND DAN "SHOE" HSU, WHO ALWAYS ASKED THE TOUGH QUESTIONS.
—CB

Here's WHY you will LOVE these BOOKS, too!

Each one features 5,000 AWESOME FACTS (about everything!)

NATIONAL GEOGRAPHIC KIDS

AVAILABLE WHEREVER BOOKS ARE SOLD • Discover more at **kids.nationalgeographic.com**